NO LAND, NO MOTHER

ACKNOWLEDGEMENTS:

The editors wish to thank the following for permission to reprint the articles listed below:

Tobias Döring: 'Turning the Colonial Gaze: Re-Visions of Terror in Dabydeen's *Turner*', *Third Text*, No. 38 (1997) and *Caribbean-English Passages* (Routledge, 2002).

Lee M. Jenkins: 'On Not Being Tony Harrison: Tradition and the Individual Talent of David Dabydeen', *Ariel*, Volume 32, No. 2, April 2001.

Mark Stein: 'Writing Place: The Perception of Landscape and Architecture in V.S. Naipaul's *The Enigma of Arrival* and David Dabydeen's *Disappearance*', *Acolit Sonderheft* 1, (1995)

Another version of Aleid Fokkema's article was previously published in J. Arnold, *A History of Literature in the Caribbean*, (John Benjamins, 1997)

NO LAND, NO MOTHER

ESSAYS ON THE WORK OF DAVID DABYDEEN

EDITED BY
KAMPTA KARRAN & LYNNE MACEDO

PEEPAL TREE

First published in Great Britain in 2007
Peepal Tree Press Ltd
17 King's Avenue
Leeds LS6 1QS
UK

ISBN 1 84523 020 5
ISBN13: 9781845230203

 Peepal Tree gratefully acknowledges Arts Council support

In memory of Gilbert P. Bartholomew,
for his great love and shared joy for literature,
and his tiresome grandchild.

CONTENTS

INTRODUCTION

Dialogue across diversity is perhaps the dominant characteristic of David Dabydeen's prose and poetry. His Guyanese Indian/West Indian heritage and his long location in the heart of British society have combined to produce a hybrid, cosmopolitan personality that manifests itself strongly in his writing. Throughout his work, haunting recollections of a receding Guyanese past blend with a constantly changing postmodern/postcolonial present to release a fertile imagination that ranges freely from the local to the universal. The abrasive and lyrical Creole of the rural peasant folk, together with the imperial structures of Standard English, were the twin beasts of burden that carried his distinctive voice in his earliest writing. Thereafter, through the transgression of linguistic and ethnic boundaries, historical griefs have been reconfigured in liberatory, though never easily redemptive ways in both his poetry and fiction.

The simultaneous habitation of multiple arenas and the refusal to surrender to the dictates of any single loyalty or to be boxed in by time and space are dominant features of current postmodernity. Yet these impulses often collide with a stubborn emotional need for belonging or even some form of racialised solidarity. Dabydeen himself acknowledges a responsibility to confront such issues and engages in a dialogue in his writing between the roles of the cultural custodian and that of the eclectic cosmopolitan. The dialectic between conflict and co-operation, change and continuity provides the moral underpinning for much of his work, whether it revisits slavery and indentureship in a past century or deals with a present day Sita in concert with the enemy.

This book presents the latest collection of critical studies that attempt to engage with the complexities of Dabydeen's writing. It complements the earlier *The Art of David Dabydeen* (Peepal Tree, 1997, ed. K. Grant) in several ways. Whilst looking again at texts discussed in the earlier work, *No Land, No Mother* extends the critical coverage to Dabydeen's third and fourth novels, *The Counting House* (1997) and *A Harlot's Progress* (1999). And, in looking again at the earlier work, these essays provide stimulating rereadings that are not only in dialogue with the essays in the earlier book, but revisit the earlier work in the light both of Dabydeen's continuing development and the continuing evolution of critical theory. Whilst each of the essayists engages with this body of work from different perspectives, there are a number of common themes. These include Dabydeen's explorations of how to imagine the unimaginable and his subversive relationship to literary tradition. Taking clues from the explicit intertextual references in his work, Dabydeen's writing has been linked to, amongst others, T.S. Eliot, Walcott, Tony Harrison, V.S. Naipaul, Conrad, Sterne, and Wilson Harris. Yet neither a search for particular influences or a focus on the undeniably foregrounded role of intertextuality in his work permits any convenient pigeonholing of the nature of his talent. The value of the essays in this book is not that they engage in a fruitless exercise of classification but that they reveal and celebrate Dabydeen's gift of raising questions, entertaining and provoking thought.

The book has been divided into five sub-sections, each containing two essays that are thematically linked in their engagement with some aspect of Dabydeen's work. Part One focuses in detail on his epic poem *Turner* and theorises the links between this work and the neo-classicist and Romantic concepts of the sublime. It positions the ambiguous nature of the poem within a wider postcolonial struggle to resist the illusion of representation as transparent and reliable and to subvert the cultural authority of hegemonic tropes of Englishness. In the first of these two essays, Aleid Fokkema reads *Turner* within a wider Caribbean tradition of (re)writing epic poetry. She compares Dabydeen's work with that of three other Caribbean writers who have also published epic poems – Derek Walcott, Édouard Glissant and Frank Martinus Arion – and suggests that each of their epics has an intimate linkage to the historically located aesthetics of the sublime. In focusing on thematic preoccupations with issues of exile, wandering and transportation, Fokkema demonstrates how each poem struggles to represent the paradoxical nature of Caribbean identity. In place of the unitary concept of roots as a metaphor for identity, she makes use of the multidimensional concept of the rhizome as a more fruitful way of comparing the treatment of these issues in these poems. In particular, she reads them (and *Turner*) through the doubleness of the trope of transportation. In this way she connects the central matter of these poems, the actual physical transport of slaves' bodies, to the discourse of the sublime. In exploring the respective treatments of the consoling possibilities of spiritual transport (involving, for instance, the loss of self in communication with the gods) she notes how Dabydeen's *Turner*, denies such consolations in the way the poem constantly negates its own thematic substance: 'no land, no words, no community,/ No mother.'

The following essay by Tobias Döring elaborates upon the use of the sublime in art and focuses in particular on the representation of terror in both Dabydeen's poem *Turner* and in Turner's painting: '*Slave Ship*'. By reference to both Edmund Burke's eighteenth century treatise on the 'sublime and beautiful' and Frantz Fanon's classic works on colonialism, Döring articulates the connections between terror and the exercise of imperial power, and examines their role in the above mentioned painting and poem respectively. He demonstrates that a morbid fascination with aspects of terror was embodied in both the Romantic and, in particular, the neo-Gothic aesthetic of the sublime and shows that this aesthetic was inextricably linked to the discourse of imperialism. Döring then argues that although the characters in *Turner* are ultimately unable to escape their earlier representation as victims, Dabydeen's incisive engagement with Turner's painting still manages to subvert the power of the colonial gaze. By focusing on the necessary role of the spectator in the aesthetic construction of the sublime, Döring shows how Dabydeen engages the reader in a self-reflexive examination of their 'spectating' role.

The essays in Part Two continue the focus on Dabydeen's poetry and expand and complement a number of the theoretical ideas raised in Part One. However, rather than concentrating on the sublime effects employed in *Turner*, the first of these essays attempts a more formal interrogation of the work's poetic form, as well as assessing its properties as an act of cultural reappropriation.

Heike Härting discusses *Turner* as both a diasporic and a postcolonial discourse, locating it in the gaps between 'nation and empire' and as a critique of earlier attempts by Caribbean writers (especially Walcott) to reinvent Caribbean history through processes of amnesiac reconciliation and transfiguration. In particular she looks at how in *Turner* Dabydeen deconstructs the nature of metaphor as a transfigurative device by tracing its role as a rhetorical device embedded in the discourse of empire and representations of race and sexuality. In her rich and complex reading of *Turner*, Härting enlarges our awareness of the multiple possible relationships between Dabydeen's poem, the painting it uses as its starting point and the historical figure of J.M.W. Turner. She shows that Dabydeen disinters the cultural icon 'J.M.W. Turner' from its deadness as a sign of Englishness, cleansed of all cultural and racial ambiguities and deviant desires. Instead of operating as a designator of cultural superiority, she shows how metaphor in *Turner* has been transformed into a trope of imperial crisis.

Madina Tlostanova's essay also explores the ways in which cultural redefinition has been handled in Dabydeen's poetry and shows how his writing both deconstructs and subverts imperial forms of representation through the utilisation of an aesthetics that involves 'unpredictable' and transgressive combinations of the traditional and the modern. She shows how his work serves to undermine the very existence of boundaries and thus removes any notions of stability that may have once been contained within the concepts of 'race' or 'belonging'. In addition to *Turner*, her essay also considers a number of Dabydeen's earlier poems in which she identifies the journey 'cronotope' as one of their main features. In ranging across the themes of intertextuality, boundary crossing, hybridity, imaginative geographies and metamorphosis, Tlostanova's essay most valuably reads Dabydeen's work in the context of a number of other diasporic writers, including Bharati Mukherjee, Abdelwahab Meddeb and, most rewardingly, Audre Lorde's *Zami: A New Spelling of My Name*.

Part Three continues the exploration of Dabydeen's poetic output both in terms of its intertextuality, and through a consideration of his ambivalent relationship to a number of literary texts from both past and present. Lee Jenkins' essay pinpoints a network of (often self-confessed) linkages between Dabydeen's writing and the poetry of both T.S. Eliot and Tony Harrison. Whilst acknowledging that Dabydeen resists being assimilated into too close a relationship with either of these poets, Jenkins demonstrates that similarities do exist between a number of their thematic preoccupations. In comparing Dabydeen's 'Coolie Odyssey' with Harrison's 'On Not Being Milton' she argues that parallels can be seen in the way that both poems draw attention to their status as poetry, and as a discourse which is remote from the world of the subject matter of the poem, and she contrasts the precise nature of their deployment of specific inter- and counter-texts. In the case of Dabydeen's relationship to Eliot, Jenkins examines both the more explicit references to *The Waste Land* that can be traced in sections of *Turner* and highlights the ways in which both poets have made subversive use of 'explanatory' notes to a number of their poems. She concludes that whilst Dabydeen may justifiably feel uneasy about his links with Western literary traditions, such connections are nevertheless 'unavoidable'. Finally, in commenting on the theme of transformation explored in several of the essays, Jenkins notes that what interests Dabydeen is not the illusion of a redemptive blurring of the interests of the former colonised and former coloniser, but the 'endless transformations' that offer freedom from any fixed identity.

Pumla Dineo Gqola's essay complements that of Jenkins by continuing the exploration of aspects of intertextuality in Dabydeen's writing and his (often deliberately misleading) authorial commentaries on a number of his poems. The essay focuses mainly on Dabydeen's first collection of poems – *Slave Song* – and its gender politics. In particular, Gqola explores Dabydeen's treatment of the theme of black male desire for the white woman, both in the context of historical discourses about slavery and sexuality, and contemporary theoretical discourses on the gendering of sexual desire in writing. She shows how the poet's deconstructive play with various modes of representation successfully subverts stereotypical images of the black male body. She also demonstrates how the addition of 'explanatory' notes to the poems in *Slave Song* serves not to elucidate but to destabilize, to alert the reader to resist immediate, fixed or monolithic interpretation.

The final two Parts of the book are devoted to an examination of three of Dabydeen's novels – *Disappearance*, *The Counting House* and *A Harlot's Progress*. Both of the essays in Part Four situate *Disappearance* within the wider context of writing about the immigrant experience, and with characters who must deal with the dilemma of being both present yet absent ('disappearing' from view) in the imperial 'centre' in which they find themselves located. Michael Mitchell's essay shows how Dabydeen utilises a number of narrative techniques to disrupt the reader's expectations about what the novel will ultimately reveal or conceal. As Mitchell shows, not only does the novel revel in the absence of the name of the narrator but this 'missing' character is involved in a quest that is clearly never going to achieve the goal of pinning down an elusive, disappearing 'truth'. Mitchell identifies and explores the significance of the overt intertextuality in *Disappearance* in a way that contrasts with the more sceptical reading by Mark McWatt in an essay in *The Art of David Dabydeen*. Mitchell's sustained reading and evident enjoyment of the dialogue with Wilson Harris, V.S. Naipaul, Conrad and T.S. Eliot makes the case that intertextuality is 'less a device than a mode in which *Disappearance* is written'.

Mark Stein's essay provides a more detailed examination of the ways in which Dabydeen's *Disappearance* relates to one of those 'absent' texts to which it refers: V.S. Naipaul's novel *The Enigma of Arrival*. By comparing both their narrative structures and their thematic preoccupations with notions of exile, alienation and the constructed nature of identity, Stein argues that *Disappearance* can in part be read as a re-working of Naipaul's earlier novel. His essay focuses in particular upon perceptions of landscape and Englishness in each novel and demonstrates how both texts subvert preconceived ideas about the ability of language to produce a stable, uniform meaning for coloniser and colonised alike. Stein explores the ways in which both narrators resist assimilation into the cultural 'centre' by insisting on the fluidity of their respective identities. Stein concludes that as a result of the ambivalent and tenuous positions that they are forced to occupy, a reading of both narratives reveals the fraudulent and artificially constructed nature of the English identity that would wish to represent itself as a 'national' essence.

The final section of the book contains two essays on Dabydeen's narrative techniques for dealing with the paradox of attempting to represent the unrepresentable. Christine Pagnoulle's discussion of *A Harlot's Progress* begins with a consideration of the relationship between Hogarth's engravings of the same title and the novel's narrative structure. She argues that the use of fragments from Hogarth's plates as epigraphs for each part of the novel signals the necessarily fragmentary nature of acts of historical reclamation. She shows how the ambiguous nature of the narrator's identity and the presentation of deliberately confusing alternative versions of events continually draws the reader's attention to the novel's fictional construction and the impossibility of presenting the 'truth' about the past. Pagnoulle shows how these deliberately destabilising acts are part of a dialogue enacted in the relationship between the anti-slavery campaigner, Pringle, and Mungo, the aged African. Whilst the former is trying to co-opt Mungo's story into *his* whitewashed narrative of Christian redemption, Mungo's freedom with 'the facts' is precisely that: an assertion of the freedom of the imagination as the writer's true province.

The concluding essay by Gail Low, a sustained reading of *The Counting House*, shows that instead of engaging in the convention of 'imaginative reconstruction', as do novels such as Caryl Phillips's *Cambridge,* and *Crossing the River* or Fred D'Aguiar's *The Longest Memory* and *Feeding the Ghosts*, Dabydeen's novel frustrates all sense of redeeming the past or offering some cathartic recovery of the voices of those previously hidden in the partial records of history. As she notes, the epilogue of *The Counting House* is full of negations, and her essay is devoted to exploring why this should be so. With its unpredictable shifts in time and location, coupled with the ruthless nature of its main protagonists, she argues that the novel revels in its own contradictory and pessimistic outlook. However, despite the inherent difficulties in interpretation, her concluding remarks suggest that *The Counting House* can nevertheless offer a salutary lesson to those who would reduce the sufferings of others to just another sanitised commodity for mass consumption.

Collectively, these essays help the reader to make sense of Dabydeen's multidimensional response to the intersecting worlds he inhabits. In approaching Dabydeen's work in ways that foreground its always questioning, ambivalent, resistant relationships to its multiple points of connection – to Guyana, to a Guyanese Hindu Indianness, to the Caribbean, to Christian doctrine, to Britishness, Black Britishness, to the English literary/cultural canon, to global postcoloniality – these essays make a valuable contribution to seeing Dabydeen's work in a genuinely holistic way. It is hoped that the essays in this book will inspire future research that is dedicated to bridging the divide between those disparate experiences.

Kampta Karren & Lynne Macedo

CHAPTER ONE
CARIBBEAN SUBLIME:
TRANSPORTING THE SLAVE, TRANSPORTING
THE SPIRIT

ALEID FOKKEMA

At a moment in literary history when a poem rarely runs longer than a page, we see in the Caribbean a sudden revival of the long poem, indeed, of poems of epic length and scope. An obvious example is Derek Walcott's *Omeros*, 1990, an epic of some 8,500 lines that centres on the (partly imagined) contemporary and historical realities of his native St. Lucia; but, significantly enough, that work is not an isolated effort.[1] Another recent work that, at 783 lines, well extends beyond the popular short poem is David Dabydeen's *Turner*, 1994.[2] Dabydeen's poem is less specific than *Omeros* in that it does not set out to record and imagine a particular place, such as the author's place of birth (Guyana, in this case). Instead it focuses on the wider dimensions of migration, the making of the Caribbean and, in particular, on the relation between coloniser and transported slave. The two poems have a number of things in common that designates them as epics. Using the trope of the wanderer, they deploy in various ways the theme of the journey – literal, spiritual, and symbolic – a theme that is of course central to the idea of an epic. This form is thus eminently suitable for recording and creating a history of the Caribbean where journeys have been so crucial. In both poems, history is not merely recorded but also imagined, just as the Homeric epic thrives on a mixture of fact and fiction: history, in Walcott's and Dabydeen's poems, 'a forgotten, insomniac night', is an alloy of facts, lore, myths and allegory.[3] (We might note in passing how that phrase echoes the famous exclamation 'history, a nightmare from which I try to escape', in yet another contemporary epic, Joyce's *Ulysses*.) In addition, both poems are highly crafted works of art, dense with references to other works, with Dabydeen employing a loose but sustained form of blank verse, and Walcott doing the impossible with the Dantean *terza rima*. It is also such craftsmanship that makes 'epic' an appropriate epithet.

When such parallels between two different recent works are suggested, the curiosity of the comparative critic is raised, and one looks for more. Perhaps, indeed, we can speak of a Caribbean (sub)genre, when we consider two earlier works. Édouard Glissant's *Les Indes* (The Indies), 1955, is again a poem of about 600 lines, with one canto in prose.[4] Like *Turner*, this poem is not concerned with the local history of Martinique but tackles subjects with a wider implication for the Caribbean, beginning with the crossing of Columbus. Its style is purposefully elevated, if not at times a little obscure, its form as wrought as that of the other two poems. And two years later the Curaçaoan writer Frank Martinus Arion published a poem in fifty-four cantos and 1,200 short lines, *Stemmen uit Afrika* (Voices from Africa), 1957.[5] The subject is once again a journey, and the poem chants a history that is unspecific and mythologized. This poem is different though from the other three in its obvious poetics of negritude: the journey is one to an authentic Africa. Yet *Stemmen*, too, aspires to the formidable style that characterises the epic. With such epic scope in theme and form, all four poems are in what is conventionally known as the sublime mode, and that, I think, comes as a surprise, considering the characterisation of Caribbean poetry in recent criticism as concerned with discarding whatever was deemed to belong to the aesthetics of the former coloniser. In the introduction to her excellent anthology of Caribbean poetry in English, for example, Paula Burnett typically contrasts a European high culture with both New World popular culture and African roots. She maintains that in the last fifty years or so, Caribbean poetry has been celebrating survival and 'the inheritance of place, tongue and tradition'.[6] She offers overwhelming evidence – in jubilant excursions that no reader can ignore – of poems written in creole-inflected language that deal with cultural experiences as far removed from the memories and cultural traditions of the former coloniser as possible; a poetry of direct, precise cultural confrontation. Who, then, would expect to find the sublime in postwar Caribbean poetry? The sublime, surely, is a concept located in 'high' European culture, in a poetry, indeed, of Empire. Whether in the earlier eighteenth century version characterised by visual tropes of grandeur, elevation or terror, or in the later Romantic construct of the sublime as a form of sensibility that involved the loss of self or the blurring of the boundaries between self and nature, the sheer notion of the sublime would seem radically at odds with the existential commitment to uncovering concrete realities that is, in the view of much critical writing, the dominant characteristic of contemporary Caribbean poetry. Even the postmodern revival of the sublime, as introduced in the early 1980s by Jean François Lyotard, would appear to be no option: it is all about the unpresentable, about 'impart[ing] no knowledge about reality', and that would seem to be light years away from the struggle over representation that characterizes the postcolonial arena.[7] The sublime, in other words, would seem to belong to an aesthetic doctrine that a Caribbean poet might be expected to reject.

Yet I will argue that these Caribbean epics are shot through with both the sublimity of the Enlightenment and that of Romanticism. What is more, they even display the postmodernist sublime's fascination with the unpresentable. In fact, these poems flaunt the aesthetics of the sublime. Their classic forebear, the Homeric epic, was considered to be the epitome of sublimity by Longinus, whose treatise on the sublime (not translated until the seventeenth century) deeply influenced aesthetic thinking in early modern Europe.[8] The sublime became a mode of writing that combined an elevated style and form with a sense of grandeur and divine inspiration, causing the reader to be moved beyond himself, to be, as it were, transported.[9] This elevation of style and form is, as I shall argue, wholly appropriate to these Caribbean epics.

This idea of spiritual transport underlies, as we shall see, many of the more obscure passages in the four poems under consideration.

It is also linked thematically and literally with the physical transportation of slaves, colonisers, and other migrants that characterizes the history of the Caribbean. In true epic fashion, that literal transport is embodied in the figure of the wanderer. In this way, the history of displacement acquires a reverberating depth in the (e)motion of the sublime.

Migration is a stock theme in Caribbean literature. In the first volume of *A History of Literature in the Caribbean*, Randolph Hezekiah makes the point that the works of writers in Martinique and Guadeloupe (and, I would argue the Caribbean as a whole) explore 'the feeling of spatiotemporal dislocation experienced by a people transplanted from a vast and distant continent to the confinement of a small island and subjected to an alien culture'.[10] Dabydeen, Glissant, and Walcott, in addition, also chart the white coloniser's journeyings to the new world in the West. The transportation, 'from the mid-sixteenth century on of millions of free, indentured, and enslaved bodies across thousands of miles of water', is of course the essence of the Caribbean experience,[11] the common denominator in communities of disparate origins. That much of Caribbean writing explores the voyage out, the journey within, and the search for roots of a deracinated people is only to be expected.

Les Indes, Stemmen, Omeros, and *Turner* all use the intertext of epics to focus on the trope of the wanderer, a wanderer, let it be clear, who is neither rootless nor lost, and manifests a relational, multi-rooted identity, much like the rhizome, that useful concept launched by Gilles Deleuze and Felix Guattari.[12] It is striking that Glissant, thirty-five years after the publication of *Les Indes*, should so warmly recommend the metaphor of rhizome (a concept also discussed by Sprouse and De la Campa[13]) as opposed to the more fixed idea of 'roots' as a way of characterising the issue of identity, of creating a 'poetics of relating' for the Caribbean.[14] It is significant that Glissant refers explicitly to epic literature, the fundamental literature of any civilization, as 'books on exile and wandering' whose main characteristic is to explore how rootlessness does not necessarily undermine identity.[15] Homeric, Virgilian, or Old Testament exile does not lead to 'the expansion of territory

20

[…] but rather to scrutinising the Other'.[16] Thus, Major Plunkett dreams of embarking on 'a masochistic odyssey through the Empire, / to watch it go in the dusk' (90), and, indeed, the heroes of Walcott's epic, for example, fit more easily into the model of the rhizome than into that of uniform roots. The St. Lucian fisherman Achille visits the underworld of ghosts in Africa, but on his return to St. Lucia he is acutely aware of his Arawak roots as well.

Identity is not established in terms of belonging to unitary roots but in belonging to a place, the Caribbean island in all its diversity, even across ostensible colonial barriers. Thus, Walcott's narrator, for example, can salute the Other in the representatives of the white colonisers, Major Plunkett and his wife Maud, by establishing a rhizomatic relation: 'There was Plunkett in my father, much as there was / my mother in Maud'; this is a relation, moreover, that draws on the trope of the epic wanderer, because the canto continues to draw a parallel between Plunkett, 'that khaki Ulysses', and the narrator, 'a changing shadow of Telemachus' (263).

Indeed, in his own *Les Indes*, Glissant explored the idea of the rhizome before he developed his theoretical concept. The idea of a relational identity is linked in the poem to the theme of the epic journey and to writing a history of the Caribbean. The visionary speaker creates a pageant of the past and sees in the pattern of history an 'Indes in eternity'.[17] The beauty of the poem lies in the evocation of the first long, anxious, thirsty voyages to the West Indies, that by implication, through the repeated phrase 'time passes', become a journey into and *through* history.[18] The speaker merges with both coloniser and victim, and identifies them with heroic 'discoverers' such as Columbus or Pizarro and with nameless seamen, with the unnamed black seer punished by the church for his visions, and with black liberators such as Toussaint L'Ouverture or Delgrès. The process of evoking and merging historical personae highlights, by implication, the rhizomatic relations among Caribbean peoples.

Similarly, the nameless speaker of Dabydeen's *Turner*, who adopts the persona of the slave cast overboard in the impressive painting *Slave Ship (Slavers Throwing Overboard the Dead and Dying – Typhoon Coming On)* by the English late romantic painter J. M. W. Turner, has a relational, rather than a unified, single identity. His head is submerged, but that lack is filled up with an identity that draws on memories of Africa, India, England, and the New World, collapsing tamarinds, yams, savannahs, cola seeds, plantains, and even English oaks into one truly rhizomatic identity. This illustrates what Walcott means when he wrote of the act of lovingly reassembling 'our African and Asiatic fragments, the cracked heirloom whose restoration shows its white scars'.[19]

In contrast to the three poems discussed so far, the poet-guide who takes his audience to the roots of African culture in *Stemmen uit Afrika* seeks uniformity in the concept of roots, keeping up, or indeed reinforcing, the barriers between a black and a white world (where the world of whites is portrayed as considerably poorer in cultural potential). Black Caribbean identity has nothing to do with whites; the coloniser and the slave do not merge or relate in this poem. The idea of roots functions strictly to affirm a continuous African identity that may have been dispersed through diaspora, but has not dissolved. Here *Stemmen* is fundamentally and ideologically different from the other three poems under consideration. Yet, in calling for a return to roots, this poem also dwells on the nature of the Caribbean colonial subject, whose origins lie elsewhere, who has been transported.

All four works, then, are centred on the historical fact of transportation. In each the sublime style enhances the construction of a metaphysical transport as a counterpoint to migration as a material displacement, as a loss of self. This is no mere play on words, as spiritual transport and material transportation share a common ground in rhizomatic identity: in saluting otherness one can also become Other and hence experience a loss of self. In addition, transportation, although the essence of the colonial experience, risks becoming a vacant, meaningless symbol unless recorded in the concrete and specific history of transported persons – and this is mostly missing from the official, statistically abstracting record. The emphasis on spiritual transport restores the inner drama to the history of the removal of the material body from one place to another.

The later romantic notion of the sublime – the loss of self

into something larger and grander – is also employed in the Caribbean epic as a way of avoiding routine or trivial treatments of the material fact of transportation. Sketching, evoking, imagining the history of any one act of transportation, the poet has access to literary tropes that constitute the 'collective unconscious' of the Caribbean.[20] One slave ship emblematically stands for all, one journey back to Africa denotes all the journeys back, one boat embarking from Genoa all the root of all imperialism, etc. Triviality is avoided through the effect of the sublime. The romantic idea of the sublime is that the ordinary is precluded, or 'the essential claim of the sublime [is that] it allows us passage past "trivial thought"; it takes us to a new order of experience and then returns us to our enlightened selves'.[21] Transport, therefore, has this double sense: it extends metonymically to the loss of selves involved in the actual transportation of slaves, criminals, and official colonisers; it also subscribes to a larger spiritual drama, that of the sublime. For 'transport' as a trope not only stands for the heightened sensation of the sublime, it also *produces* sublimity'.[22]

Related to the romantic sublime is a more postmodern version that emphasizes the impossibility of representation, the lack of a historical reality that can be reliably represented. History, the postmoderns claim, is narrative. But when history becomes 'unpresentable', as Lyotard calls it, it becomes poetry.[23] In the Caribbean epics under consideration here, the transparency of events gives way to the opacity of images: 'All of the Antilles, every island, is an effort of memory; every mind, every racial biography, culminating in amnesia and fog'.[24] The pretension of the historical real is given up for a disclosure of the unreal, of Wittgenstein's that-which-cannot-be-spoken-about, of the uncanny, or the unpresentable: in other words, the sublime. The lack of reliable history is exposed, paradoxically, as a pertinent constitutive element of Caribbean historical identity.

Frank Martinus Arion's *Stemmen uit Afrika* is the least opaque of the four poems discussed here. Martinus Arion, who has spent his life between his native Curaçao and Holland, has published poetry, critical works, and novels in Dutch and Papiamentu, and is an outspoken activist for Antillean culture. *Stemmen* expresses the aesthetics and politics of negritude.[25] In its fifty-four cantos, a black poet takes a group of white tourists on a guided tour of Africa. The idea is to give a corrective picture of blacks while contrasting their communal culture with the capitalist bleakness of white society. The Africa of the poem has no geographical specificity, and it is both a place of the present and of a halcyon past. The politics are simple, if not naïve: in short, terse, three and four-beat lines, intended to imitate African drumming, it celebrates a pre-lapsarian civilization, of the 'Negro / loving in raw purity', as primitive man who 'can intensely experience unspoilt beauty; who is naïve, childlike, guileless and without shame', and who knows neither law nor ownership.[26] The poetic model is in fact closer to Aimé Césaire's epic of negritude *Cahier d'un retour au pays natal* (Notebook of a return to the native land), 1947, than to Glissant's, Dabydeen's, or Walcott's poems. (See Arnold, 1997, on the francophone negritude poets.[27])

Yet despite its location in the explicit politics of negritude, *Stemmen* does not *narrate* the African diaspora, but evokes states of being in poetic vignettes. Transport, in the spiritual sense, both as sheer movement and as its counterpart, the still point within movement, receives more poetic attention than the actual physical transportation of slaves, which merits only one fleeting reference in Canto IX. The point, in other words, is not to reclaim an irretrievable history but to bring about a state of consciousness that can be immersed in that forgotten past. In the heart of Africa, in the heart of history, time is suspended, because 'here the turning earth reached its still point, here rays condensed into a dark center'.[28] Within that still point, however, there is also the frenzy of dance that literally moves dancer and spectator into a state beyond themselves 'till the roar of the world is consumed in trance by hot dance and song'.[29] In this image Arion both suggests a point outside history to which the crushed victim of transportation can return – to a still point in time as Eliot describes – and provides a consolatory framework for contemplating the loss of self that slavery entailed. If in the Africa to which the poem returns, Africans through dance and trance experienced a loss of self into something larger – communication with the gods

– that sublime transport remains a spiritual resource even after the dislocations of slavery.

In Book III of Walcott's *Omeros*, Achille undertakes a journey to Africa. Again it is a primitive Africa represented at a time that just predates slavery. Arion may very well be conscious that his Africa is a-historical, but he does not foreground that fact. By contrast, Walcott makes explicit the fact that he has no access to an authentic historical past: Achille's visions are simulacra, 'images that flickered into real mirages' (133), a mixture of childhood fantasy, movies, and pictures. Tribal dancing is not reclaimed from a lost past, as in *Stemmen*, but is identical to festive dances performed by the grandchildren of slaves in St. Lucia. Roots are unfixed, unstable, mere reflections even, resembling, on the border of the river, 'naked mangroves walking beside him, knotted logs / wriggling into the water' (133) – an echo, of course, of Glissant's rhizomes. The journey is not one of discovery but of memory. Still conscious of the future that awaits his ancestral village, Achille is thus cast in the role of Tiresias in Book XI of the Odyssey, known as The Book of the Dead, where Odysseus visits the underworld.

With more detail than *Stemmen* or indeed *Turner* and *Les Indes*, the ancestral memory of transportation comes to life in Achille's visions. Walcott works from the specific to the type, from the village of Achille's 'father' Afolabe, to the peoples of Ashanti, Mandingo, Ibo and Guinea; and Achille's recollection of the raiding of the African villages makes a terrifying impact. Adding to the terror of that recollection is Walcott's employment of the mode of the uncanny: Achille, both here and there, seeing countless parallels between his own world and this Homeric underworld, is explicitly in a state of transport, a spirit removed from a body that lies, all the time, unconscious from sunstroke, in his little fishing craft.[30] When 'far out' (127) at sea, Achille is terrified and mesmerized by a sea-swift (or tern), like Coleridge's albatross 'the bait of the gods' (126). Losing his sense of self, at the centre of motion, or 'in the stasis of his sunstroke' (129), he becomes the swift and returns to Africa: here Walcott draws on a popular Caribbean myth about slaves escaping as birds back to Africa.[31] It is interesting that the sensation of transport is duplicated in the speaker who, near the end of Book III, visits as 'Derek' his aged mother and describes that vision in words that allude to the epic scene of Odysseus in the underworld, where he sees his mother's ghost: 'She floated so lightly' (165). And then he, too, is visited by unrecollected memories, feeling 'transported,/ past shops smelling of cod to a place I had lost' (167).

The self in transport gains access to history as a sequence of obscure images, not trite, but sublime, because they are uncanny, terrifying, mysterious. The sublime is also known for splendour, both in neoclassical and romantic aesthetics;[32] and Walcott appears to allude to this when he celebrates the survival of the former slaves, remarking that 'there is the epical splendour' (149). Édouard Glissant explores the possibilities of splendour by creating a deliberately dazzling effect that sometimes borders on a deliberate opacity of meaning. He does not shun the rhetoric of exclamation marks, ellipses, evocative 'O's, and the grand gesture of baroque metaphor, as even the first lines of his epic demonstrate. His repetitions mesmerize; his speaker is a prophet who has seen, tasted, and known all.[33] The poetic effect of the mode of splendour is thrown into relief by the Fourth Canto. Here the subject is the death and destruction of the slave trade, and the poet opts for the more sobering mode of prose, a style he apparently finds more suitable to describe horrors, although it is still quite ornate. 'Splendour is but a dream', the narrator says, envisioning the slaves' bodies 'bleeding and naked, of burnt blood, senseless nakedness'.[34] At the end of this canto, Glissant celebrates survival, just as Walcott did, thus paving the way for a return to elevated poetry. The remaining two cantos are dedicated to the praise of the goddess of liberty, and to the (West) Indies as the locus of splendour and mystery.[35]

Much of what is lofty in Glissant's epic actually obscures meaning; but that opacity is clearly part of the poetic programme to create the effect of splendour, to create the experience of the sublime. Acknowledging the presence of that opacity has to be part of any reading of this work. Although *Les Indes* is a stunning achievement, it is also baffling and, to my taste, even a little tiresome, or as another critic put it more politely, and in support of my earlier remark about the incompatibility that some critics have found between the sublime style of the epic and political commitment: it is 'hermetic and complex [...] and does not evince the characteristics of a committed writer'.[36]

Glissant sees opacity as a function of literature precisely because the writer aims at transparency, clarity, and sublimity. 'Writing', he says, 'is relative in relation to that absoluteness, making it actually opaque, an accomplice of language'.[37] But opacity is no negative value, nor is it mere obscurity: it is, he argues, the irreducible that excludes full understanding, or rather reminds us that full understanding is always impossible.[38] Without mentioning it, Glissant seems to assume Roland Barthe's distinction between a *lisible* (authoritarian) and *scriptible* (libertarian) text – and prefers the latter: opacity, therefore, escapes the limiting forces of ownership or even colonization that are implied in the power dynamics of understanding, creating a zone of free trade in meaning.

Focusing on the submerged, unknown, but irreducible and unerasable head of the drowned slave in Turner's painting *Slave Ship*, David Dabydeen's ekphrastic poem brings together all the elements of the sublime that I have discussed so far. As I have argued above, Dabydeen restores identity to the drowned slave, filling him up with memories of a youth spent in Africa, India, the West Indies, passages that alternate with reflections on the captain of the slave ship, on Turner, and on the identity of the stillborn white child that is also tossed overboard and floats towards him, also named Turner. Like *Omeros*, *Turner* is a palimpsest of earlier sublime works: as a sea poem of mystery and wonder, it inevitably refers to the *Rime of the Ancient Mariner*, as for instance to Coleridge's lines 'where terror is transformed into / Comedy'. In *Turner*, the depth of the sea is filled with 'Jaws that gulped in shoals, demons of the universe / now grin like clowns' (21). Shakespeare's *The Tempest* is another inevitable pre-text in a poem that is not only about a painting that has a 'typhoon coming on' in its title, but also a Caliban, the 'abhorred slave' as Miranda calls him, or 'nigger' as the baby identifies him (16, 28, 39). The power relation between master and slave can, the poem suggests, perhaps be disrupted, for this Caliban will lovingly 'ransack / For pearls and coral beads to drape around / Its body' (28), which is redolent of the 'sea-change' of Ariel's song, where corals and pearls figure as well.

Turner also employs the techniques of opacity. Opacity is figured in the submerged, unknowable head of the black slave whose body is visible but whose head has been 'drowned in Turner's (and other artists') sea for centuries' (ix) as Dabydeen writes in the preface. Reproductions of the painting are included in the Cape edition of *Turner*, showing a composition with a centre that is a still point of a vortex on whose violent edges a ship moves to the left of the painting (westward), whereas in the bottom right corner, much as in Brueghel's *Fall of Icarus*, one dark shackled leg and part of a body are tossed about by the waves. Moving to the right, back to Africa, the body's head actually disappears beyond the edge of the painting. So as to present the unpresentable, the poem ascribes to that head a nascent consciousness through imagery that includes the bellies of ships, cows, and mothers giving birth, guided by the fertile pull of the moon, to a stillborn baby, the suppressed (collective) unconscious that is, paradoxically, not a deep-rooted self but that rhizomatic, white other that names the slave – who tries to mother the infant – 'nigger'. The allegory of the birth of a self serves to ladle up memories of origins and prophecies of destruction, which are, like the imagining of an England 'of hedgerows that stalked the edge of fields' (23) based on images or historical vignettes. As with Derek Walcott's Achille, the retrieval of memory can never be more than the usage of simulacra, a self-conscious recirculation of images. The poem is ambiguous about whether such memories can lead to a fresh start, or whether the self and its unconscious other will merge: the baby persists in calling the slave 'nigger' and eventually floats away, unable to 'bear the future' (39). The poem concludes by winding up all these memories and denying their existence.

Creating and, it would appear, subsequently denying a stock of memories that inform the identity of the drowned slave, the poem actually performs the motion from stillness to transport and back again. That such a dynamic should occur in an ekphrastic poem

28

on Turner's *Slave Ship* is wholly appropriate. As I have indicated above, the painting displays a similar dialectic: a dynamic vortex with a still centre. The spectator / reader is involved in that movement, or as one critic puts it: 'We are in the eye of the storm, in the eye of vision [...and the still manacled body of the slave] jolts us from our assumptions of distance and space, it makes us part of that vortex'.[39] In that respect, *Turner* is reminiscent of Martinus Arion's *Stemmen uit Afrika*, where, I have argued, both the frenzy of dance and the still centre of an ancient world composed the vortex of transport. Dabydeen is, however, evidently more resistant to the implications of this sense of transport, of the loss of self, and therefore he will not wholeheartedly create the effect of the sublime that it features.

I have argued that the other three poems manifest a quality of the sublime, traditionally associated with the epic, that has a function in matching the politics of dislocation to the poetics of spiritual transport. *Turner*, although etched on the palimpsest of traditional sublime works and featuring terror, prophetic dreams and the splendour of attempted reconciliation, is in the end ambiguous (and therefore intriguing and moving) in its position vis à vis the sublime. In the penultimate canto, the slave tells how Turner (the prototype of the coloniser) suppressed their speech and instilled English, 'And we repeated in a trance the words / That shuddered from him: *blessed, angelic, / Sublime*' (38). Perhaps the sublime is rejected as false consciousness. Otherwise, the trance of transport refers to a Caribbean sublime that combines commitment to politics with a commitment to literature as a cross-cultural artefact, stopping nowhere, belonging to no one domain.

Notes to Chapter One

1.   Derek Walcott, *Omeros* (London: Faber & Faber, 1990). Following references are included in the main text. See also Fred D'Aguiar's *Bill of Rights* (1998) and *Bloodlines* (2000) as Caribbean narrative

poems, and Kwame Dawes's *Prophets* (1995) and *Jacko Jacobus* (1996), verse epics which explore both Biblical and more popular aesthetic modes.

2. David Dabydeen, *Turner* (London: Cape, 1994). Following references are included in the main text.

3. Derek Walcott, 'The Antilles, Fragments of Epic Memory: The 1992 Nobel Lecture', *World Literature Today*, 67. 2 (1993), 261-67 (p. 265).

4. Édouard Glissant, *Les Indes: Poèmes* (Paris: Seuil, [1955] 1965).

5. Frank Martinus Arion, *Stemmen uit Africa* (Rotterdam: Flamboyant, [1957] 1978).

6. *The Penguin Book of Caribbean Verse*, ed. by Paula Burnett (Harmondsworth: Penguin, 1986), p. xxiii.

7. Jean-François Lyotard, 'Answering the Question: What is Postmodernism?', in *Innovation / Renovation: New Perspectives on the Humanities*, ed. by Ihat and Sally Hassan (Madison, WI: The University of Wisconsin Press, 1983) pp. 329-41 (p. 337).

8. M. H. Abrams, *The Mirror and the Lamp* (New York: Oxford University Press, 1953), pp. 72-4.

9. Peter De Bolla, *The Discourse of the Sublime: Readings in History, Aesthetics, and the Subject* (Oxford: Blackwell, 1989), p. 36.

10. Randolph Hezekiah, 'Martinique and Guadeloupe: Time and Space', in *A History of Literature in the Caribbean*, 3 Vols, *Hispanic and Francophone Regions*, ed. by A. James Arnold et al., (Amsterdam: John Benjamins, 1994), I, pp. 379-87 (p. 382).

11. Benedict Anderson, 'Exodus', *Critical Inquiry*, 20 (1994), 315-27 (p. 316).

12. See Gilles Deleuze and Felix Guattari, *A Thousand Plateaus: Capitalism and Schizophrenia*, University of Minnesota Press, 1987.

13. See, *A History of Literature in the Caribbean*, 3 Vols, ed. by A James Arnold (Amsterdam: John Benjamins, 1997), I.

14. Édouard Glissant, *Poétique de la relation* (Paris: Gallimard, 1990), p. 31.

15. *Poétique de la relation*, 'des livres d'exil et souvent d'errance', p. 27. The second quotation is from p. 31.

16. *Poétique de la relation*, 'non pas comme une expansion de territoire [...] mais comme une recherche de l'Autre', p. 30.

17. *Les Indes*, 'Les Indes sont éternité', p. 88.

18. *Les Indes*, 'Passe le temps', pp. 104, 108 and passim.

19. 'The Antilles, Fragments of Epic Memory', 261-67 (p. 262).

20. Juris Silenieks, 'Glissant's Prophetic Vision of the Past', *African*

Literature Today, 11 (1980), 161-68 (p. 162).

21. James B. Twitchell, *Romantic Horizons: Aspects of the Sublime in English Poetry and Painting, 1770-1850* (Columbia, MO: University of Missouri Press, 1983), p. 85.

22. *The Discourse of the Sublime*, p. 37.

23. 'Answering the Question: What is Postmodernism', 329-41 (p. 337).

24. 'The Antilles, Fragments of Epic Memory', 261-67 (p. 266).

25. See, Wim Rutgers, *Schrijven is zilver is goud: Oratuur, auratuur en literatuur van de Nederlandse Antillen en Aruba* (Utrecht: n. p., 1994), p. 216.

26. *Stemmen*, 'warr de neger / in zijn ruige reinheid mint [...] alleen de oermens kan dit schone / zo intens beleven, in al zign on-/ bedorvenheid: hij, naief, kinderlijk, / en argeloos en schaamteloos, p. 27, 29.

27. *A History of Literature in the Caribbean*, Vol. 1., pp. 479-84.

28. *Stemmen*, 'hier draaide de aarde stil. / vloeiden stralen samen / tot een donker middlepunt', p. 32.

29. *Stemmen*, 'totdat in trance en hete en lied vergaat 's wereld woest en ongetemd geluid', p. 43.

30. Craft also signifying, as implied by the dedication of *Omeros* to 'my shipmates in this craft', the art of writing poetry. In this sense, the loss of self in the craft could, perhaps, be compared with T. S. Eliot's theorem of the poet's escape from personality, or self, into tradition through writing. See *Eliot*, Stephen Spender (Glasgow: Fontana Press, 1975), pp. 71-89.

31. Aart G. Broek, *Het Zilt van de Passaten: Caribische letteren van verzet* (Haarlem: In de Knipscheer, 1988), p. 111.

32. See *Romantic Horizons*, p. 14.

33. *Les Indes*, pp. 90-1.

34. *Les Indes*, 'Qui rêve de splendeur? [...] Sangland et nu, de sang brûlé, nudité folle', p. 141, 140.

35. *Les Indes*, p. 171.

36. 'Glissant's Prophetic Vision of the Past', 161-68 (p. 163).

37. *Poétique de la relation*, p. 129.

38. See, *Poétique de la relation*, pp. 205-6.

39. *Romantic Horizons*, p. 107.

CHAPTER TWO
TURNING THE COLONIAL GAZE: RE-VISIONS OF
TERROR IN DABYDEEN'S *TURNER*

TOBIAS DÖRING

The postcolonial project turns on reviewing imperial scenarios and envisioning an alternative future to their past, a project paradoxically shaped by both the gaze at history and the need to reverse this gaze and turn it back. For all the various forms and strategies that such a project may pursue – cultural articulation, political action or physical resistance – violence, inevitably, is implicated in the process. It was Frantz Fanon who, in *The Wretched of the Earth* (1961), declared decolonisation always a violent phenomenon and traced the genealogy of this violence from the ordering of the colonial world to the point where it 'will be claimed and taken over by the native at the moment when, deciding to embody history in his own person, he surges into the forbidden quarters'.[1] Significantly though, such violent insurgencies arise out of what Fanon had earlier described as 'the fact of blackness' and analysed as resulting from the encounter with the white man's eyes. In *Black Skin, White Masks* (1952) the colonial scene is reconstructed as a violence of viewing and the coloniser's power linked to the terror of his gaze. 'Look, a Negro!' goes the phrase by which, in Fanon's narration, white views imposed themselves on the black body, until 'the corporeal schema crumbled, its place taken by a racial epidermal schema [...] and I was battered down by tom-toms, cannibalism, intellectual deficiency, fetishism, racial effects, slave ships'.[2] But how may such a view be countered? This essay sets out to explore the postcolonial legacies of gazing by focusing on terror in the visual-verbal interactions of poetry and painting.

32

My key concern is with a recent text (1994) by the Guyanese-British poet David Dabydeen, an epic poem entitled *Turner* which writes itself into the vacant spaces of a celebrated painting by J.M.W. Turner, *Slave Ship (Slavers Throwing Overboard the Dead and Dying – Typhoon Coming On)*.[3] This canvas, first exhibited in the Royal Academy in 1840 and ranking among Turner's best known works, invests in the iconography of the slave trade while, at the same time, engaging the beholder's eye with an ecstasy of light and colour, culminating in the central image of a blindingly white sun. The painting derives its power and effect through the visual rhetoric of the sublime which pervades both the theme and its execution and which, on a linguistic level, also figures prominently in the imagery of Dabydeen's poem. Dabydeen's *Turner* and Turner's *Slave Ship*, therefore, would seem to sketch out an arena of discursive forces which lends itself to analysing the politics of imperial eyes as well as postcolonial vistas. My main interest lies in establishing the aesthetic strategies by which terror becomes a social energy that confers with the imperial project. As a framework for discussion I shall draw on Edmund Burke's classic *Philosophical Enquiry into the Origin of our Ideas on the Sublime and the Beautiful* (first published in 1757) to address the question of what effects terror wields in a colonising culture, how these may become commodified and who takes the profits from them. In what follows I shall raise some salient points from Burke's treatise, then look at *Turner* in more detail and finally consider what bearings the poem might have on postcolonial views of terror.

I

It may be useful, however, to start with a definition. For this purpose I shall avail myself of the erudition and wit of Stephen Dedalus who, in the fifth chapter of Joyce's *Portrait of the Artist as a Young Man*, has the following to say about the nature of terror:

> Terror is the feeling which arrests the mind in the presence of whatsoever is grave and constant in human sufferings and unites it with the secret cause.[4]

33

The context here is a debate about tragedy in the classic Aristotelian framework, with *eleos* (pity) and *phobos* (terror, fear) as key terms describing the effects that tragedy has on its spectators. It is important to note that terror is thus placed into the theatrical space, a space defined by the interactions of script with performance, enactment with spectacle, and at the same time a space most prominently organised by the activity of communal viewing. Terror in the theatre means terror that meets the eye. When Stephen Dedalus defines it as a feeling 'which arrests the mind in the presence of whatsoever is grave and constant in human sufferings', we should realise that this is first and foremost a visual presence: the spectator's vision is affected most of all. It may even be possible to generalise from the specific context of tragedy and suggest that the function of spectatorship is integral to all operations of terror. As a matter of fact, in most articulations on the subject the function of some audience is regularly assumed as an integral part in the analysis of terror. Terror seems to engage in some kind of performance which, to be effective, needs spectators, onlookers, beholders. Terror, clearly, works through gaze.

There is a further point in Stephen Dedalus's pronouncement which is worth remembering: the cryptic ending of his definition (being, in fact, the feature that distinguishes between terror and pity; the definition of pity ends, 'and unites it with the secret cause'). What it suggests is a covert identification on the spectator's part with the causes of the terror they behold. Such an act would clearly cut across the lines of division, normally assumed in discussions of this subject, between agents and victims of terror, the latter being the ones with whom we identify through empathy, while the former are cast into the role of unknown Others whose minds we can penetrate but dimly. Stephen's dictum clearly cuts across such a delimitation by insinuating some kind of secret and possibly illicit union between the perpetrators and connoisseurs of terror. Spectators are here being placed within a double bind, making common cause with a terrorist power that also threatens to destroy their privileged position. What aesthetic pleasures and political profits might be gained from such a union?

This is, in actual fact, a paraphrase of the key question which was often raised and widely discussed in eighteenth century discourses on the aesthetics of the terrible: why do spectators take pleasure in terror? The tradition may be exemplified here with reference to John and Anna Laetitia Aiken's essay 'On the Pleasures derived from Objects of Terror' (1773), which tries to explain the popular appeal of the terrible, and to Burke's famous *Enquiry*, which provided the philosophical argument which transformed the old rhetorical category of the sublime, derived from classical times, into a full-fledged aesthetic paradigm for the rise of romanticism. As could be shown in many passages from Burke's *Enquiry*, the operation of terror is integral to the sublime.

> Whatever is fitted in any sort to excite the ideas of pain and danger, that is to say, whatever is in any sort terrible, or is conversant about terrible objects, or operates in a manner analogous to terror, is a source of the sublime; that is, it is productive of the strongest emotion which the mind is capable of feeling [...] Indeed, terror is in all cases whatsoever, whether more openly or latently, the ruling principle of the sublime.[5]

While it has long been established in critical literature that the aesthetic investment in violent emotions aroused by representations of terror forms an integral part of the philosophy of the romantic sublime as well as the Gothic genre, it needs to be equally clearly established that this eighteenth century discourse is deeply informed by the rhetoric of Empire. As my subsequent examples attempt to argue, we can trace a discursively sustained and pragmatically grounded relation, on the level of cultural politics and their social energies, between sublime aesthetics and colonial desires. What eighteenth century philosophers and aesthetic writers were discussing in terms of the adventures of the imagination and its forays into fields of unknown terror, provided a rhetoric underpinning the imperial ventures of the same period. Representations of the sublime and the politics of imperialism engage in the same discourse.

To substantiate this claim, consider the following quotations. In their essay, John and Anna Laetitia Aiken write at length about the pleasure provided by objects of terror:

35

This is the pleasure constantly attached to the excitement of surprise from new and wonderful objects. A strange and unexpected event awakens the mind, and keeps it on the stretch; and where the agency of invisible beings is introduced, of 'forms unseen, and mightier far than we', our imagination, darting forth, *explores with rapture the new world* which is laid open to its view, and rejoices in *the expansion of the powers*. Passion and fancy co-operating elevate the soul to its highest pitch; and the pain of terror is lost in amazement.[6]

Their argument utilised the experience of the wonderful (Greenblatt's genealogy of wonder and the marvellous) which surmounts, as it were, the initial feeling of terror triggered by the view of 'forms unseen, and mightier far than we'. But their rhetorical reliance on figures of exploration and colonisation ('new world […] laid open to its view') and imperial expansion ('expansion of the powers') would indeed seem to suggest that our pleasures in terror derive from the gratification of domesticating a threat by subjecting it to our power.

In Burke's treatise, too, terror and the sublime are functionally linked with the operation of power. In Part II, Section V, Burke declares 'that power derives all its sublimity from the terror with which it is generally accompanied', thus emphasising the need to invest in terror as a means to represent power and make it effective.[7] That this chiefly concerns imperial power, is suggested through the images and narrative examples Burke chooses to illustrate his philosophical claims. The destruction of the imperial metropolis of London is, albeit hypothetically, cited to provide a spectacle of terror to the analysing eyes, the fall of empire and the crumbling away of imperial power thus serving as discursive figures of displacement to act out colonial anxieties on the stage of the sublime.[8] Burke thoroughly embeds his new aesthetic paradigm in the contemporary imperial idiom while representing the operation of the sublime as parallel to the structure of colonialism with subjection, overpowerment, and enslavement as the crucial functions. This analysis is indebted to Sara Suleri who argues that the sublime 'functions as a conduit between the delusional aspects of empire-building or breaking and the very solidity of history', and concludes that 'the functioning of the sublime is dependent on the spectator's guilty recognition of his complicity in the rise and the decline of the process of empowerment'.[9] The final point, incidentally, refers us back to Stephen Dedalus and his insistence on the spectator's union with the secret cause of terror.

But Burke, even while stabilising the functional interrelationship between power and visions of terror, also encounters a crucial problem which concerns the representation of the terrible. Even if power, as quoted earlier, is in constant need of terror to represent itself, that is, to become present, visible, effective and sensuous, terror still remains essentially elusive. It eludes its own representation, rendering most efforts to this effect ridiculous. As Burke well recognises, the vision of terror often becomes a version of comedy, verging on grotesquery and producing the opposite effect on the spectators by causing laughter and hilarity. True terror, Burke shrewdly observes, must be kept obscure in its representations, for sublimity can only work its power on the basis of 'the terrible uncertainty of the thing described'.[10] The cultural representation of terror is thus caught up in an ambiguity: designed, on the one hand, to produce visible manifestations of imperial power, terror must, on the other hand, pursue a strategy of obscurity which constantly dissolves the vision it tries to establish.

Significantly, Burke here explicitly refers to painting and the visual arts when he explains the ambiguous process of representing terror:

> When painters have attempted to give us clear representations of those very fanciful and terrible ideas, they have I think almost always failed; in so much that I have been at a loss in all the pictures I have seen of hell, whether the painter did not intend something ludicrous.[11]

The full, clear and detailed representation of the terrible fails when it succeeds too fully. The aesthetics of terror is thus undercut by the very significatory process which should give it visual representation. If power needs terror to become effective, terror is haunted by the power of comedy, even while trying to establish these very effects. This ambivalence is not an idiosyncratic observation on Burke's part. The same claim was, in fact, made about Turner's *Slave Ship* almost a hundred years later. Writing for *Frazer's* magazine (under the pen-name Michael Angelo Titmarsh) W.M. Thackeray considered the painting to be 'the most tremendous piece of colour that ever was seen', even though he could not be sure whether it was 'sublime or ridiculous' in its effect.[12]

II

Against the background of the foregoing discussion consider the following quote:

> I should have sunk
> To these depths, where terror is transformed into
> Comedy, where the sea, with an undertaker's
> Touch, soothes and erases pain from the faces
> Of drowned sailors. (21)

These lines seem to speak of such a transformation process, turning terror into comedy, and they do so within a context specifically related to the politics of sublime painting. They are from a central passage of David Dabydeen's epic poem *Turner*. Their deictic reference to the first person singular signifies the poetic persona and fictional subjectivity which can be reconstructed from the poem's complex layers of memory and desire, fantasy and frustration. What emerges is a voice that speaks out of a constitutive blank in Turner's art, reinventing the body and history of a submerged African slave, tossed overboard during the Middle Passage, drowning in the shark-infested sea and figuring as a dismembered presence in the foreground of the painting.

As a matter of fact, Turner's *Slave Ship* depicts an actual scene from the archives of the British slave trade: the case of the *Zong* of 1783, a slave ship whose cargo was so badly affected by an epidemic that Captain Collingwood used the opportunity of an oncoming storm to throw 122 sick men and women into the sea. The reasoning for this was a financial calculation: he could claim insurance for Africans lost at sea, but not for those dying of disease.

The case was tried in England (but no criminal charges brought against the *Zong's* masters) and became a stock example in abolitionist campaigns (only a year before Turner's painting was exhibited, Clarkson's *History of the Abolition of Slave Trade*, in which the story is told, was republished).

Turner painted the scene, a culmination of the trade's cruelties, shortly after slavery had been officially abolished in the British territories, but as Marina Warner aptly puts it:

> his approach sublimates the theme: the drownings scarcely appear. One black leg shackled at the ankle, breaks the surface of the seething water like a splintered spar in the foreground; alongside, pairs of hands are raised to make imploring gestures which rhyme – with ghastly irony – with the fins of many fish cresting the waves as they arrive for the feast. Huge links of chain thrash in the water, rather implausibly, but marking the position of submerged bodies below.[13]

In an act of marine archaeology, Dabydeen's text sets out to excavate what has been culturally submerged in the sea of the sublime: the presence of the African. As the poet writes in his preface:

> It has been drowned in Turner's (and other artists') sea for centuries. When it awakens it can only partially recall the sources of its life, so it invents a body, a biography, and peoples an imagined landscape. (ix)

With such inventions recasting the figures of a fragmented history and creating imaginative spaces between amnesia and memory, this poem continues the cultural project of Dabydeen's work so far (two collections of poetry, five novels, and a number of scholarly books, among them a study of Hogarth's blacks), a project which he refers to as 'the pornography of Empire'.

More specifically, the poem engages in a critique of the cultural commodifications by which the terrors of the trade have become transfigured as aesthetic objects produced for the delectation of spectators and perceived as icons within English identity construction. Turner's painting has been made a central agent for this process through the championship of John Ruskin, who in the first volume of *Modern Painters* declared the picture an unsurpassable masterpiece: 'If I were to rest Turner's immortality upon any single work, I should choose this.'[14] In a famous eulogy, Ruskin went on to celebrate 'its daring conception', its 'absolutely perfect' colour, and its dedication 'to the most sublime of subjects and impressions [...] the power, majesty, and deathfulness of the open, illimitable sea', but not once giving a single indication of what the painting represents on a historical level.[15] The drowning of the slaves is relegated to a brief footnote, 'an afterthought, something tossed overboard' (ix). In this way, Ruskin's enthusiastic appreciation translates the terrible subject of Turner's painting into an aesthetic of non-representation, effacing the historical powers at work and establishing the very covert complicity between terror and the connoisseur that has been pointed out earlier in this essay. While slavery is drowned in the sublime seascape, visual diffuseness and obscurity prevail, culminating in the terrible nothingness of the white sun. Turner's painting of the Middle Passage, as well as Ruskin's eulogy, reap the profits of compassion. Dabydeen's poem brilliantly captures this aesthetic attitude with the phrase 'anchored in compassion / And for profit's sake' (1).

In a long and searching process of poetic reconfiguration (extending over 25 stanzas and 783 lines), *Turner* traces the cultural undercurrents of sublime representation and, through the presence of language, retrieves some of the historical power lost in Turner's sea. But the poem does not do so, as it were, by rattling the chains of slavery. It does not engage in discourses of victimhood, but transgresses the dichotomies imposed by terror through a complex strategy of doubling imagery and multiple inscribed meanings. How, then, can *Turner* avoid getting trapped in the simple reproduction of imperial desires and anxieties? Can the text reinvent at all a voice submerged by colonial iconography without immersing itself in the very idiom it sets out to revise? The answer is that the postcolonial poem does both: it proceeds in a deeply ambiguous fashion, with a contradictory reliance on and resistance to the cultural authority that historically preceded and discursively dominated the very position which it must now reclaim.

Formally, this ambiguity is evident in the consistent use of iambic pentameter as the basic metric pattern, which aligns the Caribbean poem's shape with the conventions of English writing and would seem to defy Kamau Brathwaite's famous statement regarding Caribbean poetry, that 'the hurricane does not howl in pentameters'.[16] Its apparent formal disregard for Creole oratory and Caribbean rhythm, however, only points to the poem's precarious position at the eye of the storm, so to speak, which it constructs for itself at the discursive intersection of Old and New World voices. Dabydeen's poem evokes a storm that does not howl like Brathwaite's Caribbean hurricane; its voice has crossed the English echo-chamber and speaks of a typhoon so thoroughly English that it comes close to the 'plague-wind and plague-cloud' which Ruskin, in his later life, noted with gloomy resignation. In 1884 Ruskin lectured to a London audience on 'The Storm-Cloud of the Nineteenth Century', relating his meteorological observations on new disturbing phenomenon in English weather (claiming 'had the weather when I was young been such as it is now, no books such as *Modern Painters* ever would have been written') and, from the inventory of metaphors of heat and wind that he assembled, intimating the entropic end of Empire, he declared that 'the Empire of England, on which formerly the sun never set, has become one on which it never rises'.[17] The oncoming storm that Turner's painting refers to in its title may indeed blow from the same direction.

The same ambiguity which characterises *Turner*'s metric shape also informs the central image of the sea which pervades the whole poem and provides both the topos of terror (celebrated by Ruskin in *Modern Painters*) and the counter-trope of cleansing and renewal. The sea is an active agent for much of the poem's imagery; the sea divides and unites (6), decorates and violates (9), cleanses and bleaches (14), paints and disguises (14-16), gives and erases pain (21); with such ambivalent characterisations recreating the terror of the trade as well as the desire of memory to remake the historical experience.

The double inscription of imagery is already operative in the very first lines of the poem:

41

Stillborn from all the signs. First a woman sobs
Above the creaking of the timbers and the cleaving
Of the sea, sobs from the depths of true
Hurt and grief, as you will never hear
But from woman giving birth, belly
Blown and flapping loose and torn like sails,
Rough sailor's hands jerking and tugging
At ropes of veins, to no avail. Blood vessels
Burst asunder, all below-deck are drowned.
Afterwards, stillness (1)

This may be read as a twofold layer of meanings through images superimposed and emerging from a figurative structure that re-enacts the historical dynamics in the trade and trauma of the Middle Passage. On one level, what is being evoked are the pains of a labouring mother at the moment of abortive birth. On another level, the imagery is derived from the inventory of navigation: expressions such as 'creak of timber', 'cleaving of the sea' or 'jerking and tugging', signify moments in the process of giving birth, just as they refer to seafaring experience. With the phrase 'belly blown and flapping loose and torn like sails' the rhetorical operation of simile shows how the language of birth is displaced by the language of navigation; the two vocabularies are not so much fused as jarringly juxtaposed. Most evidently, the different semantic and symbolic levels of mothering and sailing are mutually subjected to condensation and displacement in the term 'blood-vessels', which signifies, metaphorically, the ship that carries slaves as well as, metonymically, the veins that carry blood.

In this way, the very opening of the poem symbolically contrasts and unites the two sides of historical slave experience and opens up the terrible tension between them. The *topos* 'Mother', on the one hand, comprises claims of origin and belonging, of home and Africa; the *topos* 'Ship', on the other hand, stands for passage and loss, alienation and cultural displacement. The power that unites the two *topoi*, in the language of the poem, is the image of the sea which, on the one hand, signifies the amniotic fluids of the motherly womb while, on the other hand, representing the medium of the Middle Passage, the agent of terror and trade.

Floating bodiless in the sea, the lyrical persona of the poem longs to reunite with its invented origins of an idyllic African childhood, memories of which constantly surface in the streams of the text. It attempts 'to begin anew in the sea' (39) by imaginatively conjuring up a history unburdened by the pain of displacement. Yet its desire is finally frustrated, because it cannot, as Dabydeen writes in the preface, escape Turner's representation as 'exotic and sublime victim'; nor can it describe itself anew, but is 'indelibly stained by Turner's language and imagery' (x). Thus is the effect of the beholder's gaze, of our gaze, by which the slave is being tossed and held in the sea.

It is only consistent, therefore, that the poem ends not with an affirmative triumph of liberation but with a long sequence of negations that all revoke the *topos* of motherhood, which formally structured the thematic substance of the slave's memory. The final lines read:

> No savannah, moon, gods, magicians
> To heal or curse, harvests, ceremonies,
> No men to plough, corn to fatten the herds,
> No stars, no land, no words, no community,
> No mother. (39)

With this conclusion the poem re-enacts the predicament of postcolonial cultures of the Caribbean, historically shaped by European image-making and, in a revisionary effort, now trying to move beyond the representations provided for them from elsewhere. But a simple substitution of African dreams for colonial nightmares will not do either. For the New World memory, the slave trade forms the link to as well as the severance from the cultural past. What remains when the sea of recollection has subsided is the journey as a figure of transition. It is on this that a postcolonial Caribbean-British text like *Turner* must stake its claims. Nor would Dabydeen seem to be the only New World/Old World writer working in the precarious space sketched out by these ambiguous forces. It was the Martinican poet Édouard Glissant who argued that the slave trade 'has fixed us in the unceasing tug of Africa against which we must paradoxically struggle in order to take root in our rightful land. The motherland is also for us the inaccessible land'.[18]

Where, then, does this lead us with regard to investigating the culture of colonial terror? After my brief interpretation of Dabydeen's poem, the question now remains what its postcolonial strategies of rhetorical revision imply for the aesthetic views of the terrible. In this final section I will therefore take up some points raised at the beginning of this essay and consider them in the framework provided by *Turner*.

If my reading of Burke suggested that terror turns out to be uncannily unrepresentable so that it can only work through obscurity and darkness, it may now be possible to venture some discursive explanation. The aesthetics of the sublime rely on strategies of invisibility because the representation of terror proceeds from the politics of slavery. This is, at any rate, suggested by a closer look at the 1840s which provides the relevant historical context. What we find at this point in English culture, shortly after the abolition of slavery, is the intersection of two discourses: the abolitionist rhetoric of liberal humanism and the aesthetics of terrible emotions searched for by romanticism. My claim is that slavery as a topic of discourse, whilst historically belonging to the former, became an integral part of the latter.

In 1840, the same year that Turner exhibited his *Slave Ship*, the leading abolitionist of the period, Fowler Buxton, published a treatise entitled *The African Slave Ship and its Remedy* in which he argued that the evil of slavery had to be tackled at its real roots, namely in Africa, whence all the abominations originated in the practice of indigenous societies – a host of horrors which, now that the legislative home battle had been won, was urgently in need of British enlightenment and moral correction. As Patrick Brantlinger has comprehensively documented, the *topos* of 'Africa as the Dark Continent' was constructed through the abolitionist culture of blame and its displacement upon Africa as the *prima causa* of slavery.[19] For decades, these campaigns invested in a rhetoric of abomination which, while ostensibly attacking the horrors of the trade, produced new protagonists of terror: the dark, inhuman African. This, in turn, was transformed into the cultural productions of the time. The point is made by Dabydeen when he, in a recent interview, explains that:

> there is something very voyeuristic about Turner's response to all that blood and mayhem, in the same way that slavery provided the horror that fed into the Gothic novel at the turn of the 18th century: all that horror and Neo-Gothicism partly fed on the descriptions of slavery, the shark, the broken nigger, the blood.[20]

Significantly though, this cultural transformation was prefigured and prepared by the aesthetic discourse of the 18th century and can, in fact, be traced even in the *Enquiry*. For in Burke's philosophical construction it appears that the sublime is racially encoded. One of his key examples involves an African as the prime conduit for what he argues is a naturally induced experience of terror. In Part IV, Section XV (entitled 'Darkness terrible in its own nature'), Burke relates the story of a boy born blind and having later regained his sight who, 'upon accidentally seeing a negro woman, was struck with great horror', the implication being that blackness is inherently terrible to the human nature, prior to any cultural associations.[21]

Against the background of the foregoing discussion, however, it might be plausible to reverse this argument. Since Africans, for the culture of colonialism, had to be socially invalidated and muted, they were consistently rendered invisible to the European gaze. What developed from this was, firstly, the aesthetics of the obscure and indistinct as evinced in Turner's *Slave Ship*, and secondly, the rhetoric of the unspeakable, leading directly to Marlow's 'unspeakable rites' and the horrors of the *Heart of Darkness*. The only licence for blacks to claim a visible presence on the colonial stage was to act as comic characters, as stock types in the tradition of the minstrel show: terror transformed into comedy.

Burke identifies the terrible effect of black bodies as resulting from their visual vacuity which disturbs the sense of sight because our gaze falls into nothingness.[22] In Dabydeen's *Turner*, such vacant spaces turn out to be aesthetically constructed as passive victims, invisible presences which suddenly become invested with a cultural agency as they return our terrorising gaze even in the act of reading.

Notes to Chapter Two

1. Frantz Fanon, *The Wretched of the Earth* (London: MacGibbon & Kee, 1986), p. 33.
2. Frantz Fanon, *Black Skin, White Masks* (London: Pluto Press, 1986), p. 112.
3. David Dabydeen, *Turner: New and Selected Poems*, (London: Cape, 1994). Further references will be included in the main text of the essay.
4. James Joyce, *A Portrait of the Artist as a Young Man* (London: Paladin, 1988), p. 209.
5. Edmund Burke, *A Philosophical Enquiry into the Origin of our Ideas of the Sublime and the Beautiful*, ed. by A. Philips (Oxford: Oxford University Press, 1990), pp. 34, 54.
6. John & Anna Laetitia Aikin, 'On the Pleasures derived from Objects of Terror', in *Miscellaneous Pieces in Prose* (London, 1773), p. 125, emphasis added.
7. *A Philosophical Enquiry*, p. 60.
8. Ibid., see p. 44.
9. Sara Suleri, *The Rhetoric of English India* (Chicago and London: University of Chicago Press, 1993), p. 38.
10. *A Philosophical Enquiry*, p. 58.
11. Ibid., p. 58.
12. Quoted according to Robert K Wallace, *Melville and Turner: Spheres of Love and Fright* (Athens and London: University of Georgia Press, 1992), p. 68.
13. Marina Warner, 'Cannibal Tales: The Hunger for Conquest', in *Managing Monsters: Six Myths of our Times*, The Reith Lectures (London: Virago, 1994), p. 66.
14. John Ruskin, 'Of Water as Painted by Turner', in *Modern Painters*, ed. by David Barrie (London: Deutch, 1978), p. 160.
15. Ibid.

16. Edward Kamau Brathwaite, *History of the Voice: The Development of Nation Language in Anglophone Caribbean Poetry* (London: New Beacon Books, 1984), p. 10.

17. John Ruskin, 'The Storm-Cloud of the Nineteenth Century', in *The Norton Anthology of English Literature*, 5th edn, (New York and London: Norton, 1986), p. 1353.

18. Edouard Glissant, *Caribbean Discourses: Selected Essays*, trans. by J. Michael Dash (Ithaca and London: Cornell University Press, 1988), p. 177.

19. See Patrick Brantlinger, *Rule of Darkness: British Literature and Imperialism, 1830-1914* (Ithaca and London: Cornell University Press, 1988), p. 177.

20. Tobias Döring and Heike Härting, 'Amphibian Hermaphrodites: Marina Warner and David Dabydeen in Dialogue', *Third Text*, 30 (Spring 1995), p.43.

21. *A Philosophical Enquiry*, p. 131.

22. Ibid., see Part IV, Section XVII, p. 133.

CHAPTER THREE

PAINTING, PERVERSION, AND THE POLITICS OF CULTURAL TRANSFIGURATION IN DAVID DABYDEEN'S *TURNER*

HEIKE H. HÄRTING

In her lecture 'History and Imagination: Writing *At the Full and Change of the Moon*', the Caribbean Canadian writer Dionne Brand remarked enigmatically that 'Walcott's line 'The sea is History' is a poem he has not yet written'[1] – enigmatic given that 'The Sea is History' is the title of Walcott's seminal and perhaps most frequently quoted poem. Brand goes on to draw attention to the historical, cultural, and aesthetic significance of the sea metaphor in Caribbean writing and literary history. If Walcott's generation helped translate the sea's imperial inscriptions of dispossession and the Middle Passage into a symbolic space of new beginnings, the younger generation of Caribbean writers now inhabits this space and submits it to a critical revision. Unlike Walcott, however, Brand and Dabydeen are reluctant to keep faith with the transformative power of historical amnesia. Instead, they locate their narratives of postcolonial histories and identities in the gaps between 'nation and empire'.[2] From different diasporic perspectives, their works advance an intricate critique of both cultural originality, and the imperial tenets that continue to shape the political and national unconscious of Western modernity.

Such a critique, as Dabydeen's long poem *Turner* suggests, at once acknowledges and positions itself against earlier Caribbean writers' attempts at reinventing Caribbean history and identity through processes of cultural transfiguration and reconciliation.[3] With its Christian connotations and promise of historical redemption, the idea of transfiguration commonly refers to a ritual process of transforming and synthesizing conflicting identities through metaphorical operations of substitution and transference. Dabydeen's *Turner*, I propose, invites us to examine the ways in which the conceptual links between metaphor and transfiguration constitute practices of representation embedded in imperialism. More specifically, in *Turner*, Dabydeen uses metaphor in a way that cannot be reduced to a rhetorical device of imperial mastery and identity formation. Instead, by elucidating the contradictory practices of imperial and national representations of race and sexuality, metaphor functions as a trope of cultural crisis. Furthermore, while I agree in part with critics such as Paula Burnett, who argues that recent Caribbean writing deals primarily with 'deconstructing history as rape and sadism', I also believe that a critique of *Turner* cannot be restricted to an analysis of slavery's atrocities.[4] Rather, it must account for both the ideological continuities between empire and England's modern narrative of the nation, and for the historical construction of imperial subjects inside and outside England's national boundaries.

This essay is divided into four parts, the first of which discusses *Turner*'s preface in the context of recent postcolonial discourses concerning cultural transfiguration, and examines the effects that the preface may have on the reader. In order to illustrate how *Turner*'s metaphorical orchestration intervenes in England's normative practices of imperial and national self-consolidation, the following three parts discuss *Turner*'s organizing metaphors of the moon, the child, and the prostitute. However, my analytical focus on *Turner*'s metaphors should not be mistaken for a formalist reading of Dabydeen's text. On the contrary, I argue that the aesthetic configurations of *Turner* denote and, to a large degree, facilitate the poem's political project: by harnessing the ambivalence of metaphor, of being at once an overdetermined and self-subversive trope, to the discursive refractions of empire, Dabydeen's poem demonstrates that the desire for cultural transfiguration is itself embedded in the discourse of imperialism and that this renders direct and unmediated forms of self-reinvention impossible.

In the preface to *Turner*, Dabydeen provides his readers with an explanation of his own text. The poem, he writes, gives voice to the 'submerged head of the African in the foreground of Turner's painting' (xi); *Slave Ship (Slavers Throwing Overboard the Dead and Dying, Typhoon Coming on)* (1840). However, in 'Turner's (and other artists') sea' the African's attempts at self-reinvention fail; his 'real desire' is for an absolute cultural originality. Yet, realizing that he cannot position himself outside of history, he is forced to 'recogni[ze] himself as "nigger"'. The desire for transfiguration or newness or creative amnesia is frustrated' (x). His wish to mother another stillborn child tossed overboard 'from a future ship' is equally frustrated because '[n]either can escape Turner's representation of them as exotic and sublime victims. Neither can describe themselves anew but are indelibly stained by Turner's language and imagery' (x). The repetition of 'neither' as a negative subject prompts us to ask to what extent it is possible to resist imperially shaped and historically naturalized forms of cultural representation. How can one write in the ambiguous space of modernity, a space which, in the context of the poem, refers to the '"colonial" disjunction of modern times and colonial and slave histories, where the reinvention of the self and the remaking of the social are strictly out of joint'.[5]

By prefacing *Turner* with an apparently authoritative reading of his own text, Dabydeen invites the reader to acknowledge his presumably authentic and representative status as a postcolonial writer. The invitation seems alluring insofar as it appears to assign the reader of postcolonial texts a number of hidden expectations and then questions them. More precisely, the preface alludes to such reading practices that perceive an unquestioned truth-value in the voice of the oppressed and make the postcolonial writer the representative mouthpiece of an supposedly racially and culturally homogenized collective. Reading practices of this sort risk obscuring the role and position of the reader as well as the numerous conflicts and tensions entailed in the production of cultural difference. These practices, as Gayatri Spivak reminds us, tend to evaluate postcolonial texts not on their own terms but on the grounds of the reader's own 'interested desire to conserve the subject of the West, or the West as Subject'.[6] Furthermore, to read postcolonial texts merely through their assumed cultural marginalization reinforces the binarisms of victim and aggressor, colonized and coloniser, blame and guilt, and subsequently reproduces imperial power relations. The preface and the poem, then, throw the reader back onto his or her own unacknowledged reading desires, and make him or her complicit with some of the regulatory discourses of empire. Indeed, given that the refracting and domesticating strategies of imperialism have made an absolute division into Self and Other impossible, the reader or/and critic is always already implicated in the hegemonic discourses she seeks to dismantle.[7]

By making the reader a complicit actor in the theatre of imperialism, the preface positions the reader as a spectator, aligning the reader of *Turner* with the viewer of Turner's sublime painting. In much the same way as the techniques of Greek tragedy, the aesthetic effects of the sublime, namely the generation of emotions of terror, pity, and catharsis, depend on evoking the spectator's empathy. In his essay 'Turning the Colonial Gaze: Re-Visions of Terror in Dabydeen's *Turner*', Tobias Döring explains that terror chiefly works through the technologies of 'the gaze', and needs spectators to operate effectively. Taking his cue from James Joyce's articulation of terror,[8] Döring suggests that dramatizations of terror effect 'a covert identification by the spectators with the causes of terror they behold' so that 'spectators are [...] being placed within a double bind, making common cause with a terrorist power that also threatens to destroy their privileged position'.[9] By casting its readers in the position of spectators, literally before the poem/painting, Dabydeen's preface draws the reader into the operations of terror and indicates the reader's complicit identification with the humanist causes and contradictions of both empire and modernity.[10]

If the act of reading enables a form of agency, we need to examine our own colonizing and colonized reading desires in terms of a critical politics of transfiguration. I would like to distinguish three forms of transfiguration pertinent to a reading of metaphor in

Turner: imperial self-transfiguration, plural, and self-affirmative forms of transfiguration. Along with critics such as Gayatri Spivak, Edward Said and Simon Gikandi, I understand imperial self-transfiguration as a process of Othering. This process establishes a continuity between imperial ideologies of cultural control and English nation formation through the construction of race as a universal (i.e. 'everybody has a race') and particular (i.e. 'everybody belongs to a specific race and must be evaluated accordingly') phenomenon. In the discourse of nation formation, this division between the universal and the particular, as Benedict Anderson observes, enables the building and defence of national boundaries. In imperial discourses of identity formation, the division produces a dominant imperial Self against a disavowed black Other. The colonial Other, as Gikandi convincingly argues, has a supplemental and symbolic function, 'endow[ing] England with a romantic notion of its own powers' and 'provid[ing] the figures of alterity that would reinforce the civilizing authority of Englishness' during moments of national crisis.[11] Indeed, by criticizing the moral decay brought about by nineteenth century British predatory capitalism through the representational vehicle of the slave trade, Turner's *Slave Ship* employs blackness as a metaphorical mirror for the degenerated imperial self. One may argue that the painting's own mission is to remind the viewer of England's former majestic power, and thus to overcome the moment of national crisis. The painting, then, employs a critique of empire in order to facilitate a practice of imperial self-transfiguration. *Turner*, in contrast, suggests we read this moment of crisis as an integral and constitutive force of England's national narrative.

The pluralist notion of transfiguration refers to a specific but not uncommon critical response to Dabydeen's poem, or to what Aleid Fokkema generally terms 'Caribbean epic writing'.[12] In her article 'Caribbean Sublime: Transporting the slave; transporting the spirit', Fokkema classifies Walcott's *Omeros* and Dabydeen's *Turner* as 'Caribbean epics'. While Fokkema admits that the sublime would appear to have nothing to offer to the postcolonial 'struggle over representation', she contends that these Caribbean epics are 'shot through with both the sublimity of the Enlightenment and that of Romanticism' and 'display a postmodern fascination with the unpresentable'. If the sublime strives for a 'spiritual transport' or movement of the reader, Fokkema argues, then the Caribbean sublime connects this spiritual experience with the literal transport of slaves and envisions a Caribbean wanderer without unitary roots but not without identity. Drawing from Deleuze's and Guattari's notion of the rhizome, Fokkema suggests that the Caribbean sublime generally articulates a 'truly rhizomatic [Caribbean] identity', combining 'commitment to politics with a commitment to literature as a cross-cultural artefact, stopping nowhere, belonging to no one domain'.[13] In other words, Fokkema suggests a relational and plural concept of a cross-cultural Caribbean identity.

What, we may ask, are the ideological implications of combining the notion of the rhizome with the aesthetic of the sublime in a postcolonial context? Fokkema and other Caribbean critics read the rhizome as an assemblage of infinitely combinative fragments that do not dispense with the notion of identity. Yet a rhizomatic identity also posits all of its fragments in equal relation to one another and emphasizes movements and states rather than bodily fixity as the condition of identity formation. In this context, the notion of the rhizome erases the particular memories and histories inscribed in and constitutive of gendered and racialized bodies in favour of a more universal notion of becoming. In contrast to Fokkema, I will argue that the sublime equally invests in the erasure of bodies to produce gothic landscapes, and in an appropriation of racialized bodies as representational vehicles to inspire awe and terror in the beholder or reader of sublime art. The absence of a living body in *Turner* indicates that the presumed unrepresentableness of the sublime cannot be read outside the violation of the black body: it is precisely this violation of the body which has become unrepresentable and naturalized in the aesthetic configurations of the sublime. Neither the drowned African nor the stillborn child can assemble an identity out of fragments that are steeped in specific historical discourses of representation. If we understand a rhizomatic identity as a combined series of largely dehistoricized differences, then the desire for such an identity also embodies a pluralist vision of identity that transcends historical contradictions. In order to formulate cross-culturalism in terms which do not dispense with cultural conflict, it is necessary to investigate representations of moments of imperial crisis and the ways in which they produce and abuse colonial spaces of alterity as a foil for contemporary images of racial Otherness. In contrast to Fokkema, I argue that Dabydeen's *Turner* does not draw on the conventions of the sublime in order to construct a rhizomatic cultural identity. Rather, the poem dramatizes the ways in which the sublime eroticizes violence and sublimates the repressed sexual anxieties and desires that fuel the pornographic fantasies of empire.

Unlike Fokkema's notion of transfiguration, Paul Gilroy's advocacy for a critical politics of transfiguration suggests a self-affirmative approach towards the articulation of black British art and identity. Gilroy points out that the 'politics of transfiguration' does not refer to 'a counter discourse but a counter culture that defiantly constructs its own critical, intellectual and moral genealogy anew in a partially hidden public sphere of its own. The politics of transfiguration therefore reveals the internal problems in the concept of modernity'.[14] Critically, Gilroy acknowledges that 'The Other Story', the story of the former slave and racialised Other, cannot be neatly separated from the imperial formations of the English nation. Elsewhere Gilroy maintains that there is the 'desire to make art out of being both black and English' so as to recode the 'cultural core of national life'.[15] Yet his understanding of the 'politics of transfiguration' rarely considers the ways in which imperialism produces its Others within England. For example, in his discussion of Turner's *Slave Ship*, Gilroy traces the ambiguous reception of the painting, ranging from Ruskin's national idolatry, to his later disavowal of the painting, to its defamation as an 'absurd rather than sublime' work of art.[16] Gilroy concludes that it is the painting's 'strange history' that 'pose[s] a challenge to the black English today. It demands that we strive to integrate the different dimensions of our hybrid cultural heritage more effectively'. However, Gilroy's analysis does not address J. M. W. Turner's alienated and marginalized position within Victorian society; a position which is, as Dabydeen's *Turner* suggests, at once linked to and separate from postcolonial concerns of identity formation. More specifically, it is the conflict between the desire to integrate disparate histories and the impossibility of doing so which links Turner's painting to postcolonial concerns. Moreover, Dabydeen's dramatization of *Slave Ship* illustrates the ways in which the techniques of imperial normalization of England's domestic life intersect with Britain's colonial enterprise. In contrast to Turner's painting, however, Dabydeen's poem implies that the desire to integrate or harmonize historical contradictions is fallacious. This does not imply that we should abandon Turner's art: on the contrary, as an ambiguous artist of empire, Turner needs to be claimed as an element of England's racially hybrid narrative of nation.

A critical politics of transfiguration can then neither do away with the violent reality of racism, nor make this reality the sole ground to which postcolonial cultural representations must return. At the same time, it must examine how the aesthetic particularities of postcolonial texts inform their political concerns. What I am interested in, therefore, is the different ways in which *Turner* dramatizes the incessant erasures and reinscriptions of metaphorical meaning in order to forestall facile processes of cultural transfiguration. Upon encountering another 'part-born' child 'tossed overboard' (1) from another slave ship, the dead African, the narrative voice of Dabydeen's poem, 'name[s] it Turner' (1). He hopes 'to begin anew in the sea' (39), and wants to craft and shape 'this creature's bone and cell and word beyond / Memory of obscene human form' (28). But the stillborn child refuses to be the receptacle of the African's hope for new beginnings: '"Nigger!" it cried, seeing / Through the sea's disguise as only children can, / Recognizing [him] below [his] skin long since / washed clean of the colour of sin' (16). '"Nigger," it cries, naming [him] from some hoard / Of superior knowledge [...] "Nigger", / It cries, sensing its own deformity' (28). In this passage the endless repetition of history inhibits transfigurative processes and makes it impossible for the stillborn child to locate itself outside of history. Names are no longer unique, and metaphors are no longer brilliant inventions, but clusters of obscured and defiled histories, stalling cultural reinvention. The child refuses to make this history of loss and victimization the agent of change, for this strategy of resistance often works within the Manichean operations of dominant historiography.[17] Rather than discovering the hoped for possibility of new origins, the African contemplates resistance in terms of either nativist self-invention, or assimilationist strategies, through which he 'should have sunk / To these depths, where terror is transformed into / Comedy' (21).[18] The African soon realizes that all of these strategies merely mimic the master's voice, and repeat 'the ancient formulae of Empire' (28) in its self-consolidating practices of naming, classifying, and controlling the cultural Other.

The child, who acts as both the African's unconscious and an agent of history, asserts its authority by uttering its fragmented memory of violence through the language of metaphor: it interpellates, to use Althusser's term, the African into history by naming him 'Nigger', and thus forces him to acknowledge that his unconscious and his historical origins are subject to discursive formations of power. However, the partly disembodied condition of the child points to a process of physical erosion, a process that is also characteristic of metaphorical operations. According to Jacques Derrida's understanding of metaphor, it is the effacement of a physical image inscribed in metaphor that enables metaphorical operations of substitution and sublimation. If an idealist concept of metaphor erases the trope's physical ground by synthesizing metaphor's tenor and vehicle, Dabydeen's poem, to use another metaphor, experiments with a sort of rhetorical disfigurement. More specifically, the metaphor of the stillborn child is possibly a metaphor without ground; a metaphor that denies its constitutive bodily inscriptions and thereby impedes metaphor's synthesizing operations. From a postcolonial perspective, such a reading of metaphor enables us to see that metaphor can never advance from a natural, unhampered physical ground, for it is the violated black body that conditions metaphor as a representational vehicle of the various aesthetic and political narratives of empire. The metaphor of the stillborn child, then, historicizes what seems to be natural in metaphorical operations and thus guards against a transfiguration of representational violence.

II

In order to understand the desire for cultural transfiguration as a product of imperial techniques of cultural representation, we need to examine the ways in which *Turner*, first, orchestrates the paradoxical effects of metaphor, and second, employs the metaphor of the moon to foreground the contradictory narratives of empire inscribed in J.M.W. Turner's earlier painting *The Parting of Hero and Leander*, which is discussed below. Fragment XII of the poem begins with the African's awareness that '[t]he sea has brought [him] tribute from many lands', and yet 'mocked and beggared' (17) him. The 'tribute' is quickly recognized as 'counterfeit goods'. '[S]crolls in different letterings' and 'the babbling / Of dying sailors' become a 'means to languages / And the wisdom of other tribes' (17). A grave of sailors and slaves, the sea contains a second Tower of Babel where languages have lost their familiar reference systems in the history of slavery. Obliterated, mixed, and assembled from different countries, from old and new traditions, the creolized languages of the Caribbean, to paraphrase Kamau Brathwaite, function as tool and tomb, reflecting the historical discontinuities and paradoxes of Caribbean history. In *Turner*, the imperial legacies of language the African finds in the sea appear as a paradox and generate a silence marked by terror, a negative space without 'land' and 'voice' (17).

This space of absence and paradox first occurs in *Turner*'s opening line: 'Stillborn from all the signs' (1).[19] The brokenness and silence of the phrase and image of the stillbirth contrasts with the abundance of signs and words, of language and representation. On the one hand, the profusion of existing representations of Otherness symbolically forecloses the possibilities of newness and originality conventionally associated with the image of birth. On the other hand, reading the poem out loud creates a paradoxical blurring of meaning between 'stillborn' and 'still born', between death and birth. The figure of the paradox situates Dabydeen's poem in the liminal traditions of Caribbean writing: according to Wilson

57

Harris, a paradox works primarily through metaphor and defies closure. It refers to parallel time zones and historically unfinished shapes of reality that give access to the half-remembered and half-forgotten traumas of history.[20] The double inscription of 'Still/born', then, indicates that Dabydeen's poem articulates identities through various histories, through a play of lack (stillbirth) and excess (multiplicity of signs) that assigns neither originality nor wholeness to the process of identity formation.

In Fragment XII the paradoxical meanings of the stillbirth metaphor recur in the metaphor of the moon, an image taken from a fragment of Turner's painting *The Parting of Hero and Leander* (1837). In *Turner*, the moon shines as the 'silent / Full eye' (17), indicating simultaneous silence and fullness, lack and excess. In other words, the paradoxical capacities of the moon metaphor add meaning (fullness), and supplement a lack (silence). Fullness and silence, however, are configurations of both the African's and J. M. W. Turner's linked visions of identity. Silence invokes the African's longing for calmness and peace, but actually designates a lack of language that incurs terror. In this instance, the African's desire for new beginnings is inspired by the 'silent / Full eye' of the moon, which he takes as a true sign of nature, unvisited by imperial representations. Yet, derived from a displaced fragment of Turner's painting *The Parting of Hero and Leander*, the silence of the moon is deceptive, and obscures the fact that its origins once again lead back to Turner's visual representations of empire. Given that the moon is a component of Turner's painting and the African's memory both before and after the Middle Passage, the fullness of the moon summons the image of an all-seeing eye that will always say more than both Turner's and the African's self-consciousness can perceive.

The split moon metaphor, then, explores the ambivalence of metaphor; its violent operations of naming, and its differential, self-destructive effects. Investigating the space between lack and excess, deferral and difference, the moon metaphor suggests that the infinite self-reproduction of metaphorical operations may either wear out their own subversive potential or produce, in Dabydeen's slightly romanticizing vision, 'the possibility of total

58

originality'.[21] In the context of postcolonial theory, Bhabha makes use of the supplementary space between metaphorical lack and excess to articulate his notion of cultural difference and hybridity. Both of these concepts work rhetorically through strategies of repetition which 'terrorize [...] authority with the *ruse* of recognition, its mimicry, its mockery'.[22] This notion of mimicry implies that the processes of identity formation are guided by self-conscious and strategic choices that work from within colonial representations of Otherness. The '*ruse* of recognition' presupposes that an act of self-recognition has already taken place and can be used in the service of subversive mimicry. Fragment XII of *Turner*, however, dramatizes the impossibility of strategic choice and implies that the contradictions within the discourse of empire are constitutive of what Spivak calls the 'domesticated other', and the regeneration of imperial ideology.[23] The interactive relation between the verbal and the visual image of the moon shows the ways in which the dead African is entangled in and co-opted by the multiple discourses of imperialism in advance of any possible act of self-recognition. In this sense, the metaphor of the moon suggests that the desire for cultural transfiguration can be fulfilled neither by imperial nor postcolonial concepts of identity.

To the African the watchful eye of the moon promises the last resort of comfort and serene peacefulness during an existence of utter loss and isolation. The moon's 'loneliness and grief' are also the African's loneliness. For years he courted the moon for salvation and memory so that his 'dazed mind' could hope to reach 'across a distance big beyond even / Turner's grasp'. Only the moon still hears his 'whisper' (17) of hope for a creative amnesia. He begs the moon for relief from those fragments of memory that bring back abduction and rape. In the end the African has 'even forgotten the words. / Only the moon remains, watchful and loving' (18). While the moon metaphor supplements the lack of memory and provides a foil of identification for the African, it is also marked by an excess of meaning which the African cannot decipher. The play of lack and excess appears in the fragment of Turner's *The Parting of Hero and Leander*, reproduced on the page opposite to Fragment XII. The correspondence between the verbal and the visual image of the moon implies that both images function as a simulacrum of each other. The possibility of a creative amnesia or transfiguration quickly fails because, unlike Walcott's sea, Dabydeen's is not a space bereft of cultural inscriptions, of Turner's mark and brush. Indeed, if we recontextualize the fragment of Turner's painting in its occluded whole, we see that what the African reads as a vast negative space of emptiness and loss harbours imperial and Western literary history.

As with his *Slave Ship*, Turner's *Parting of Hero and Leander* comments on the materialist corruption and greed which, according to Turner, cause the decay of empires. The painting is divided into halves, one of which shows an empty ancient city sinking into darkness and a sea of clouds. The other half depicts gigantic waves populated with mythic sea sprites. The waves tower over the harbour front, caught in the moment before collapse. The right middle-section of the painting represents the moon hiding behind clouds but illuminating a narrow harbour passage that leads into an open, storm-tossed sea. In the foreground of the painting we see Hero who holds up lanterns to guide her lover Leander back home. The dark and light contrasts of the painting and suspended chaos of the sea forebode Leander's tragic drowning. The painting's threatening movement of impending collapse and darkness is only interrupted by the moon's ray of light, which creates a unity in perspective and controls the composition of the painting.

Dabydeen's *Turner* reprints this image of moonlight, with its impression of momentary stillness, and illusion of wholeness and order. The reproduction of the fragment implies a change from the signs of decay and collapse into an almost pastoral staging of the sea, reflecting the African's 'fallacious hope', to appropriate Turner's phrase, of originality and blissful belonging.[24] This edited reprint of Turner's initial narrative of turmoil and destruction in *Turner* cites Ruskin's editing practices in his reading of *Slave Ship*.[25] Yet, it seems to me that *Turner* is less concerned with Ruskin's racist colour blindness than with his attempt at naturalizing both Turner's critique of empire and the artist's sufferings which speak through his paintings. Ruskin's appropriation of Turner's *Slave Ship* implies that the conservative establishment of Victorian society regulated social outsiders like J.M.W. Turner.[26] *Turner*'s reproduction of *The Parting of Hero and Leander* reminds us that the technologies of imperial control linked the regulation of social outcasts within Victorian society with the management of slavery outside England's domestic borders.

If the fragment of *The Parting of Hero and Leander* signals the erasure of heterogeneous narratives of empire, we may ask what other narratives are submerged in Turner's painting and were subsequently omitted from both the painting's reproduction in *Turner* and indirectly from the African's consciousness. An answer to this question opens the Pandora's box of English literary history: the myth of Hero and Leander has been told and adapted throughout the history of Western literature and painting, by artists and writers such as Rubens, Ovid, Virgil, Musaeus, Keats, Housman, and Marlowe. With regard to *Turner*'s 'Hero and Leander'-fragment, Marlowe's *Hero and Leander* (1598) designates one of the narratives which may have influenced both Turner's painting and Dabydeen's long poem. While *Turner* is indebted to the generic features of Marlowe's mythographic and erotic brief epic, Turner's painting takes up Marlowe's satirical narrative of commodified sexual and human relationships. We may also argue that Marlowe's erotic metaphors of economic exchange and blackness illustrate the ways in which early modern English identity concepts emerged in conjunction with the commodification of sexuality and its deployment in power discourses. This political legacy of intersecting discourses of sex, power, and race, resurfaces in Turner's depiction of the Hero and Leander myth and also in the perverted and abusive desires of Turner, the captain of *Turner*'s slaver. My point, though, is not to trace *Turner*'s intertextual references, but to show that the dead African's unconscious, his fantasy of new and original beginnings, is shaped by a chain of existing representations of Otherness. As a normalizing trope of substitution and sameness, metaphor always returns to the same origins in the discourse of empire. More specifically, the metaphorical overdetermination of the moon leads the African back to 'Turner's (and other artists')' (xi) practice of using blackness as a representational vehicle for decay, chaos, and corruption.

61

Both of Turner's paintings, *The Parting of Hero and Leander* and *Slave Ship*, emphasize the destruction of empires through a linear and progressive narrative of history. Similarly to other Romantic works of art, as Karl Kroeber points out, Turner's paintings speak about the present British Empire in terms of ancient empires. Turner, Kroeber writes, knows that 'the British Empire is no more [...] at the moment of the Empire's burgeoning [...] He foresees the British Empire vanishing into a continuity of history'.[27] Thus, rather than criticizing the idea of empire, Turner transforms it into a natural phenomenon of humanity's 'universal' history. His image of drowning slaves symbolizes and sublimates Victorian anxieties of social and cultural change while condemning the violent excesses of empire. Yet Turner's relativist views of history prevent him from imagining an alternative to the idea of empire. In fact, his paintings present the viewer, as Gilroy points out, with 'images of black suffering' whose purpose it is to help 'England [...] make sense of itself and its destiny'.[28] If Turner's *Slave Ship* and *The Parting of Hero and Leander* endorse imperialism's overall mission of civilization, is it possible, we may ask, to read the African's identification with the moon in ways that destabilize Turner's notion of empire? What can we gain from conceptualizing J.M.W. Turner as a figure who was himself subjected to the imperial regimentation of sexuality?

III

As a surveying and observing eye, the moon metaphor primarily operates to regulate the dead African's conscious and unconscious fantasies of originality and transfiguration. The metaphor of the eye, however, has already occurred in Fragment II of the sequence. In this section the ambiguous connotations of the eye metaphor not only establish links with metaphors of childhood but also evoke the vision of a pastoral African past and undermine the African's longing for historical continuity.[29] Following his encounter with the stillborn child, the African wants to invent a 'fable' (1) of happy family and childhood memories. Yet, he fails to map his memory with new names for landscapes and animals because this strategy mimics the empiricist science which the African has learnt 'since Turner's days' (2). Further, the African cannot clearly recall concrete events, names, and places. Instead, he remembers the 'sound' of milking a cow 'that still haunts' him and 'survives the roar [...] Of waves' (2). This moment of an apparently genuine and solid memory of the past also disrupts the African's pastoral fantasy because he remembers the cow as being both a titillating playmate and protectoress. In this passage the poem introduces the metaphor of the eye in ambiguously sexual terms: the cow 'watches' and 'winks' at the children with 'covetous eyes', or 'a harlot's eye' (3). Linked to children's games, the image of the prostitute foreshadows the pederast lust of Turner, the captain of *Turner*'s slaver and the painter, and interrupts the linear flow of modern temporality.[30] Lying underneath the cow's 'belly', the children feel protected while waiting for the European intruders to 'burn the huts, stampede the goats, / Drag girls away by ropes' (3) like cattle. The abrupt turn from play to violence, from epic splendour to the crude enumeration of violent acts, recalls the disruptive experience of the Middle Passage. The contradictory association of the cow's 'harlot's eye' with its protective belly destabilizes the African's vision of continuous historical time.

Writing from within the disjunctive time frame of postcolonial modernity, *Turner* examines the ways in which the sexual energies of Turner's sublime paintings and the construction of cultural difference intersect. While classical as well as recent critics of the sublime agree that the aesthetic effects of the sublime largely depend on what appears to be unrepresentable, postcolonial critics argue that the unrepresentable of the sublime both embodies and erases the violence of the Middle Passage from the dominant narratives of modernity.[31] Paul Gilroy conceptualizes the temporal gap in the discourse of modernity as a specific 'diaspora temporality' he calls the 'Slave Sublime'.[32] 'The modern world', he writes, is:

> fragmented along axes constituted by racial conflict and [can] accommodate non-synchronous, heterocultural modes of social life in close proximity... [Black artists'] conceptions of modernity [...] were founded on the catastrophic rupture of the middle passage rather than the dream of revolutionary transformation. They were

punctuated by the processes of acculturation and terror that followed that catastrophe and by the countercultural aspirations towards freedom, citizenship, and autonomy that developed after it among slaves and their descendants.[33]

The common denominator of Gilroy's notion of the 'Slave Sublime' and classical concepts of the sublime is the experience of terror. In contrast to the classical idea that terror is an effect of the sublime, Gilroy understands racist terror as both the cause of the sublime and the central element of a black conceptualization of modernity. Although Gilroy's 'Slave Sublime' illustrates the ways in which racial terror informs the classical aesthetic of the sublime, it does not fully explain the seductive and, frequently, erotic power which sublime representations of terror, despite their perverted violence, exercise on readers and viewers.

Furthermore, Gilroy's analysis gives little consideration to the ways in which the sexual energies inscribed in the aesthetic of the sublime mirror the Victorian project of colonizing bodies and minds inside and outside England's national boundaries during the beginning stages of modernity. In her study *Race and the Education of Desire*, Ann Stoler criticizes Foucault's *History of Sexuality* for 'short-circuiting empire'.[34] She argues that the construction of bourgeois identities must be read through a discourse of sexuality that 'cannot be charted in Europe alone': that through contrast the 'racialized' colonial body defined the 'healthy, vigorous, bourgeois body' (7). More importantly, discourses of sexuality were racially coded and defined 'marginal members of the [Victorian] body politic' in order to articulate who had, and did not have, the right to claim a certain national and middle-class identity. In other words, prostitutes, hysterical women, and people suffering from a mental illness were often described in abject sexual and racial terms and drew what Stoler calls the 'interior frontiers' (7) of national communities. Thus, the idea of a unified bourgeois self could only be articulated against the role 'Europe's external and internal "others" played' (194) in the interwoven discourses of race, sexuality, and empire. In *Turner*, the reiteration of the child metaphor and Turner's name examines the ways in which J.M.W. Turner's progressive critique of empire remains tied to racial and social classifications of national identity. The reiteration demonstrates the perverted and painful logic through which Turner's *Slave Ship* translates the terror of both the sexual regulation and racialization of empire's 'historical others' (195) into the aesthetic of the sublime.

The various textual circulations of the name 'Turner' produce a number of 'historical Others'. In his interview with Maya Jaggi, Dabydeen says he 'made Turner symbolically a child abuser. [...] It's a metaphor for dependency and power'.[35] Conceptualized as a metaphor for child abuse, the name Turner refers to the paternalistic and abusive power relations between the mother country and its various colonies, perceived as children, and the representation of the slave as a child. *Turner* dramatizes the dependency relations that govern the Victorian slave/child metaphor through the sado-masochistic sexual violations Captain Turner inflicts upon the black children aboard his slaver. The poem's multiple reiterations of the name 'Turner' stage the ways in which the slave/child metaphor can be used to identify and manage colonial desire. In *Turner*, the name Turner belongs to the painter, to Dabydeen's poem, to the stillborn child, to all 'the one's / With golden hair' (8), and to Christ who is 'Turner nailed to a tree' (25). Similarly to the African's 'father' who 'count[s] beads at the end of each day', Turner the captain of the slaver 'multip[lies] percentages' (18) to count his profits from the slave trade. In several ways, the name 'Turner' embodies the law-of-the-father and that of colonial violence and order. For example, the African can still distinguish the men '[w]ith golden hair' from other drowned men because the silver of their boot buckles survives the transformative properties of the sea. In fact, the silver boot buckles not only evoke images of military discipline, violent blows, and kicking feet, but also suggest that the perpetuation of racist violence obstructs all hopes for symbolic or cultural transfiguration. Furthermore, playing on the word 'return' and the idiom 'to turn a profit', the name 'Turner' clearly alludes to the postcolonial predicament of exile and home as well as to the neocolonial cultural and economic exploitation of non-white people.

The memory of violence establishes a link between past and present racialized and sexualized discourses of the nation. Referring to the stillborn child and a child abuser, the name Turner alludes to the Victorian practice of controlling children's sexuality and regulating deviant forms of sexuality to constitute a racially homogenous bourgeois national self. J.M.W. Turner's documented preference for children's company may reflect both the symbolic objectification of children in the discourse of national identity formation and Turner's own attempt at sublimating and concurrently aborting his sexual desires. The slave/child metaphor reflects both of these normalizing practices, the idealization and objectification of children. In a perverted way, the slave/child metaphor at once incorporates and translates the paternalistic Romantic utopia of children being the fathers of men into an imperial utopia of white supremacy. Yet, children's autoerotic sexuality and their close contact with servants, as Stoler suggests, also threatened to undermine this utopia, posing a potential danger of social and racial pollution. Thus, children and slaves were disciplined for their own benefit as well as for the greater good of society, and the success of empire's civilizing mission. While J.M.W. Turner's paintings testify to the painter's belief in this mission, the reiteration of his name in *Turner* allows us to read the various intersecting psychological and discursive elements that made this belief possible.

The portrayal of J.M.W. Turner as a sado-masochistic slave trader and pederast (see Dabydeen's introduction) recalls Turner's miserliness and his love for children with whom, according to Lindsay's biography, he got along better than with adults. Turner's fondness of children connects with the image of the benevolent and paternalistic colonial master; and further points to Turner's own unresolved social and sexual desires which made him an Other in Victorian society. Lindsay observes that Turner's 'images of natural violence can be related to the world outside, [... but] also represent the demented mother in her spasms of hate and torment' (95). Turner's attitude towards art and sexuality was riven, as Lindsay explains, by 'a keen anxiety and [by the fact] that he had to keep on driving down or evading a fear of madness'

(94). He suffered a 'repressed guilt-sense' for having hospitalized his mother, as well as for coming from a family plagued and destroyed by his mother's mental disintegration.[36] He sublimated his guilt and anxiety by replacing his physical mother with the symbolic mother of the Royal Academy, 'on whom he continued passionately to beget his countless art children' (94). Having expelled the abject body of his mother, and thus his own body, from his consciousness, Turner was unable to form viable relationships with women. Instead, as Lindsay suggests, he found 'satisfaction only in a socially-guilty (adulterous or promiscuous) connection' (94). His fear of anxiety seems to have been strongly regulated by a death drive through which Turner imagined himself to be the 'art mother finally', buried together with his paintings, his 'art children'.[37] This fantasy, I think, depicts the nodal point at which the figures of Turner the painter, and Turner the child-abusing captain of the slaver, converge. In the sado-masochistic pleasure of imagining the joint death of himself (as the disembodied mother) with his (her) art children, Turner at once undertakes an act of sexual self-disciplining and transgression, making children the object of his incestuous desire to merge with what he has created. Through this misogynist fantasy of death, as Lindsay suggests, Turner achieved '[t]he escape from a difficult and disturbing reality [...]. Womb had become tomb, and vice versa. The desired relationship of harmony and peace had been won, but at the cost of giving up all struggle. The self-sufficient sphere was complete and finally isolated' (95), and the regimented Victorian body was successfully installed. Lindsay's critical biography of Turner, then, helps us situate Turner as one of England's 'historical Others' who returns in Dabydeen's poem to refract the dominant narrative of the English nation, not from the margins, but from the centre of English art.

Lindsay's biography, which Dabydeen mentions in his 'Acknowledgments', implicitly relates Turner's life to the Victorian technologies of sexuality and power. As Foucault argued, sexuality, rather than being repressed, was an omnipresent discourse that constructed objects of knowledge and imposed a system of self-discipline that established class, gender, and psychological hierarchies within Victorian society. According to Foucault, images such as those of the mad hysteric, the prostitute, or any individual with 'deviant' desires, mark these figures as a threat to a homogeneously conceived national community. Sexuality, as Foucault argues, is 'not [...] an exterior domain to which power is applied' but 'a result and instrument of power's design'.[38] In this context, Turner's fear of madness expresses a fear of being socially marginalised at the same time as he was constantly striving to escape from his own impoverished background. More importantly, Lindsay's biography suggests that Turner's anxiety and sense of guilt entailed self-disciplining acts that normalized the body as a site of subjection and power production. Turner's own 'deviant' desires, then, perhaps did not merely symbolize a repressed sexuality, but rather suggested an attempt to conform to the norms of a 'healthy', clean, bourgeois body through acts of self-beratement and disavowal, both essential elements of the psychological dynamics of cultural transfiguration.

The price Turner had to pay for this domesticated bourgeois self, was, Lindsay suggests, 'complete and final[] isolat[ion]' (95). This socially sanctified disavowal of the body led not only to utter isolation and self-denial, but also generated a violent psychic excess that informs Turner's techniques of cultural representation. More specifically, in the splitting of Turner's bourgeois self, the body, in Francis Barker's words, is censored as a 'rootless thing of madness and scandal' and forced into an object position which can then be 'pressed into [the] service' of artistic sublimation.[39] Barker argues, moreover, that the regulatory practice of censoring the body as a site of identification also generates an excess of meaning that lies beyond conscious legibility. In contrast to Barker, however, Stoler argues that the biopolitics of Victorian sexuality cannot be read outside the racialized grammar it employs and generates. Thus, Turner's attempts to escape social marginalization and discipline his body, cannot be read simply as an act of repression, but rather as contributions to the construction and ordering of imperial class and race relations.

Although the discourse of empire normalizes both the deviant Victorian and the black body, this should not lead to the conclusion that these bodies were in any way equal. In *Turner* the effects of disciplining the body are not, as Robert Hyam suggests, merely transferred into and excessively realized in the colonies.[40] Such an argument presupposes the repression of sexual drives as the main incentive for colonial expansion and assumes a clear separation between colonial and non-colonial spaces. The governing discourses of imperialism, as *Turner* shows, are played out both inside and outside England's national boundaries and are based on the successful integration of desire into the imperial project. This assumes that 'people themselves believed in the sexual codes of the moralizing state [and that] personal affect and sentiments could be harnessed to national projects and priorities for racial regeneration' (Stoler 136).

If Turner's paintings display the successful integration of colonial desire into the national mission of empire, then this process of integration, as *Turner* dramatizes it, also signifies a violent sexual transgression enacted through and on the black body. At night on board the slaver, Captain Turner physically and mentally coerces the slave boys into complete submission:

He gave selflessly the nipple
Of his tongue until we learnt to say profitably
In his own language, *we desire you, we love*
You, we forgive you. He whispered eloquently
Into our ears even as we wriggled beneath him,
Breathless with pain [...]
          He fished us patiently,
Obsessively until our stubbornness gave way
To an exhaustion more complete than Manu's [...]
And we repeated in a trance the words
That shuddered from him: *blessed, angelic,*
Sublime; words that seemed to flow endlessly
From him, filling our mouths and bellies
Endlessly. (38)

In this passage acts of physical and representational violence link Turner, the captain of the slaver, with Turner, the painter.

The violent imposition of the English language through the language of the sublime transforms Captain Turner's slave children into the painter's art children, literally inseminating them with both the painter's and the imperialist's fantasy of a primitive utopia.

J.M.W. Turner's desire to begin again beyond the corruption of civilization, beyond the fallacies of hope, perfectly translates into the child/slave metaphor. Saturated with the Romantic discourse of childhood, his desire, like that of earlier English explorers and conquerors of the Americas, is for a new beginning of human history built on innocence, naïve wisdom, and the unfettered imagination. Simultaneously, the mythologies of childhood, as Marina Warner observes, assign children 'all kinds of transgressive pleasures, including above all the sado-masochistic thrills of fear'.[41] For the Turner of Dabydeen's poem, inflicting violence can be legitimized as a civilizing act which, in his imagination, causes necessary pain and is rewarded with the pleasures of enlightenment and cultural refinement. What is equally important, however, is that Turner successfully integrates his own sentiments into the national project of imperial civilization. In this combined national and aesthetic project, slave children can turn into 'art children' who, in Stoler's words, become 'heirs' not only to their parents (the legacy of J.M.W. Turner) but also to 'the national patrimony and the race' (144). Today, the latter characterizes the iconographic value of Turner's painting in the dominant narrative of the English nation.

By demanding a repeated confirmation of affection from his victims, Captain Turner seeks to legitimize and to naturalize the violent authority he exercises. This strategy recalls the Foucauldian notion that political authority does not designate a given state but a discourse that draws from and defers its own legitimacy to an irretrievable past. By requesting the children to reiterate his own 'teachings', Turner submits and links his authority, initially based on violent coercion, to the aesthetic strategies of sublime art. J.M.W. Turner, we remember, considered the sublime as an artistic expression of the eternal and natural repetitions of the history of antique and modern empires, a history that can be captured on canvas only be making its presumably idealist and moral ambitions appear to be unrepresentable. This transference of authority from physical violation to aesthetic sublimation mirrors the substituting operations of metaphor and causes a deliberate forgetting of history.[42] While this process of forgetting constitutes what we usually call 'dead metaphors', it is by no means an innocent process. On the contrary, dead metaphors mark historical sites of violence and social conflict. Though seemingly neutral, they reveal how identities are produced over time through a process of remembering and forgetting, a process that facilitates nation narration. For example, in the context of Dabydeen's poem, we might argue that in the English imagination the name 'Turner' functions as a dead metaphor both of England's imperial art and of a homogeneously conceived national identity. *Turner*'s repetitions and conceptual displacements of the name 'Turner', however, allow us to read the social contradictions that had to be erased from the name 'Turner' in order to make it an effective icon of English nationhood. As a dead metaphor, the name 'Turner' enters the discourse of nation narration cleansed from all cultural ambiguities, from all of J.M.W. Turner's deviant desires, delirious acts, and unacknowledged sufferings. What is at stake in *Turner* is both the reconstruction of England's imaginary and the dismantling, not necessarily of Turner's art, but of its violent laws of cultural representation.

While we may argue that imperial practices of cultural representation perform acts of symbolic violence, in the history of racism symbolic violence and the internalization of defiled images of blackness effect and underpin racially motivated physical assaults. For this reason, *Turner* refuses to provide its readers with the comfort of a clear boundary between symbolic and physical acts of violence. In the poem, the figure of Turner, the artist, merges with Turner the sado-masochistic captain of the slave ship who gains satisfaction from violating black children. As a sexual and psychic practice of subjection, the sadist seeks to absorb the body of the Other in order to discover his own. His object is the willing surrender and incorporation of the Other into the Self. Captain Turner's pleasures, therefore, consist in exorcising difference and consuming guilt and conflict. These practices of sadistic incorporation and transfiguration of the Other into the

Self correspond to J.M.W. Turner's techniques of the sublime. While Turner's paintings harmonize the contradictions of empire, Dabydeen's *Turner* makes them legible. In fact, if we consider that according to the drowned African the sea produces merely 'counterfeit goods' (17), we can read J.M.W. Turner's imperial paintings as forged representations of the imperial Self and colonial Other. Similarly to Captain Turner's slave boys, these representations have been 'fished [...] patiently' (38) and profitably from the sea of slavery. Dabydeen's dramatization of *Slave Ship*, then, illustrates that the harmonizing effects of Turner's art, part of Britain's most cherished cultural capital, are deceptive. For these effects are produced through the pornographic fantasies of empire, the simultaneous fetishization and violation of the black body.

If Turner's paintings fuse the fragmented political and psychological conditions of imperial identity formation into a transcendental image of the arbitrary and eternal power of nature, Dabydeen's poem discloses Turner's notion of the sublime as a Western master narrative which legitimates and constructs the enslaved black body. Through the techniques of the sublime, the obliterated black body returns in an aestheticized and sublimated version to construct harmony out of the ambiguous effects entailed in managing colonial desire. The sadistic pleasures that form the core of this operation cause the effects of awe and terror the beholder of a sublime painting experiences and identifies with. To create harmony out of his own sense of guilt and psychic traumas, J.M.W. Turner hoped to end all struggle with the regulatory power apparatus of Victorian England by envisioning his own death as a communion with his paintings. The death he wished for, however, was a death that happened elsewhere, on the slavers and in the colonies of empire. The vision of his own death and that of slaves on the sea spurred Turner's imagination and allowed him to contain the otherwise unmanageable contradictions of the Self and the nation's socio-political life. *Turner*, then, brilliantly captures the dynamics of the imperial imagination by translating Turner's 'art children' into abused black children.[43]

Turner's configurations of the moon and child/slave metaphors emphasise that in the discourse of empire metaphor functions as a historically and politically overdetermined trope. At the same time, these metaphors reveal the instability of imperial power relations. For example, if both of these metaphors produce a narrative of sexually and racially normalized identities, they also show that the imperial technologies of sexuality and race produce historical Others who threaten to undermine the perceived homogeneity of the newly constructed Victorian bourgeois national Self. For this reason, metaphor provides a useful device through which to read the contradictions and crises of both colonial and postcolonial forms of representation. Furthermore, Dabydeen's poem reminds us of the fact that we can speak about metaphor only in terms of metaphor, so that no conceptualization of metaphor (including mine) can escape the hegemonic effects of metaphor as historically inscribed. Instead of offering us an easy escape from the vicissitudes of metaphor, *Turner* enables us to read the ways in which metaphor's historical production has been inflected by specific discourses on race and gender.

The moon metaphor, as I have discussed earlier, appears in the dead African's fabricated childhood memories as the cow's 'harlot's eye' (3) and gains further sexualized inflections through its circulation in the discourse of imperial violence. In *Turner*'s narrative, the theme of the harlot or prostitute recurs in several configurations in which the body functions as a surface, rather than as a vehicle of depth and truth that awaits discovery. As a frequently used meta-metaphor in the classical discourses of rhetoric, the metaphor of the prostitute designates a crucial site of *Turner*'s critique of imperial cultural representation. Furthermore, insofar as both J.M.W. Turner and the figure of the prostitute embody those Victorian Others who were socially regulated yet instrumental for the formation of the self-disciplined Victorian bourgeois subject, the metaphor of the prostitute intersects with the governing discourses of *Turner*. The metaphor of the prostitute initially emerges from the African's invented memories and signifies his misconceived identification with Turner. Inventing '[w]ords of his own dreaming and those that Turner / Primed in [his] mouth', the African's mind becomes a 'garment of invention'. One of the birds circling around him strikes him as 'arrogant in beauty feathers / Blown loose', and he names it 'Tanje after the strumpet / Of [his] village' (14). The memory of Tanje, whether invented or real, triggers a short moment of self-recognition in which the African names himself and turns the notion of historical depth or content into an image of bodily surfaces. The sea, the force of history, has 'bleached [him…] of colour, / Painted [him] gaudy, dabs of ebony, / an arabesque of blues and vermilions, / Sea-quats cling to [his] body like gorgeous / Ornaments. [He] has become the sea's whore, / Yielding' (14). Similar to the techniques of priming a canvas, imperial representations of the Other have already 'primed' the African's mind, establishing an invisible but functional depth of historical meaning. More specifically, the dead African functions as an aesthetic feature in Turner's painting, as a vehicle of hidden meanings which are coded in terms of the racialized body. The African's body has been reduced to an 'ornament', a decorative emblem and conduit in the imperial discourse of art and race: it can be traded as an object of imperial desire, as the 'sea's whore' who pools and transfers unspoken and forbidden sexual and aesthetic pleasures.

In their earliest conception, ornaments were called *grotteska* and showed animals, plants, and human images without adhering to realist conventions of representation. They presented unfinished forms in an unstable world, an incomplete metamorphosis of birth and death.[44] Later, in the early Renaissance, the notion of 'transformation', and thus of the ornament as an object with the capacity for change, was associated with sexual mutilation and the bisexual body of Hermaphroditos. *Turner*'s metaphors of the 'sea's whore' and the 'ornament' explicitly emphasise the fact that these processes of transformation are violent yet unfinished. Perceived as a 'garment of invention', the racialized body, we may argue, functions as a receptacle of imperial fantasies and desires. Given that the racialized and gendered body historically served as the chief locus of imperial and colonial oppression, we may also argue that in *Turner*'s dramatization of the body as a 'garment of invention', the body can no longer function as the conceptual ground of imperial representations. While such an understanding of the body risks overlooking the ways in which gender, race and class markers construct particular bodies, it also facilitates a non-foundationalist reading of the body as a productive site of historical power relations. More specifically, through their association with surfaces and physical violence, the metaphors of the ornament and the prostitute symbolically enact cultural and physical crises. By foregrounding the ways in which classical discourses of the body and rhetoric inform each other, these metaphors cite and reinscribe the functions of metaphor itself.

As Tzvetan Todorov and Paul de Man have argued at length, from Quintilian to John Locke, classical rhetoricians considered metaphors as dangerous tropes because their self-subversive and self-reproductive tendencies destabilize the discourses in which they are employed and which they produce. As a corollary, rhetoricians excluded metaphor from the dominant practices of rhetoric and thereby not only introduced a division between literal and poetic functions of language but, in Todorov's words, exercised rhetoric 'henceforth with a guilty conscience'.[45] However, the exclusion of metaphor from the order of rhetoric disrupts the order in the form of a moralizing, gendered, and racialized discourse on metaphor, in which the operative modes and properties of metaphor are likened to those of a prostitute. This particular discourse of rhetoric articulates its own critique of metaphor through another metaphor, by arguing that the instability and ambiguity of metaphor equals the presumed moral and sexual promiscuity of a prostitute. Like a prostitute, a woman, or a slave, metaphor must be restrained and pressed into the service of unequivocal meaning production. The explicitly sexual and racist language that characterizes the rhetorical analogy between metaphor and prostitute also speaks of a different 'guilty consciousness' of the classical rhetoricians, namely, of their failure to fully control the racial and sexual Other their discourse produces.

The analogy between a metaphor and a prostitute, then, depends on establishing a relationship between the functions of language and of the body through a binary division and valorization of content versus form, insides (thoughts, ideas) versus outsides (words). The analogy evolves from the classical aesthetic notion of beauty in which a natural unadorned body gives more pleasure than an ornamented body so that, as Cicero puts it, 'only elegance and neatness will remain' (qtd. in Todorov 74). In the same vein, only unadorned speech achieves the clarity that is true to the idea or the thought it tries to convey. 'Rhetorical ornaments', Todorov writes, correspond to 'the adornments of the body. […] Ideas are like bones and veins; words, like flesh, fluids, and skin' (73). In this sense, metaphor both clothes and unveils the body in a gesture of control. In *Turner*'s metaphor of the 'sea's whore' we can read this double movement of metaphor differently. History prostitutes the African, signalling the traffic in colonial desires and economic exploitation. Yet, the poem transfers this act of metaphorisation onto both the African's dead and the stillborn child's absent body. Subsequently, the power of metaphor to reveal a deep-seated truth, namely the authority of imperial representation, is frustrated. The absence of the body does not necessarily suggest an absence of metaphor. Rather, the absent body symbolically refuses metaphorical synthesis and divests metaphor of its inscribed historical meanings: thus, metaphorical transfiguration turns into the dis*figure*ment of metaphor. This kind of incomplete metamorphosis, however, is not a mere process of literalization because, as *Turner*'s metaphors of the 'sea's whore' and the 'ornament' illustrate, there is no original, literal meaning hidden, waiting to be discovered by metaphor. We do not find interior and internalized ideals and truths of history. Instead, the surfaces of forms produce meaning and dissolve metaphor's binary divisions into inside and outside, tenor and vehicle.

The metaphor of the 'sea's whore' activates a discourse of metaphor in which metaphor itself is subject to moral regulation and obliteration. The 'perversion' of metaphor, its promiscuity of meaning, emerges from two consecutive arguments in the classical discourse of rhetoric. Both arguments suggest that normative conceptualizations of metaphor cannot be severed from a white, male practice of rhetoric. The first states that metaphor or ornamented discourse is an expression of moral decay and sexual licentiousness. In classical rhetoric, according to Todorov, 'ornamented discourse is the male courtesan', a cross-dressing man, parading in the 'glaring make-up' of an 'easy woman' (Kant qtd. in Todorov 74). Envisioned as an effeminized man, as the stereotypical image of both male slaves and East Indian men, metaphor also refers to a rhetorical style of 'bombastic, Asiatic, redundant [, and ...] excessive repetition[s]' (Quintilian qtd. in Todorov 75). By way of contrast the discursive production of metaphor symbolically aligns classical rhetoric with a healthy, white, male body. Thus, the sexualized and racialized meta-metaphor of the prostitute safeguards the notion of rhetoric as a discourse committed to the production of truth, forthrightness, and masculine virility, the assumed qualities of Victorian empire building. The second argument, linked to such rhetoricians as Augustine, compares the act of reading metaphors with that of undressing women. In this context, the value of the woman/metaphor consists in being guaranteed 'to arrive in the end at the body itself' (Todorov 76). The desire to remove clothing, or to decipher metaphorical meanings posits the body as the object and container of hidden truths that must be revealed: and here both arguments converge, for the unveiled woman/metaphor is an indecent woman, a prostitute.

The underlying fear of these attempts at negating and defaming metaphor is, as Todorov remarks, that '[r]hetorical ornamentation changes the sex of discourse' (75) and that metaphor may come to function as a 'transvestite' (74) who disturbs the given orders of authority in the dominant discourses of representation. Subsequently, the normative effects of metaphor depend on presupposing that truth is generated through the hiding and revealing of specific meanings, through the construction and erasure of a natural body as carrier of metaphorical operations. *Turner's* metaphor of the 'sea's whore', however, refuses to yield this preconceived body on which to project endless representations of Self and Other. Instead, it emphasizes both metaphor and the body as surfaces that dispense with received divisions into internal meaning and outward appearance, content and form, depth and shallowness. In this way, the discursive production of metaphor and of the African's body become legible as artifices of history. This transference of identity formation from the site of nature to that of artifice 'has the effect', as Rey Chow argues, 'of emptying "meaning" from its conventional space – the core, the depth, or the inside waiting to be seen and articulated – and reconstructing it in a new locus – the locus of the surface, which not only shines but *glosses*; which looks, stares, and speaks'.[46] By naming himself the 'sea's whore', then, the African reinscribes the ornamental functions of metaphor without giving them a structure of depth, thereby making previous ascriptions of gender and race accessible to resignification.

In *Turner*'s Fragment XXI, Manu, the hapless magician, contemplates how one can learn to live with a future that has symbolically already been written by imperial history. '[I]n the future time', we read, 'each must learn to live / Beadless in a foreign land; or perish. / Or each must learn to make new jouti, / Arrange them by instinct, imagination' (33). Manu's advice seems alluring. In the light of my discussion of *Turner*, however, it should be evident by now that Manu's words reflect a desire for cultural transfiguration, for new beginnings, that may be restrictive rather than productive. What is at issue is not a life 'barren of ancestral memory' (33), but the claim to a cross-cultural memory, a national imaginary written through the disjunctures and continuities between 'empire and nation'.[47] In contrast to many postcolonial concepts of identity, *Turner* suggests that identity formation is not solely a cultural process but inseparable from the sexual and racial politics of empire and the English nation state. Rather than 'mak[ing] new jouti' and relying on 'instinct [and] imagination', Dabydeen's poem examines the various legacies of both Turner's and Walcott's sea, and makes us rethink the fundamental operations of metaphor and cultural representation in terms of political and cultural crisis.

1. Brand delivered her lecture on October 11, 2000 at the University of Victoria, Canada.
2. Simon Gikandi, *Maps of Englishness: Writing Identity in the Culture of Colonialism* (New York: Columbia University Press, 1996), p. 49.
3. David Dabydeen, *Turner: New and Selected Poems* (London: Cape, 1994). Following references are included in the main text of the essay.
4. Paula Burnett, 'Where else to row, but backward? Addressing Caribbean Futures through Re-Visions of the Past', *Ariel*, 30:1 (January 1990), 11-37 (p. 34).
5. Homi K. Bhabha, *The Location of Culture* (London, New York: Routledge, 1994), p. 244.
6. Gayatri Spivak, 'Can the Subaltern Speak?', in *Colonial Discourse and Post-Colonial Theory: A Reader*, ed. by Patrick Williams and Laura Chrisman (New York: Columbia University Press, 1989), pp. 66-111 (p. 66).
7. For a discussion of this issue, see Gayatri Spivak, 'Three Women's Texts and a Critique of Imperialism', in *The Feminist Reader: Essays in Gender and Literary Criticism*, ed. by Catherine Belsey and Jane Moore (London: MacMillan, 1989), pp. 175-195.
8. In Joyce's *A Portrait of the Artist as a Young Man*, ed. by Thomas Crofts (1916; New York: Dover Publications, 1994), Stephen Dedalus contemplates the complicity between the beholders of terror and the causes of terror: 'Terror is the feeling which arrests the mind in the presence of whatsoever is grave and constant in human suffering and unites it with the secret cause' (p. 148). In this context we may also remember the significance of the various levels of audience that structure Conrad's *Heart of Darkness,* ed. by Stanley Appelbaum (1902; New York: Dover, 1990) and make the reader/listener a complicit party to Marlowe's tale of terror. In particular, both Marlowe's desire to draw his listeners into his story and his observation that Kurtz was desperate for an audience indicate the active role the audience plays in bringing about the terror it nevertheless appears to relish from a distance.
9. See Chapter Two: Tobias Döring, 'Turning the Colonial Gaze: Re-visions of Terror in Dabydeen's *Turner*', pp. 32-47.
10. I use the term modernity to emphasize that Turner's painting dates

back to 1840, to the dawn of modernity around 1850. Although the painting cannot be strictly classified as a modern work of art, it is concerned with form and colour experiments rather than with figurative representation. Further, *The Slave Ship* expresses Turner's critique of both England's moral decay and the disintegration of imperial history. Dabydeen's rewriting of the painting suggests that the effects of imperialism and Turner's paradigmatic disenchantment with England's civilizing mission constitute seminal elements of England's march toward nation and artistic modernity. Further, in my reading of Dabydeen's poem, the term also indicates that Turner's desire to resolve historical contradictions through art reflects the tendency of modern art to transcend increasingly incompatible world views through artistic form. In the context of postcolonial studies, modernity, as I have defined it earlier, refers to the inherent violence of such ideologies as 'progress' and 'enlightenment' that served to 'civilize' and thus to subject and construct empire's cultural Other.

11. *Maps of Englishness*, p. 74.
12. See Chapter One: Aleid Fokkema, 'Caribbean Sublime: Transporting the Slave, Transporting the Spirit', pp. 17-31.
13. Ibid., p. 29.
14. Paul Gilroy, 'It Ain't Where You're From, It's Where You're At...The Dialectics of Diasporic Identification', *Third Text*, 13 (Winter 1991), 45-52 (p. 11-12).
15. From November 28, 1989 to February 5, 1990, the London Hayward Gallery ran an exhibition called 'The Other Story: Asian, African and Caribbean Artists in Post-War Britain'. The following quotation is from: 'Art of Darkness: Black Art and the Problem of Belonging to England', *Third Text*, 10 (Spring 1990), 45-52 (p. 46).
16. 'It Ain't Where You're From', 45-52 (p. 50, 51).
17. As the only word the stillborn child speaks, 'Nigger', I suggest, also inverts the only three words 'Massa, he dead', spoken by an African in Conrad's novella *Heart of Darkness*. In this way, *Turner* makes clear that it is impossible to write outside of history while simultaneously pointing to the dangers of holding on to the pains and losses of history. Here Dabydeen's poem makes an argument similar to Toni Morrison's *Beloved*, namely of the necessity of forgetting the atrocities of slavery but of remembering the moment of historical forgetting.
18. The poem may allude to the Paddy Dignam burial scene in Joyce's *Ulysses*. In this scene death itself connotes terror and becomes part

of a grotesque discourse on human decay. In Dabydeen's poem, however, terror results from J. M. W. Turner's aesthetic elevation of the slave trade's violence through the sublime. Death does not occur naturally and cannot simply enter into a universal discourse on the *condition humaine*. Döring notes that, after all, '[t]he only licence for blacks to claim a visible presence on the colonial stage was to act as comic characters, as stock types in the tradition of the minstrel show: terror transformed into comedy': Chapter Two: 'Turning the Colonial Gaze', p.45.

19. Karen McIntyre's essay, 'Necrophilia or Stillbirth? David Dabydeen's *Turner* as the Embodiment of Postcolonial Creative Decolonisation', in *The Art of David Dabydeen*, ed. by Kevin Grant (Leeds: Peepal Tree, 1997) rightly suggests that 'stillborn' can be read as both stillborn and still born. However, McIntyre does not provide a theoretical reading of the sign's doubling, seeing it as a configuration of the past through which 'creativity is *still*born' p. 148.

20. See Wilson Harris, 'Metaphor and Myth', in *Myth and Metaphor*, ed. by Robert Sellick (Adelaide: Centre for Research in the Literatures in English, 1982), and also Wilson Harris, 'An Interview with Wilson Harris', *Kunapipi*, 2:1 (1980), 100-106.

21. In 'Interview', *Configurations of Exile: South Asian Writers and Their Word*, ed. by Chelva Kanaganayakam, (Toronto: TSAR, 1995) pp. 26-33, (p. 29), David Dabydeen talks about the metaphor of the sea in *Turner*. His argument is located within and beyond the Derridean notion of difference.

22. *Location of Culture*, p. 115.

23. In 'Three Women's Texts' Spivak points out that '[n]o perspective *critical* of imperialism can turn the other into a self, because the project of imperialism has always already historically refracted what might have been the absolutely other into a domesticated other that consolidates the imperialist self' p. 186. It is this process of internalizing the enunciatory split inherent in the discourse of imperialism, of becoming the 'domesticated other', that shapes colonial desire in both the colonizer and the colonized. In his introduction to his poetry collection *Slave Song* (Oxford: Dangaroo, 1984), Dabydeen articulates this desire as the 'erotic energies of the colonial experience' (p. 10). In *Turner* these energies become the focal point for an investigation into the operations of postcolonial subjection.

24. Turner's phrase refers to his materialist and humanist critique of slavery articulated in his incomplete long poem 'The Fallacies of

Hope'. Turner used the following passage as an addendum to the title of *Slave Ship*:

> Aloft all hands, strike the top-masts and belay;
> Yon angry setting sun and fierce-edged clouds
> Declare the Typhoon's coming.
> Before it sweeps your decks, throw overboard
> The dead and dying – ne'er heed their chains.
> Hope, Hope, fallacious Hope!
> Where is thy market now? (Lindsay, *Sunset Ship*, p. 86).

25. For a discussion of James Thomson's, Byron's, and Coleridge's influence on Turner's art and critique of empire, see chapters five and fifteen in Jack Lindsay's *J.M.W. Turner: His Life and Work: A Critical Biography* (New York: NY Graphic Society, 1996). Further references to Lindsay are included in the main text of the essay. See John Ruskin, 'Of Water, As Painted by Turner', *Modern Painters*, 2nd edn (London: George Allen, Sunnyside, Orpington, 1897) I, pp. 376-406.

26. In Maya Jaggi, 'Out of the Torrid Waters of Colonial Culture: Writer David Dabydeen Talks to Maya Jaggi about his New Reading of the Enigmatic Turner', *Guardian*, 23 April 1994, p. 28; Dabydeen explains that Turner 'has become a symbol of genteel English identity in the same way that John Major talks about old maids bicycling off in the mist to hold communion [...] Yet the intensity of [*The Slave Ship*] suggests that he must have suffered traumas and lusts and disgusts. I wanted to recover his humanity – however perverse – from that neck-tied establishment conservatism.'

27. Karl Kroeber, 'Experience As History: Shelley's Venice, Turner's Carthage', *English Literary History*, 41 (1974), 321-339 (p. 325).

28. 'Art of Darkness', 45-52 (p. 51).

29. To conjure a Golden African age signifies a further correspondence between the African's and the Romantic longing for a pre-industrial and unspoiled English past. Both longings participate in an imperial as well as modernist narrative of history by constructing a continuity between antiquity and the present. For a discussion of how the nation imagines itself as at once ancient and modern see Benedict Anderson, *Imagined Communities: Reflections on the Origin and Spread of Nationalism* (London, New York: Verso, 1991).

30. In Dabydeen's poem the magician Manu explains that 'time future was neither time past/ Nor time present, but a rupture' (*Turner*,

33). With this quotation from Eliot's 'Burnt Norton', *Turner* replaces the modern notion of repetitive and circular time frames with that of discontinuous time zones. In the context of postcolonial concepts of time, the rupture of the Middle Passage marks the disjunctive temporality of modernity.

31. Immanuel Kant and Edmund Burke provide the classical discussion of the sublime. While Burke suggests that every natural object that 'excite[s]' terror 'operates in a manner analogous to terror, is a source of the Sublime', *A Philosophical Inquiry into the Origin of our Ideas of the Sublime and Beautiful*, ed. by James T. Boulton (1759; Oxford: Blackwell, 1987), p. 36, Kant argues that the sublime operates through the representation of a natural object 'which determines the mind to regard the elevation of nature beyond our reach as equivalent to a presentation of ideas', quoted in Slavoj Zizek, *The Sublime Object of Ideology* (London, New York: Verso, 1989), p. 202. In both cases the sublime is characterized by its capacity to represent what is elusive. Zizek reads Kant's definition of the sublime through Lacanian psychoanalysis, arguing that the object of the sublime is no longer the empirical 'object, but an object which occupies the place, replaces, fills out the empty place of the Thing as the void, as the pure Nothing of absolute negativity' p. 206. Zizek implies that the sublime corresponds to the Lacanian Real and thereby also locates the sublime in the realm of the unrepresentable. Jean Francois Lyotard, however, situates the sublime in the politics of visuality and language. He argues that in sublime art 'the art object no longer bends itself to models but tries to present the fact that there is an unpresentable; it no longer imitates nature, but is, in Burke, the actualization of a figure potentially there in language' p. 206. It is this erased yet potentially present figure postcolonial critics identify with the sublimated dead slave body in Turner's paintings. Critics such as Sara Suleri and Paul Gilroy contextualize the sublime in the history of empire and colonialism. For example, Suleri argues that the sublime 'functions as a conduit between the delusional aspect of empire-building or breaking and the very solidity of history', emphasizing the fictitious quality of historical narratives: *The Rhetoric of English India* (Chicago: Chicago University Press, 1993), p. 37.

32. *Black Atlantic*, p. 191.

33. Ibid., p. 197.

34. Ann Laura Stoler, *Race and the Education of Desire: Foucault's History of Sexuality and the Colonial Order of Things* (Cambridge: Cambridge

University Press, 1997), p. 7. Following references are included in the main text of the essay.

35. 'Out of the Torrid Waters of Colonial Culture', p. 28.

36. Turner's mother died in 1804, thirty-three years before the official beginning of Victorianism. However, I discuss Turner in the context of those discourses of sexuality and power that, according to Foucault, made and regimented Victorian society and its sites of knowledge production. Francis Barker and Ann Stoler point out that Foucault's analysis cannot be restricted to the actual historical period of Victorianism, but that it also applies to the late eighteenth and early nineteenth century. This period sees the intersection of various sites of modern knowledge production; the onset of industrialization; Enclosure Acts which changed the face and order of the English countryside and its traditional life; and the construction of a bourgeois identity based on the transformation of a body in pain into a body in subjection. Turner's life time, 1775-1851, covers the crucial social, economic and political changes within English society at the peak of imperialism, and thus lends itself to a Foucaultian reading.

37. From 1838 onwards, Turner's work was criticized for 'running riot into [...] frenzies', for 'rising almost to insanity, and occasionally sinking into imbecility', for being 'wonderful fruits of a diseased and reckless hand'. Thackeray, for example, wrote that 'Turner's exhibits 'are not a whit more natural, or less mad': all quoted in *J.M.W. Turner*, p. 97.

38. Michel Foucault, *The History of Sexuality*, trans. by Robert Hurley, 3 vols (New York: Vintage, 1978), I, p. 152.

39. Francis Barker, *The Tremulous Private Body: Essays on Subjection* (London: Methuen, Cambridge University Press, 1984), p. 67.

40. See Robert Hyam, *Empire and Sexuality: The British Experience* (Manchester: Manchester University Press, 1990).

41. Marina Warner, *Managing Monsters: Six Myths of Our Time: The 1994 Reith Lectures* (London: Verso, 1994), p. 40.

42. I refer to Derrida's notion that metaphor functions as 'white mythology'; in the discourse of Western philosophy, we can say that every metaphorical operation substitutes a sensory or corporeal image for an idea. In the course of metaphor's circulation in various philosophical discourses, however, the original violence of metaphor, the erasure of the corporeal image, falls into oblivion. See Jacques Derrida, 'White Mythology: Metaphor in the Text of Philosophy', *New Literary History*, 6:1 (Autumn 1974), 5-74.

43. The imperial imagination, as Toni Morrison argues in *Playing in the Dark: Whiteness and the Literary Imagination* (London: Picador, 1992), was rooted in the violent 'sexual dynamics', in the 'rawness and savagery' that provided the blueprint for the white literary and visual imagination, p. 44.

44. For a discussion of the discovery and function of the specific Roman ornament *grotteska*, see Mikhail Bakhtin, *Rabelais and His World*, trans. Helene Iswolsky (Massachusetts: MIT Press, 1968) pp. 24-32.

45. Tzvetan Tordorov, *Theories of the Symbol*, trans. by Catherine Potter (New York: Cornell University Press, 1997), p. 73. Following references are included in the main text of the essay.

46. Rey Chow, *Primitive Passions: Visuality, Sexuality, Ethnography, and Contemporary Chinese Cinema* (New York: Columbia University Press, 1995), p. 150.

47. *Maps of Englishness*, p. 49.

CHAPTER FOUR

A PERMANENT TRANSIT: TRANSGRESSION AND METAMORPHOSES IN DAVID DABYDEEN'S ART.

MADINA TLOSTANOVA

The borderline work of culture demands an encounter with newness that is not part of past and present. It creates a sense of the new as an insurgent act of cultural translation. Such art does not merely recall the past as social cause or aesthetic precedent; it renews the past, re-figuring it as a contingent 'in-between' space, that innovates and interrupts the performance of the present.

Homi Bhabha, *The Location of Culture*

The silence of Friday is a helpless silence. He is the child of his silence, a child unborn, a child waiting to be born that can not be born.

J.M. Coetzee, *Foe*

Among the substantial number of transcultural writers who have, in the last decades, come to acquire a visible space in the decentred and largely de-hierarchised body of world literature, David Dabydeen holds a very special place. His art escapes easy definitions and he evades straightforward classification, in a political, cultural, regional or aesthetic sense, as a postcolonial, Caribbean, or postmodern author. Although all these elements are present in his work, they mingle in fluid ways. Meaning in his writing is not predetermined or fixed, but always in the process of becoming, giving birth to a new aesthetics of transgression and metamorphosis. The Dominican-American writer Julia Alvarez pointed out in a recent interview:

'I get nervous when people ask me to define myself as a writer. I hear the cage of a definition close around me with its "Latino subject matter", "Latino style", "Latino concerns". I find that the best way to define myself is through the stories and poems that do not limit me to a simple label, a choice. Maybe after years of feeling caught between being "a real Dominican" and being American, I shy away from simplistic choices that will leave out an important part of who I am or what my work is about'.[1]

While trying to avoid putting Dabydeen's art in such a 'cage of definitions', I think it is profitable to look at how such constructs as the possibility/impossibility of cultural translation, or hybridity and inbetweenness and homelessness are being creatively redefined and deconstructed in Dabydeen's work.

On the most general level of the interaction of cultural models Dabydeen plays ironically with possible ways of defining postcolonial experience in a new global multicultural situation, mixing together and transforming existing forms of cultural and aesthetic representation. For example, he critiques traditional approaches to representation, with its characteristic urge to freeze differences once and for all, in one of his best known poems, 'Coolie Odyssey' with its assault on a sentimental 'vogue' for 'peasantry'.[2] Implicit in the poem is the argument that Western culture's ways of exoticising the Other deprive him/her of his/her own voice. Even the most intimate pictures from the past, from childhood, are stereotyped by a 'reversely enchanted' consciousness, depriving the sphere of personal memory of any meaning.[3]

A critiqued use of the mode of cultural assimilation, based on the modernizing urge to resemble a super-progressive, intensive type of development, involving cultural mimicry or 'crypto-ethnicity', to use Linda Hutcheon's term, is present in many of Dabydeen's poems as well.[4] Paradoxes of assimilation and the fluidity of ethnic, racial, and cultural gradations are themes in his account of Caribbean immigrant experience in Great Britain, but these newer identities are never fixed and always shown to be fluid.

But the aesthetic model that seems to be most prevalent in Dabydeen's art lies in his play with the strange and unpredictable combination of traditional and modern elements. Between these elements there is space for a 're-newing and re-figuring', for creative instability, inner tensions and contradictions as constitutive factors.[5] The co-existence in the aesthetic work of phenomena belonging to different historical periods and cultures (Western and non-western, 'pre-literate' and 'post-literate') puts the work ontologically, aesthetically, and psychologically in a permanent situation of transit. In this model, identity formation is always postponed and dynamic, with a tendency to openness, flexibility, and non-finality. It gives birth to an unstable meaning-generating time-space, where the third and the first worlds are in a state of constant friction, 'haemorrhaging', to use Gloria Anzaldúa's visceral metaphor from her now classic *Borderlands/ La Frontera. The New Mestiza*.[6] The hyphen that often marks this 'in-between-ness' (Indo-American, Franco-Maghrebian, British-Caribbean, etc.), can become both the border of dividedness and painful 'split-ness at the root', as the American poet and essayist Adrienne Rich calls it, and an imaginary bridge, an image of connection.[7] The number of postcolonial writers who work with such an ontology and aesthetics is not vast. The mere use of postcolonial motifs or the urge to speak on questions of political and cultural suppression does not predicate the use of aesthetically innovative forms. David Dabydeen clearly belongs to a group of writers that neither hides behind a nativist cloak nor lauds complete assimilation. The postcolonial theorists' concept of homelessness becomes, in Dabydeen's works, a play between multiple homes or multiple homelessness. His attitude toward Western imperialism and colonialism is clear and, judging from a narrow and careless focus on some recurrent themes and imagery in his poetry, one could mistakenly classify him as a traditionalist, hostile to Western culture and discourse; a nationalist 'local colour' poet; or, even more narrowly, a 'West Indian poet with a Caribbean field of allusion'.[8] In reality, a closer analysis of Dabydeen's poetics clearly denies such an interpretation, showing his involvement in cultural-aesthetic hybridity on all levels: his ludic use of language(s) and discourse registers and his fondness for intertextual reference, using both Western and non-Western texts. In his case there is neither the absolute ironic negation of any tradition nor the use of any traditions as an absolute reference point. He skilfully de-constructs various discourses, estranging and questioning them in the process. This contributes to giving Dabydeen's poetry its newness and originality, a quality he shares with transcultural writers such as Maxine Hong Kingston, Bharati Mukherjee (hyphenated Americans, creatively denying their hyphens), or the Maghrebian writer Abdelwahab Meddeb, who decentres the French language to the extent that the reader becomes lost in the hybrid discursive labyrinth of his novels.

In Dabydeen's long poem, *Turner*, the reader finds a variety of cultural models, ranging from, on the one hand, an exploration of the virtues of creative amnesia about the most painful episodes of the past, and on the other, the possibility of more constructive efforts to create the world anew. These tensions are expressed in the polar, yet simultaneously doubling forms of the unborn child and the drowned slave's head, images of victims in the 'sublime' mode, suddenly coming alive, connected to each other in the shadow of empire, represented by Turner both as artist and ship's captain.[9] In *Turner*, in the attempts of the drowned slave to reconstruct African memory, the opposition between archaic tradition and Western civilization becomes one of the central themes of uncertainty. Obviously, in his descriptions of the times 'before' there are traceable elements of the existence of an archaic community that 'Turner' as representative of empire would destroy. But the very notions of before and after are no longer truly significant in the timeless universe of the slave's head. In it mingle syncretic religious beliefs, dreams, obviously invented descriptions, and interpretations of phenomena from the Western tradition by means of archaic myths (for example, the sea battle is compared with the love battle of the two gods Sensu and Zain (6)).

There is the same ambivalence concerning Shaman Manu's prophesy concerning the coming times. In the non-rational wisdom of the magician there hides a strange foreshadowing of the unfixed character of postmodern meaning-production, when the seemingly simple enumeration of what Turner will bring entangles positive imagery with negative and destructive phenomena, so that it is no longer possible to say what is going to be good or bad for the community. Godlessness, motherlessness and alienation, generated by contact with Turner's culture, become in Manu's prediction inseparable from the images of life-giving rain; of salvation from disease and evil; of learning to count and weigh, measure and rationalize; of access to new words and also to a new cult of gold, a substance that was meaningless before. In this prediction, the duality of Western culture is obviously being confronted, and for Manu there is no contradiction in the way the extremes, the oppositions, meet and coexist. He predicts that 'civilization' will bring his community into 'a rupture so complete / That pain and happiness will become one, death / And freedom, barrenness and riches' (33). Manu foresees a future life without the sacred beads, symbols of the stability and predictability of tradition, and urges the need to invent new ways of arranging them. As a colonial and postcolonial subject who must survive the conditions of new invisibility, he metaphorically formulates intermediary forms to allow cultural passage through the phases of assimilation and mimicry in order to reach the next stage of the creative meaning-production that the slave's head dreams of invoking. The unborn child is a crucial image in *Turner*, a materialization of the negative self-identity of a colonial subject. The author shows that the unborn child, who does not want to begin anew in the sea of oblivion and new possibilities, is fed only by anger and hatred, which can hardly be the source of anything positive. The creative impulse, on the contrary, lies in the slave's head who, following Manu's prediction, tries in vain to build the world anew, to give a tongueless earth a meaningful voice, not just a vaguely Shakespearean 'idiot witter/ Of wind through a dead wood' (39), or the destructive cry, 'Nigger' (28, 39). The narrator is left with a godless, motherless, bead-less nothingness, and new destructive ways of self-reflection: Turner's, 'drowning in the yolk of himself' (39). This sense of undecidability unfolds slowly in the circling, expanding images of emptiness and negation. There is 'no Savannah, moon, gods, magicians [...] No stars, no land, no words, no community' and most importantly, 'no mother' (40). 'Mother' is a key symbol of tradition in this poem, a symbol of home, salvation and rebirth and also the expression of its author's carefully hidden guilt. But nothingness can also bring a new beginning, a new quest for another image of the self. The final phase of the poem presents homelessness in its most complete form, but it also seems to assert an act of growing up and getting rid of all sentimental attachments, of wilfully and consciously accepting de-territorialization as a permanent condition.

Among the most important themes of Dabydeen's works one could point out the journey cronotope, to use Michael Bakhtin's term, and metamorphosis and transgression as all-embracing structural principles.[10] All are interrelated, so that the journey is presented as metamorphic and transgressive of various boundaries. In the introductory note to *Coolie Odyssey* Dabydeen points out:

> The first poem started on a train journey from Edinburgh to Birmingham, with further pieces written in trains from Coventry to London and in planes from London over the Atlantic to the Caribbean. [...] The poems offer glimpses into an odyssey, not a chronicle of threaded events. The journey is from India to Guyana to England, and it is as much a journey of words as deeds.[11]

The odyssey in Dabydeen's works is usually directed from a cyclical past to a linear present and future, from the third world to the first. It connects to the words of Jasmine, the main character in Bharati Mukherjee's eponymous novel, whose past happened 'many lifetimes ago'.[12] The journey, as exodus to salvation, as a quest for El Dorado, is accompanied by transgressions and crossings of boundaries, a constant wandering and changing of identities and masks, often presented as migrations from one self to an other. This theme is treated in Dabydeen's works as both a personal, or individual, and collective experience. Thus, in 'Coolie Odyssey', the group experience of Indian workers taken to Guyana is presented as the dark side of an ironically realized 'golden' El Doradean dream. The Coolies found only disappointment and death in the colourful land of light and gold, which turned out to be the gold of sugar cane fields waiting to be harvested. At one level, Guyana is thus presented as a cemetery for Indian workers' hopes and aspirations. Their story, though, is seen as problematic, not easy to catch on paper and reproduce, needing to find some other pattern than that of the rationalized Western vogue for peasantry mentioned above. The postmodern sense of the past as a text that is waiting to be written and thus is relative, variational, and always contextualised by the present, comes forward in this poem in the rendering of tradition in the images of the 'library of graves', where 'ancestors curl and dry to scrolls of parchment' and say, *'Got no story to tell'*.[13]

Dabydeen's attitude to the past and the idea of collective memory is problematic, if not downright sceptical. This past hardly exists, is waiting to be born, to be written down as a text by the children, educated in far away (Western) schools. This seems to assert that it is not possible to tell the story of the past other than in the Western tongue and mode. But then 'Coolie Odyssey' also suggests that such a discourse cannot truly represent the story or make it heard in its own voice. He echoes Maxine Hong Kingston in her reflections on the made-up, invented nature of any cultural tradition, in which the personal, the familial and the stereotypical mingle together and become inseparable.[14] Perceptions of an ubiquitous tendency to stereotypical renderings of 'tradition', and a questioning of the authenticity of representation, are constants in Dabydeen's art. There is an equal scepticism about the reception of 'working class/ peasant/ third-world' writing in the West, in which the 'poetry bubbles from peat bogs' to be consumed by the educated listening to him reading his poems 'between courses', 'sipping wine'.[15] But such ironies do not equal a simple call back to the past, to the authentic: the poet exercises a very careful, self-reflective, controlled nostalgia, a balancing act of sorts.

For all writers coming from South and Central America and the Caribbean, regions of multi/cross-cultural contact, the concept of border as 'frontera' in the widest sense, including 'boundaries of expression' becomes a crucial metaphor.[16] This is clearly the case with Dabydeen. The 'boundaries of expression', geographical, historical, cultural, social, sexual, linguistic, become for him the boundaries of transgression, including the crossing of the boundary between life and death, and various forms and states of existence. The cronotope of journey in Dabydeen's works further problematizes the concept of the border, making it constantly shift and multiply and this is reflected in the dynamics of his art. *Turner*, for instance, is characterized by the foregrounding of its 'unfinished' nature, openness, shifts in images based on apparently free associations, sentences that contain a chain of recollections, put together in a seemingly arbitrary form. The instability of narrative voice (it is not always clear who is telling the story – the author, Turner, the slave's head, the unborn child) intensifies the open, unfinished, transitory nature of the narrative.

The instability of boundaries in relation to the concept of home, is another key theme for many postcolonial writers. For example, Audre Lorde, an American with Caribbean roots, presents a journey home through bits and pieces of various myths and stories, heard from her mother and then reconstructed, leading to the creation of the world anew, with new names for everything and everyone. This is also an important theme in Dabydeen's *Turner*. But Lorde's 'biomythography' *Zami. A New Spelling of My Name* leads finally to the negation of her mother's interpretation of home and tradition, and to the final deconstruction of the Zami myth to suit the main characters' purposes. One of the narrator's invented sisters in *Turner*, Rima, with her special prophetic gifts and strange songs, which even hypnotised Turner, reminds the reader of the sexually transgressive ideal of Zami, a Carriacou name, reinvented by Lorde, for women who work together as friends.[17]

In *Zami* the Saidian principle of imaginative geography comes alive when the author juxtaposes her several conflicting ideas about home: the ungracious Harlem of the 1950s, a half-mythic Carriacou in the Caribbean, and Mexico where, for the first time, she felt herself not invisible.[18] The details of the journey in Lorde's and Dabydeen's work are of course different, but the archetypal journey from the culture of origins to the wider and less intimate modern world remains essentially the same. For Lorde, after all, her parents' journey from the Caribbean to Manhattan is not a personal experience, as the journey from Guyana to England was for Dabydeen; Lorde knows her past only through her mother's stories. However, the motif of getting to know the past through foreparents and ancestors is present in Dabydeen's poetry as well.

Both Lorde and Dabydeen mix together fragments of lost Edenic imagery (itself frequently undermined by more realistic, 'fallen', images of home) with the harsh reality of the post-Edenic existence of an un-homed self, living in 'the very house of difference rather than the security of one particular difference', in other words, in the situation of permanent transit.[19]

In Dabydeen's poetry, the principle of 'imaginative geography' is not, as in Lorde's case, connected with the literally unknowable nature of a home that cannot be captured between the pages of an atlas, but there is a similar urge to 'invent' new geographies and new locales; complete worlds with names for people, flowers, plants, birds, beasts, a nonexistent space, with a creator who by the very act of naming repeats and re-invents the age-old archetype of creating the world with the word. Imaginative, alternative geography, where the proportions are disturbed, is especially evident in the poem 'The Old Map', representing a map of the Caribbean, which comes suddenly alive, so that the hidden, the muted, the sunken ships and drowned slaves, the islands forever unborn, re-emerge under the poet's searching gaze.[20] The state of unbornness is crucial for Dabydeen's work (the unborn child in *Turner*, the unborn islands in 'The Old Map', as un-realized possibilities and never-born selves). The large and the small, the distant and the close mix and stand for each other, distorting the spatial dimensions in the alternative map that Dabydeen offers to his readers: the Coolie's mouth spitting cane and a sailor's mouth in *Turner* spitting lime seeds mirror cannonballs spat out from the mouths of ships. Whole islands, Cuba and Jamaica, are compared to small objects and living creatures, like crabs, are seen from a bird's eye view.

The lyric voice in Dabydeen's poetry, in its constantly transitory state, creates new and multiple meanings through specific, often fantastic spatial-temporal relations, thus playing on and denying the happy unity and undividedness of traditional versions of consciousness. Such ambivalence about belonging to any particular cultural and discursive tradition, as well as the ludic nature of postmodern tricksterism, are typical features of several hybrid postcolonial authors. In Dabydeen's case, however, the ludic metamorphoses tend to be sad and painful rather than happy and life-asserting, as for example those the Argentinean theorist Maria Lugones suggests in her essay 'Playfulness, World-travelling and Loving Perception'.[21] For Dabydeen, any liberation from the past, any constructive activity, is possible only in the sphere of words, in the textual collisions, where the unhomed self can finally re-territorialize. Julia Alvarez describes this specific realm as a 'comunidad of the word', the only space where it becomes possible for a many-homed writer to feel at home.[22] Dabydeen constantly asks whether he can really forget everything and start anew in the sea of oblivion, the symbol of both death and resurrection; can he overcome the 'hunger of memory'? And the answer always lies in the word, not in the world. Thus, in 'Ma Talking Words' Dabydeen juxtaposes his mother's traditional wisdom, 'World don't know word', and the lyric skills of the poet who uses the word as a powerful instrument, often erotically coloured, enabling him, for example, to 'seduce' a white woman who is 'ravished by the poetry'.[23] In the in-between world of Dabydeen's poetry, different periods of time constantly leak into each other. The present is always coloured by the past, driving the poetic consciousness back in time, granting the possibility of symbolic liberation only in the sphere of the world as text and turning the creative process into a sublimation of rage, despair, confinement, and various inferiority complexes. In *Turner*, the past and the suppressed anger of the victimized are violently materialized in the image of the unborn child. Here the poet seems to be playing on the psychoanalytic concept of the subliminal, juxtaposing it with the sublime, echoing Homi Bhabha's description of the specific psychological state of unhomelessness as a space between the sublime and the subliminal (subconscious):

> The worlding of literature lies in a critical act that attempts to grasp the sleight of hand with which literature conjures with historical specificity, using the medium of psychic uncertainty, aesthetic distancing, or the obscure signs of the spirit world, the sublime and the subliminal.[24]

In Dabydeen's *Turner*, a strange marriage of the sublime (clearly marked as a concept drawn from the Western tradition) and the subliminal (marked by the invisibility of the drowned slave's head) takes place in the ambivalent image of the unborn child, bearing the subconscious fears and burden of the past.

In the preface to *Turner*, Dabydeen skilfully brings together academic diction and discourse with the realm of the unnamed, the hinted at, the uncanny, those modes that often 'slip between' and remained unnoticed. Dabydeen ironises the basic notions of Western aesthetics by drawing attention to its clashing perspectives, focusing on the contrast between the 'sublime style' of Turner's painting, with its personification of the sea and inanimate nature, that hides the awful rather than noble (in Ruskin's terms) subject of the painting itself: the slaves, dehumanized to the state of goods lost at sea, the 'bounty' (14) around which birds circle, or 'jettisoned', as in 'The Old Map'.[25] This is clearly Dabydeen's way of redefining the metamorphic theme of animate vs inanimate: a slave is rendered in the Western tradition as an animal, as an object, forbidden to change, to take part in life-giving metamorphoses by the master, who robs him of all other possible roles and masks. This is what happens to the slave boys on Turner's ship, and the imagined sister Ellar, who is raped and molested by Turner. Beautiful words normally assigned noble meanings, '*blessed, angelic*', '*sublime*' (38) (or sometimes, with more sadistic overtones as in '*we desire you*', '*we forgive you*', etc.,) are infused with the erotic essence of Turner as a sadistic personification of the Western patriarchal tradition, and are violently divorced from their 'noble' meanings and come to signify something completely different for the slave boys, who have to repeat Turner's phrases mechanically, like trained animals or sexual automata, coming to associate sublimity with the pain of rape and humiliation. This negation of the usual meaning of words is used by Dabydeen to stress once more the incongruence of Western and non-Western cultural and aesthetic systems, and consequently the words problematize cultural translation and code-switching as important elements of all trans- and vari-cultural traditions.

Metamorphosis is used by David Dabydeen not only as a prevailing theme, but also as a device, a trope, a structural principle, allowing him to combine and hybridize traditional elements and late 20th century Western dimensions of metamorphosis as a grotesque, alienating phenomenon, a turning of the familiar into something strange and horrible. Both the non-regenerating, finalized, anti-Bakhtinian interpretation of the metamorphosis of the grotesque, as a shadow of exhausted Western culture and tradition, and the non-final, open dimension of the kind of metamorphoses found in Ovid or English Romantic writing are present in *Turner*, constantly acting against each other. This contrast is especially clear in the image of the master of metamorphoses, shaman Manu. In the Guyanese tradition, the shaman is often called 'a lookman' or 'seer', literally, the one who predicts, who foretells, the 'shapeshifter' who constantly exercises his ability to undergo metamorphoses that the Western tradition with its 'forbidden change' principle has largely lost.[26] The intervention of Western ways into the traditional system of coordinates can lead to freezing, to non-dynamic logocentric binary oppositions such as living-dead, man-woman, inner-outer, White-Black, animate-inanimate.

These are the polarities that Dabydeen gradually estranges and denies in *Turner*, making the opposites meet and mix, producing an array of intermediary forms and shades, and making them look non-absolute and relative. This specifically non-binary use of metamorphoses can be described as the intervention of the sphere of 'beyond' that Dabydeen's *Turner* is largely based on. In Stanza XVIII we find out that there are more states of being than just life and death. The narrator-creator wants to mould the unborn child (the unformed or deformed) into something new, beyond the human form. He vacillates, drifts between death and 'another mood' (28), which is never defined in the poem, but clearly denies simple life vs death oppositions. In *Turner*, the principle of metamorphosis as the expression of the unformed, 'un-settled magma', to use Bharati Mukherjee's definition, located between many worlds and many options, is clearly expressed in the image of the sea as a powerful transforming agent, a magician, a creator, a force that remoulds everything and everyone alike, depriving persons not only of social status, but also of race, sex, age, colour, etc.[27] The metamorphoses wrought by the sea do not acquire the unpleasant, macabre connotations typical of Western tradition, acting out instead its colourful, almost carnival features. The narrator says that the sea;

> has bleached me too of colour,
> Painted me gaudy, dabs of ebony,
> An arabesque of blues and vermilions,
> Sea-quats cling to my body like gorgeous
> Ornaments. (14)

In Dabydeen's art, a many-layered metamorphic self is in constant transit between various identities, which all exist simultaneously, ironically re-making each other. The image of a happy boy from a Guyanese village, who is yet unfamiliar with the sense of homelessness, flashes through the other images of a new immigrant in London, and a Western-educated professor, contemplating his own situation and exercising critical distance. In *Slave Song*, Dabydeen bridges otherwise incommensurate images and discourses, by the unique self-translation of Creole poems into English: mocking the would-be scholarly commentary to an Other-ed text, making impossible the cultural translation, which centres between and beyond the Western rational analysis and the emotional thickness and violence of the actual words, spoken by the mute or the unborn. That is why even in Dabydeen's dramatic monologues, even when formally they follow the Caribbean poetic tradition, there is nearly always a certain additional perspective present, problematizing the act of cultural translation or linkage, first of all in the linguistic sense, but also, as in *Turner*, estranging the genre of the dramatic monologue itself, assigning it not to a living person (a slave, a coolie), but to a drowned and half-decomposed head, recollecting its past and dreaming of its future. If the intermediary meaning in Dabydeen's self-translated poems in *Slave Song* lies somewhere in the silenced gap between the Creole and the English, in *Turner* he goes even further to invent a nonexistent tongue, comprehensible only to the slave's head. Here, the poet echoes Meddeb's strategy towards the language of empire, used in his novel *Phantasia,* similarly structured around French romantic paintings, representing North African Arabs in a particular, stereotyped way. Meddeb points out that 'writing in French surrenders us to the other, but we will defend ourselves with the arabesque, the subversion, the maze, the labyrinth, the incessant de-centring of the sentence and of language so that the other will get lost just as in the narrow streets of the casbash'.[28]

Turner is a good example of the interaction of Western and non-Western texts, a case of what Helen Tiffin describes as 'canonical counter discourse'.[29] It is important to note that in Dabydeen's case there are not only verbal, but also visual images from Western canon that the author makes use of, made possible by his extensive acquaintance with British fine art. Counter-canonical discourse is multilayered and polyphonic in Dabydeen's work, not concentrating on just one canonical work, as often happens (as in J.M. Coetzee's *Foe*, or Jean Rhys's *Wide Sargasso Sea*, for example.[30]) Again, *Turner* is not the only example of Dabydeen's postcolonial reading of a famous painting. His shorter ballad ('Dependence, or The Little Ballad of the Little Black Boy'), gives voice to the marginalized slave boy in Francis Wheatley's painting *Family Group and Negro Boy*.[31] The marginal image in Turner's painting also becomes the main agent in Dabydeen's poem, denying the usual logocentric division between the centre and the periphery. This unusual and contradictory transitory self is no longer the flat self of a cultural victim or an extremist, but a self which is able in a perfectly postmodern way to invent a body and a biography, and to people an imagined landscape, thus proclaiming his ability and right to create the whole world anew. The narrator incorporates bits and pieces of various traditions, old and new, coming from different cultures in his act of world-creating. The liberating motif of naming as an act of creation, connected often with poly-lingualism and sensitivity to the gap between the world and the word (often a foreign word, taken out of the non-native language, forced upon the user) is a recurrent theme of Caribbean poetry. Thus, in Derek Walcott's poetry the moment of naming, of giving birth to the world, is also closely connected with the violent nature of the Western tongue and culture that forces its words and meanings upon the muted and yet unborn places and people:

My race began as the sea began,
With no nouns and with no horizon,
With pebbles under my tongue,
With a different fix on the stars [...]
I began with no memory
I began with no future[...]
And when they named these bays
Bays,
Was it nostalgia or irony? [...]
Being men they could not live
Except they first presumed
The right of everything to be a noun.[32]

The counter-canonical discourse in Dabydeen's *Turner* is not limited to Turner's painting alone. Among its other canonical sources one could name certainly William Shakespeare's *The Tempest* and maybe, more unexpectedly, T.S. Eliot's *The Waste Land*, as well as a number of other Western texts.[33] Dabydeen's turning to *The Tempest*, a paradigmatic text for all Pan-American territories, is more predictable, but his use of Shakespeare's text is different from that of many South American and Caribbean authors and theorists. The old argument of assimilation, impersonated by Ariel, and the aggressive, non-assimilating identity, personified by Caliban, becomes largely deconstructed and estranged in Dabydeen's poetry. The erotic overtones of *The Tempest*, ironically subverted, are present in a good deal of Dabydeen's work. The empire is presented as a White woman (Miranda, Britannia), who symbolically seduces Caliban, changing roles with him. In 'The Seduction', the poet deconstructs the stereotypes of sexually violent Caliban and pure and innocent Miranda:

I cannot come to you tonight
With monstrous organ of delight
I have no claw, nor appetite
I am not Caliban but sprite
But weakness flutterance and flight
An insect scurrying from the light.[34]

The general erotic turn of much of Dabydeen's poetry, with its rendering of the sadism of empire, also leads to a specific interpretation of colonization and subjugation as driven by the need for compensations for impotence, physical and symbolic. But 'Impotence' also suggests a 'black' impotence under the focus of a 'blue-eyed' gaze. Reading across both *Turner* and 'Impotence' suggests a vision of the sterility of the cultural and racial encounter.[35]

The problematics of life/death metamorphoses and the meaninglessness of knowledge in a godless universe, as well as the images of exhaustion and fragmentation in Western culture that T.S. Eliot's *The Waste Land* was based on, are certainly present in Dabydeen's *Turner*. The motif of death by water, so important in *The Waste Land*, is repeated and redefined in *Turner* in its smallest details; the sea, picking the bones of a drowned sailor in whispers, his recollections of the past, etc. But again the emphasis shifts from the perspective of the Phoenician sailor as a free agent, a merchant, preoccupied with profit and loss, to the point of view of the live goods that give him profit, the slaves. The haunting images of eyes turning into pearls, bones becoming corals, have clearly migrated from Shakespeare's *The Tempest* through T. S. Eliot's *The Waste Land* into *Turner*, transformed and redecorated in a neo-baroque Pan-American way. The grotesque metamorphoses of the sea (in Shakespeare's text – *'a sea-change / Into something rich and strange'*[36]) in *Turner* become at once both more colourful and repulsive; 'terror is transformed into / Comedy' (21). The sea is repeatedly presented in the poem as the receptacle for the rubbish of Western civilization, but also as the powerful creator, remaking and transforming the drowned sailors, slaves, and goods into new states, a marginal theme for both Shakespeare and Eliot. Moreover, in their texts, metamorphoses are more or less final; animate forms give birth to inanimate objects. Dabydeen performs reversals of a different sort, turning the inanimate back into the animate, making new lives in new forms. For example, when he lavishly describes how sea-quats swallow the drowned men's eyes and crabs roost between the drowned women's breasts we are given terrible, but not final, and in a sense, life-giving pictures. These images of decomposition/regeneration, death/revival, as a specific rendering of the motif of metamorphosis multiply in Dabydeen's work, evoking painful, physiological metaphors of a passage towards self-identification, including artistic identification, typical of many hybrid writers (see, for instance Audre Lorde's simile for the creative process in blood gushing out from under broken skin, or G. Anzaldua's cacti needle tormenting the writer's flesh in the process of artistic creation). The motif of decomposition that is repeated in many of Dabydeen's works also has a clear metamorphic meaning in relation to the decomposing self and its messy remaking into something new, incorporating the meaning of decomposition into that of a new birth. Echoing Turner's colonizing/violating practices, which he disguises as teaching the barbarians the '*sublime*' and the '*blessed*' (38), the sea also 'decorates, [and] violates' (9) its prey, and these words are separated by only a comma in *Turner*, almost becoming synonyms in its fantastic world.

Imagery from Eliot's poem re-emerges in strange and unexpected forms in *Turner*. Blindness as clairvoyance, presented in *The Waste Land* in the image of a mythic, double-gendered Tiresias, is echoed by the drowned slave's head, also blind and clairvoyant, which multiplies and denies itself in its doppelganger, the unborn child. This leads back to the past, to the collective cultural trauma, and this sets up a counter-current to the images of revival and regeneration in the sea. It points to an intermediary limbo state between the amorphous and the clearly formed, between various elements, between life and death. The travesty of doubleness, characteristic of this poem, is clearly a part of a wider all-embracing principle of metamorphosis that Dabydeen's art is based on. In the multiplying, syncretic images of Turner (as painter, captain of the ship, the unborn child, a symbol of all Whites, even all men) Western binaries mingle with traces of traditional Caribbean notions, such as that of the Guyanese Dutchman jumbie (the dangerous, destructive spirit of an early European coloniser) producing an elusive and metamorphic postcolonial ghost of a wiped-out or never-born self, a materialization of the negative self-image of an ambivalent consciousness. The unborn child is the ultimate example of such a ghost, a frightful doppelganger, an ominous shade of the colonizing civilization, incapable of separate existence outside its coordinates. This is contrasted by the author with more obviously romantic rendering of the same subject (the unborn as symbol of life to come), acquiring cruel, sexual, physiological, sadistic overtones. The blind oracle in both Eliot's and Dabydeen's texts is a sexually transgressive creature, neither a woman, nor a man. It is indicative, though, that in Dabydeen's case this imagery is much more positive than in *The Waste Land*: it is its mothering, not sexual nature that the slave's head wants to take as its woman's side. Possible sexual/gender transgressions are divided by Dabydeen into those connected with violence and rape (as in Turner raping the boys) and those connected with (more or less) free will and liberating actions (the head is not sure of its gender, but is eager to breastfeed the unborn child).

These are only a few examples of counter-canonical discourse in Dabydeen's poetry that contributes to its transgressive and metamorphic effects. It is a realization of a hybrid, in-between aesthetic-ontological model, based not on a denial of the source texts, be they Shakespeare, Eliot, Turner's painting or the Guyanese cultural mix, but on the ironic and intricate play between these discourses and images. These allow us to link his poetics and ontology to the paradox of the 'permanent transit' and define Dabydeen as a representative of a new generation of writers: belonging to the as yet tentative and not sufficiently defined global realm of 'world literature', constantly performing a balancing act that allows the creation of new meanings to make sense of the chaos we live in with its intricate inner order, and the invention and understanding of the possible ways from (post)modernity to beyond.

Notes to Chapter Four

Epigraphs:
Homi Bhabha, *The Location of Culture* (London & New York: Routledge, 1994).
J. M. Coetzee, *Foe* (London: Penguin, 1986).

1. Julia Alvarez, 'Finding a Home in the Comunidad of Words', *Middlebury Magazine*, Fall (1998), 38-39 (p. 39).
2. David Dabydeen, 'Coolie Odyssey', *Coolie Odyssey* (Coventry: Hansib/Dangaroo, 1988), p. 9.
3. M. Maffesoli, 'La Socialidad en la Postmodernidad', *Pergola*, 8 (1989), p. 103.
4. Linda Hutcheon, 'Crypto-Ethnicity', *PMLA*, 113.1 (January 1989), 29-33 (p. 28).
5. *Location of Culture*, p. 7.
6. Gloria Anzaldúa, *Borderlands/La Frontera: The New Mestiza* (San Francisco: Aunt Lute Books, 1987).
7. Adrienne Rich, 'Split at the Root', *Blood, Bread, and Poetry* (New York: W. W. Norton & Company, 1986), pp. 100-123.
8. *Contemporary Poets*, ed. by Thomas Riggs, 6th edn, (New York: Saint James Press, 1996), p. 22; and subsequently Laurence A. Breiner, *An Introduction to West Indian Poetry*, (Cambridge: Cambridge University Press, 1998), p. 192.
9. David Dabydeen, *Turner: New & Selected Poems* (London: Cape, 1994), p. 70. Further references to *Turner* and poems collected in the same publication will be included parenthetically in the text.
10. M., Mikhail Bakhtin, *The Dialogic Imagination: Four Essays*, trans. by M. Holquist (Austin: University of Texas, 1981).
11. 'Preface', *Coolie Odyssey*.
12. Bharati Mukherjee, *Jasmine* (London: Virago, 1991), p. 3.
13. 'Coolie Odyssey', p. 12.
14. Maxine Hong Kingston, *The Woman Warrior: Memoirs of a Childhood Among Ghosts* (London: Vintage, 1989).
15. 'Coolie Odyssey', p. 9, p. 13.
16. *Introduction to West Indian Poetry*, p. 192.
17. Audre Lorde, *Zami: A New Spelling of My Name* (California: The Crossing Press/Freedom, 1997).
18. Edward W. Said, *Orientalism* (London: Routledge & Kegan Paul, 1978), pp. 54-55.
19. *Zami*, p. 226.
20. 'The Old Map', *Coolie Odyssey*, p. 14.
21. Maria Lugones, 'Playfulness, World-Travelling and Loving Perception', in *The Woman That I Am: The Literature and Culture of Contemporary Women of Colour*, ed. by D. Soyini Madison (New York: St Martin's Press 1997) pp. 626-638.
22. 'Comunidad of Words', 38-39 (p. 39).

23. 'Ma Talking Words', *Coolie Odyssey*, p. 40; 'The Sexual Word', *Coolie Odyssey*, p. 32.
24. *Location of Culture*, p. 12.
25. 'The Old Map', p. 14.
26. Elias Canetti, *Masse und Macht* (Hamburg: Claassen Verlag, 1960).
27. Bharati Mukherjee, 'A Four-Hundred-Year-Old-Woman', p. 27.
28. S. Mehrez, 'Translation and the Postcolonial Experience: The Francophone North African Text', in *Rethinking Translation* (London: Routledge, 1992), pp. 120-138 (124).
29. Helen Tiffin, 'Postcolonial Literatures and Counter-Discourse', in *Postcolonial Studies Reader*, ed. by Bill Ashcroft, Gareth Griffiths, Helen Tiffin (New York: Routledge, 1995) pp. 95-8 (p. 97).
30. J. M. Coetzee, *Foe* (London: Penguin, 1986); and Jean Rhys, *Wide Sargasso Sea* (London: Penguin, 1966).
31. 'Dependence, or The Ballad of the Little Black Boy', *Coolie Odyssey*, p. 47. His novel *A Harlot's Progress* (London: Cape, 1999) and earlier collection of poetry *Slave Song* (Denmark: Dangaroo Press, 1984) also show an interest in interplay between visual art and literature.
32. Derek Walcott, 'Names', *Collected Poems 1948-1984* (London: Faber & Faber, 1992), pp. 305-308.
33. T. S. Eliot, *The Waste Land* (New York: Boni and Liveright, 1922); and William Shakespeare, *The Tempest*, ed. by Frank Kermode, 6th edn (London, Massachusetts: Methuen, 1962).
34. 'The Seduction', *Coolie Odyssey*, p. 30.
35. 'Impotence', *Coolie Odyssey*, p. 29.
36. *The Tempest*, pp. 35-6.

CHAPTER FIVE

ON NOT BEING TONY HARRISON: TRADITION AND THE INDIVIDUAL TALENT OF DAVID DABYDEEN

LEE M. JENKINS

One of the more unusual critical responses to T.S. Eliot is surely David Dabydeen's claim that 'Eliot is the parent of Caribbean poetry.' Indeed, Dabydeen himself feels the need to qualify his remark before he makes it, when he says that Eliot assumes this parental role 'in a peculiar sense'.[1] On a thematic level, much of the work of the British-based Indo-Caribbean poet Dabydeen is to do with absent parents (the poet's actual parents, his parent country of Guyana and the Caribbean parent language, Creole. Now living in England, Dabydeen shares with Eliot the status of *metoikos,* or resident alien). On a formal level, his poetry is less a quest for origins than it is a turbulent, by turns loving and loathing, respectful and rebellious, relationship with Eliot and other literary progenitors from Homer to Tony Harrison.[2]

Dabydeen's *agon* with Eliot is evident from his first collection, *Slave Song* (1984).[3] The poet's use of Creole in this collection is, on one level, a testament of authenticity and, paradoxically given Dabydeen's title, a proclamation of emancipation from the influence of Eliot and the Western literary tradition: this black vernacular is a language which, despite its 'capacity for a savage lyricism' permits no level of abstraction, so 'you cannot have the *Four Quartets* in Creole'.[4] Notwithstanding this, what is innovative in contemporary black British and Caribbean poetry suggests a certain continuity with Eliot. Prior to these poetries, Dabydeen has argued, 'the last great innovator in British poetry this century has been T.S. Eliot'.[5] Dabydeen goes on to specify 'the brokenness of the [Creole] language', in which 'resides not just a certain barbaric energy, but also the capacity to be experimental', suggesting perhaps that Dabydeen's may be a synthetic, constructed Creole, in the sense in which the Scots of Hugh MacDiarmid's early lyrics is a synthetic Scots.[6]

Sarah Lawson Welsh's point that *Slave Song* 'is characterised by a vigorous orality but also [an...] ultimately stronger [...] textuality' is borne out by Dabydeen's subsequent collection, *Coolie Odyssey* (1988).[7] As Benita Parry remarks, 'Where *Slave Song* offers a fiction of transparency, of instant access to the authentically demotic voices of Guyana, *Coolie Odyssey* satirises the conceit of poets aspiring to retrieve a folk heritage'.[8]

Tony Harrison has also satirised such an aspiration in the conceits of *The School of Eloquence*, and as Dabydeen's citation of Harrison in the title of his essay 'On Not Being Milton: Nigger Talk in England Today' suggests, there is some contiguity between their projects.[9] Reading the Gawain poet as a student at Cambridge, Dabydeen could see 'the ancient divorce between north and south in Britain' as 'evocative of the divide between the so-called Caribbean periphery and the metropolitan centre of London' (Ricks and Michaels, 4). Dabydeen's essay goes on to complain that 'Milton's ornate, highly structured, Latinate expressions [...] are still the exemplars of English civilisation against which the barbaric, broken utterances of black people are judged' (8). Elsewhere Dabydeen reminds us that 'the term "barbarian" is derived from a Greek word meaning "to speak like a foreigner"';[10] and of course there is the grammar schoolboy-self Harrison remembers in 'Them & [uz]' being dubbed 'barbarian' by his RP-speaking teacher for his Leeds-accented rendition of Keats (20). Later in this poem Harrison remarks that 'You can tell the Receivers where to go / ... once you know / Wordsworth's *matter* / *water* are full rhymes' (21), and Dabydeen has pointed out that in Creole pronunciation, 'water' becomes 'wata' (Ricks and Michaels, 3). Over and above incidental consonances like these, Dabydeen paraphrases Wordsworth's dictum that 'poetry was the language of ordinary men', adding 'his own poetry wasn't, and my Creole isn't, because you always shape the language you use', a remark with which the wordsmith of *The School of Eloquence* would surely agree.[11]

Dabydeen's essay defines the 'barbaric, broken utterances' of 'black people' (and of poets like Harrison, as Dabydeen's self-alignment with the latter suggests) against the 'Latinate expressions' of Milton; and yet the two elements in the title of Dabydeen's essay, 'On Not Being Milton' and 'Nigger Talk in England Today', contradict, modify, qualify each other, as do the two elements in the title of his 1988 collection *Coolie Odyssey*. In both titles, allusion implicitly aligns the poet with literary tradition, while the competing use of terms such as 'Coolie' and 'Nigger' serves to racialise, to complicate, perhaps to appropriate and certainly to revise, a tradition which, despite his anterior claim of not being Milton, includes a poet such as Harrison.[12] Yet Dabydeen has in retrospect described as naïve his initial perception of an analogy between Harrison's north/south divide and antagonisms between a Caribbean periphery and English centre (Ricks and Michaels). The title poem of Dabydeen's collection *Coolie Odyssey* elaborates on his sense of displacement not only with reference to 'the metropolitan centre', but also in relation to Harrison, Seamus Heaney, Douglas Dunn and the readerly 'vogue' of 'peasantry' attendant upon their writing:[13]

> Now that peasantry is in vogue,
> Poetry bubbles up from peat bogs,
> People strain for the old folk's fatal gobs
> Coughed up in grates North or North East
> 'Tween bouts o' living dialect,
> It should be time to hymn your own wreck,
> Your house the source of ancient song:
> (*Coolie Odyssey*, 9)

The use of the conditional in 'It *should* be time to hymn your own wreck, / Your house the source of ancient song' (my emphasis) in the first verse of 'Coolie Odyssey' suggests that Dabydeen is as wary of positioning his own poetry in relation to that of Heaney and Harrison – the poem goes on to acknowledge that 'the connections [are] difficult' – as he is aware of potential readerly and critical appropriations of his poetry given that 'peasantry is in vogue'. Like a Guyanese Richard III, Dabydeen, who frequently brings into his work in standard English the Shakespearian timbre he detects in Creole, declaims, 'In a winter of England's scorn / We huddle together memories, hoard them from / The opulence of our masters' (9), 'masters' operating as a mordant pun in which the masters of the slave system are identified with Dabydeen's literary 'masters'.[14]

'Coolie Odyssey' explores dislocation from home and from origins which, in the process of rendering them as poetry, are transformed. At the end of the poem, Dabydeen's Guyanese homeland becomes 'this library of graves', where 'The ancestors curl and dry to scrolls of parchment' (12). In Harrison's 'Book Ends' from *The School of Eloquence,* a generational and cultural divide is figured in terms of writing and representation, and Dabydeen, similarly, describes parents who are 'authored' by their own offspring; Dabydeen's ancestors 'lie like texts / Waiting to be written by the children' (12). Both poets, Harrison and Dabydeen, assume an ambivalent stance toward what Harrison calls 'Littererchewer' (21) and literary tradition; and in the case of both, the writing of poems which 'go back to my roots' (Harrison 11), also signals the distance travelled (in Dabydeen's case, that distance is geographical as well as cultural), from origins. Yet while he can acknowledge analogy between his own dilemmas and those of Harrison and Heaney, Dabydeen also resists assimilation into the society of these 'Rhubarbarians'. Speaking in an interview about the 'folk grandmother' to whom his poem 'Coolie Odyssey' is dedicated, Dabydeen has said:

> I cannot write about her in the way the Irish, like Heaney, would write about their folk. And I cannot write about her the way Tony Harrison in Britain would write about their folk in the north of England. My folk is not like their folk, and there is nothing romantic or snug about my folk; they don't wear caps and don't smoke clay pipes.[15]

Dabydeen courts here the charge of special pleading, and of perpetuating stereotypes (caps and clay pipes) which have little to do with the facts of Irish or Northern experience.

Notwithstanding this, however, the issue of relationship between generations, between a poet and his or her family, forebears, father or mother country, is negotiated by the two poets, Dabydeen and Harrison, in a manner strikingly similar and yet differently inflected. Harrison opens *The School of Eloquence* with the verse epigraph 'Heredity', answering the question *'Wherever did you get your talent from?'* by referencing his 'two uncles, Joe and Harry – / one was a stammerer, the other dumb' (7). Dabydeen, likewise, brings to mind Shklovsky's argument that the 'legacy' of art, or literary tradition, 'is transmitted not from father to son, but from uncle to nephew', even if he does not present his poetic gift, as Harrison does, in terms of an unprecedented triumph over adversity. Dabydeen comments that 'one of my uncles had already gone to Oxford – straight from the bush'.[16]

'Coolie Odyssey', which begins with wry speculation about the recent 'vogue' for the 'folk', ends by considering issues of reception and audience, as the poet describes the unsatisfactory alternatives with which he feels he is faced, of writing either 'songs / Fleshed in the emptiness of folk, / Poems that scrape bowl and bone' or reading his 'fair conceits';

> To congregations of the educated
> Sipping wine, attentive between courses –
> See the applause fluttering from their white hands
> Like so many messy table napkins. (13)

These alternatives are rephrased in Dabydeen's 'On Not Being Milton: Nigger Talk in England Today': 'you cease *folking* up the literature, and you become "universal" – or else you perish in the backwater of small presses' (Ricks and Michaels, 12). Keith Tuma suggests that 'One way out of this double-bind is to move between and among modalities […] refusing to be pinned down in one or the other',[17] and although Dabydeen continues to insist that the 'immigrant [poet] in Britain lacks genuine audience', the standoff between 'folk' and 'the educated' in the last lines of 'Coolie Odyssey' presents a perhaps strategically dichotomised version of the more complex interplay between elements (between Creole and standard English, between the vernacular and literary tradition) which characterises the finest work of this poet as he does what Tuma bids him to do: 'move between and among modalities'. As Dabydeen has said of the composition of his *Slave Song,* 'the tension between the home environment [of Guyana] and the Cambridge environment just created poetry'.[18]

And yet blackness, in the closing lines of 'Coolie Odyssey', is seen in terms of 'emptiness' and lack, whiteness in terms of surfeit: neither term in this binary is sufficient, satisfying. The poet's role in relation to the 'folk' is self-ironised as redundant, even predatory – 'Fleshed in the emptiness' is Dabydeen's oxymoronic formulation for that relationship – and in relation to a white audience he is accessory in another sense: he is recreational, postprandial. Here the poem concludes with an image of the white reception of the black text as a form of consumption – Dabydeen's version of that inversion found in slave narratives and some subsequent black texts of white cannibalism.

The opening lines of Dabydeen's poem also offer possible contexts for the black poem: the black reception (Dabydeen's) of white texts, and the relationship his own writing might bear to such texts. Like Harrison's 'On Not Being Milton', the opening poem of *The School of Eloquence,* 'Coolie Odyssey', the first poem in Dabydeen's book of that title, begins with references to other texts. Both poems, then, foreground their status *as* poems, and as manifestos, the difference being that where Harrison and Heaney serve as Dabydeen's white intertexts (and countertexts), Harrison's poem deploys *black* intertexts: 'On Not Being Milton' is dedicated to two Mozambiquan poets-cum-political activists, Sergio Vieira and Armando Guebuza, and in the first verse, Harrison compares his own poem with Césaire's *Cahier d'un retour au pays natal.*

The epigraph to *The School of Eloquence,* taken from E.P. Thompson, enables Harrison to introduce his own poetry as a contemporary 'cover' for political activism, and allows him to play and pun, in the collection's first poem proper, on the idea of 'corresponding societies'.[19] 'On Not Being Milton' suggests a correspondence between working-class and black; for Harrison, 'growing black' is a way of recovering his 'roots':

111

> Read and committed to the flames, I call
> these sixteen lines that go back to my roots
> my *Cahier d'un retour au pays natal*
> my growing black enough to fit my boots. (11)

In addition to this black-and-white correspondence, Harrison's poem also suggests a correspondence between the present time of writing (the 1970s) and an earlier phase of English working-class radicalism, epitomised by the activities of the London Corresponding Society and the Cato Street Conspiracy. Harrison's black intertexts, the Mozambiquan poet-activists who are his dedicatees, and Césaire, merge militant political activism with writing, as of course did the members of the London Corresponding Society, all of these models being linked implicitly to Harrison's own project as poet. The poem ends:

> Articulation is the tongue-tied's fighting.
> In the silence round all poetry we quote
> Tidd the Cato Street conspirator who wrote:

> *Sir, I Ham a very Bad Hand at Righting.* (11)

Richard Tidd has the last word in the poem, and his is a precursor text for that of Harrison, the self-aware 'ham', who will continue, now in the broader dispensation of the first person plural, the unintended if fitting affiliation between writing and putting to rights which is the unconscious subtext of Tidd's '*righting*'.

Harrison's poem, beginning as it does with Frelimo and Césaire, and ending with Richard Tidd, involves a gradual leaching out, a bleaching, of its black referents. In the opening verse, Harrison's analogy between blackness and the working-class Northern voice results in a merger of the two: in the phrase 'growing black enough to fit my boots' black British immigration, a major concern of Harrison's later sequence *v.*, is registered only implicitly, assimilated into a local English saying. Harrison's phrase is a domestication of the black British, who are seen to be as natural, as much a resource, and at the time of writing as politically inflammatory, as the coal with which the black immigrant community is also compared. In contrast, Harrison's black intertexts remain conspicuously exotic: the title of Césaire's poem is not translated from the French and the poem's dedication is left unexplained to those less well versed than Harrison in the politics of African postcolonial struggle. (Ironically, in the face of Harrison's defiantly regionalist poetic, the poem's single footnote explains a local usage, 'Enoch'). Tidd, however, is contextualised for us, within the text of the poem itself, in his role as one of the Cato Street conspirators.

And yet, working against the poem's black-to-white trajectory, Tidd's brief text – '*Sir, I Ham a very Bad Hand at Righting*' – harbours among its (unintended?) subtexts a black reference: Harrison's own sustained license to pun means we may legitimately read Tidd's '*Ham*' not only as Harrison intends us to read it – to be ham-fisted, and / or to ham, to act or overact – but also as a nomination of blackness: Ham the son of Noah as supposed progenitor of the world's black races. And there is a further black subtext too, a black British subtext, to the Cato Street Conspiracy itself, in the form of one William Davidson (1786–1820): known as the 'Black Davidson'. He was the Anglo-Caribbean mulatto son of a Scots planter, hanged in 1820 for his part in the Cato Street plot, along with Richard Tidd, Arthur Thistlewood, James Ings and John Brunt. That one of Tidd's fellow conspirators was black we learn, in passing, from E.P. Thompson, and in considerably greater detail from Peter Fryer, and from Dabydeen and Paul Edwards, in their *Black Writers in Britain 1760 – 1890*.[20]

Another of the black British writers represented in Dabydeen's and Edwards' book, the ex-slave Olaudah Equiano, had lodged with Thomas Hardy, the founder of the London Corresponding Society in 1792, when Equiano, himself a member of the LCS, was working on a revised edition of his autobiography (first edition 1789). Thomas Hardy declared, in a letter, 'I am fully persuaded that there is no man, who is, from principle, an advocate for the liberty of the black man, but who will zealously support the rights of the white man, and *vice versa*'.[21] Harrison's poem also proposes such a model of white-and-black and black-and-white solidarity, but in spite of all the crossovers and correspondences Harrison suggests – between words, writers, historical periods of political agitation, liberation movements – his poem only partially ends the occlusion of black British history and writing. As Dabydeen says, 'black British literature is not a modern phenomenon', and figures like Davidson and Equiano represent a black sub-text to British cultural history, one which Dabydeen himself has, as part of his interrogation of origins, done much to bring to the surface of history and literary inquiry.[22]

Harrison's use of black intertexts in his 'On Not Being Milton' is answered by Dabydeen's more equivocal use of reciprocated white intertexts (including Harrison's poem) in 'Coolie Odyssey'. Dabydeen's poem, which is in one sense a reply to Harrison's, seems to suggest that black British and northern working-class British are not, in anything but Harrison's wordplay, corresponding societies. And yet, as Dabydeen has said, 'My use of [Creole, in *Slave Song*] was influenced not by living in a village in Guyana, but by being in a library in Cambridge where I was reading medieval alliterative verse'.[23] Dabydeen is playing, in his use, in *Slave Song,* of explanatory notes and translations of the Creole poems into standard English, on the notes and glosses to a modern edition of a text such as *Gawain.* At the same time, his framing materials can be seen as an uncomfortable reminder of the white affidavits which framed earlier black texts, such as slave narratives; or, as Sarah Lawson Welsh suggests, it may be that such white affidavits 'are replaced in *Slave Song* by a self-generated critical introduction which parodically 'authorises' the text for white or non-Creole-speaking consumption'.[24] Additionally, the notes to *Slave Song* may suggest that *The Waste Land* is a kind of 'master text' to which Dabydeen's text is chained. And yet Dabydeen's open acknowledgement of Eliot's influence is anything but anxious. 'It was a literary joke – hence I referred twice in *Slave Song* to T.S. Eliot, because Eliot had also joked and provided a kind of spoof gloss to *The Waste Land'*.[25] Dabydeen calls his poem 'an act of counterparody, in the way that Eliot had annotated his *Waste Land'* (Ricks and Michaels, 5), and explains that his annotations were prompted by his anticipation of 'such automatic responses' to the book as that of Peter Porter, who appears to miss the point when he complains in his review of Dabydeen's book that Creole is hard to understand (Ricks and Michaels, 5). 'Canecutters' Song' from *Slave Song* reappropriates the closing words of *The Waste Land,* Eliot's 'Shanti! Shanti! Shanti';[26] and in a wider sense, Eliot and the multiple personae of *The Waste Land* stand behind Dabydeen's comment that 'none of the poems uses the word 'I'; one inhabits a series of masks'.[27] As Welsh points out in her discussion of the use of Creole in Dabydeen's poetry, 'the literary reconstruction of this medium of vocalisation is necessarily a contrivance, an artifice, a self-conscious process [...] There are no originary voices in *Slave Song*, only reconstructed, represented, mediating ones'.[28]

A principal scene of Dabydeen's next book, *Coolie Odyssey*, is Guyana, 'the blasted land', a land laid waste by the degradations of slavery and the devastations of cane. The title poem tells us that 'The odyssey was plank between river and land,' the 'odyssey' being both Dabydeen's text itself and the history of the transport of indentured Indian labour (and subsequent Caribbean emigration to Britain). 'The odyssey was plank', too, in the sense of Homer providing Dabydeen with one of his poem's principal intertexts, another being *The Waste Land,* itself a peripatetic quest poem.

Dabydeen's 1994 poem-sequence *Turner,*[29] which takes its place in the tradition of the long poem about a painting, is also self-consciously part of the lineage of the maritime epic with which Dabydeen has already had congress in *Coolie Odyssey*, where the two terms of the title suggest that this is a literary quest which self-consciously takes its place among, even as it revises, the tradition of watery epics from Homer through to Eliot and on to Walcott's *Omeros.* Thus *Turner* is a text which accommodates both Homer and the Caribbean oral tradition, both the *Odyssey* and the African experience of diaspora.[30] And *Turner* is also a sustained rewriting of *The Waste Land.* Death by water haunts both poems; the drowned slave who is the focal figure of Dabydeen's poem is, in one of his many facets, a version of Eliot's Phlebas; and, fittingly, Dabydeen owes a stylistic debt to Section IV of *The Waste Land,* 'Death by Water', in the lyricism of the equally brief Section X of *Turner.* There is also reference to Ariel's song, one of the principal intertexts of *The Waste Land*, in Section IX, 'Words are all I have left of my

115

eyes'; and again in Section V, where 'the sea prepares / Their [the drowned slave women's] festive masks, salt crystals like a myriad / Of sequins hemmed into their flesh through golden / Threads of hair' (9).

Dabydeen's remark that *Turner* was 'a great howl of pessimism about the inability to recover anything meaningful from the past' could have been taken verbatim from any number of critical responses to Eliot's poem.[31] Both texts, Eliot's and Dabydeen's, have a mythic substructure: Manu, the Noah of Indian myth, co-ordinates Dabydeen's text, and is his Fisher King: in Section XVII, Manu 'prophesies / The stranger who will bring rain to fertilise / The crops' (26). Where Eliot's Fisher King ends amid fragments and ruins, Manu dies, his tale unfinished, with a 'broken / Word' (32). And Manu orchestrates the temporal simultaneity which Dabydeen's poem shares with Eliot's work when, in a remarkable moment which crystallises Dabydeen's complex relationship with tradition, Western and black, literary and oral, this African/Indian magician paraphrases the poet of *Four Quartets*: 'he told that time future was neither time past / Nor time present, but a rupture so complete / That pain and happiness will become one' (33).

Turner has other intertexts, too: for instance, there is the echo of Yeats' 'Leda and the Swan' in Section XXV, 'the white enfolding / Wings of Turner brooding over my body' (39), which, McIntyre says, suggests 'a complicit creativity [...] perhaps claiming solidarity with other colonised peoples'. This is notwithstanding the fact, seemingly unrecognised by McIntyre or Edward Said, that Yeats is only metonymic of 'the Irish' in a very restricted sense, and that his status as a decolonising poet is at the very least debatable. Indeed, 'Leda and the Swan' has been read as a reaction against the conservative ideology of the newly independent Irish Free State.[32] Other possible intertexts, which again invoke Eliot, are Toni Morrison's *Beloved*, a novel which not only shares with Dabydeen's poem the themes of child haunting, slavery and rememory, but according to Dabydeen also compares with Eliot in its fusion of 'the intellect and the senses';[33] and Adrienne Rich's 'Diving into the Wreck', itself, like Rich's earlier 'Snapshots of a Daughter-in-Law', a revision of *The Waste Land*.[34] Dabydeen says in his preface to *Turner* that 'the sea has transformed' the slave, has 'bleached him of colour and complicated his sense of gender.' This brings to mind Rich's lines about the androgynous 'mermaid' / 'merman' (164), while the final lines of Rich's poem, where the 'book of myths / in which / our names do not appear' figures the erasure of women from cultural history, compare with Dabydeen's remarks in the preface to *Turner* about an erased African presence in British culture, and also, more specifically, with Section XVIII of *Turner*, where the slave-speaker (and by implication Dabydeen-as-poet) is named 'Nigger' 'from some hoard of superior knowledge' yet this is a hoard which, we are told, 'I will still ransack' (28).

Turner is an extended meditation on J. M. W. Turner's 1840 painting, *Slavers throwing overboard the Dead and the Dying*, known as *Slave Ship*. In his preface, Dabydeen explains that his poem 'focuses on the submerged head of the African in the foreground of Turner's painting' and he defines his own response to the picture against that of Ruskin, its owner and dominant explicator, who consigns the content of the artwork, 'the shackling and drowning of Africans' to a 'brief footnote' which 'reads like an afterthought, something tossed overboard' (*Turner* IX). The submerged African becomes metonymic, for Dabydeen, of the Western erasure, or relegation to a footnote, of black life and black history, and by extension, black culture. According to McIntyre, for 'postcolonial' writers such as Dabydeen, 'footnotes become the lost history and culture, the 'holes' in standard representations, that once retrieved and reinserted, allow one to write and read otherwise, against the dominant order'. *Turner* is, in one sense, a poem of retrieval, as Atlantic slavery is retrieved by Dabydeen from the sub-text to which Ruskin's essay on the painting relegates it. Dabydeen retrieves the African who for the most part 'remains unseen in Turner's text. All that is visible above sea level in the painting is, fittingly, a foot'.[35]

Ruskin's interpretation of Turner's *Slave Ship* is predicated upon 'something tossed overboard', on an absence. Another of Turner's paintings, *The Golden Bough*, again owned by Ruskin, also featured a figure which, to Ruskin's consternation, quite literally 'dropped off' the canvas. The figure was that of the Sibyl of Cumae: 'at the very last moment Turner added the Sibyl herself in the foreground holding up the bough.'[36] The Sibyl foregrounds *The Waste Land*, too, just as her image and Turner's painting foreground Eliot's ur- and primary inter-text, Frazer's *Golden Bough,* the opening sentence of which asks, 'Who does not know Turner's picture of the Golden Bough?'.[37]

If Ruskin's response to Turner's *Slave Ship*, his relegation to a footnote of the painting's subject – the slave trade – privileges style over content, then, McIntyre infers, the reinsertion of that footnote, which is Dabydeen's response to the painting, revises and reverses Ruskin's priorities, stressing content over and above the demands of style and form. But representation of the history of the Atlantic slave trade, of which the individual drowned slave is metonymic, proves problematic in several ways. This is not least because as a poet Dabydeen, without compromising the ideological integrity of his project, refuses the reductiveness of that variety of literary-critical postcolonialism which construes assault upon 'the dominant order' purely in terms of overt political message. In his preface to *Turner,* Dabydeen says, of the poem's slave, 'His real desire is to begin anew in the sea, but he is too trapped by grievous memory to escape history' (ix-x), and this may be the case for Dabydeen and his text as well: 'Neither can describe themselves anew but are indelibly stained by [the] language and imagery' of others. Dabydeen comes close, here, to echoing the well-worn postcolonial paradox, that 'all experience is articulated in the forms and institutions of the Old World'; and yet the application of such a paradox does little to address the complexities of Dabydeen's poem, which negotiates a much more nuanced relationship with its Western intertexts than this postcolonial paradigm alone can register.[38]

A more resourceful critical praxis is suggested in Paul Gilroy's response to Turner's painting: the context of Gilroy's essay 'Art and Darkness. Black Art and the Problem of Belonging to England', which predates by four years the publication of Dabydeen's *Turner,* is a 1989-90 exhibition of visual art which bears the 'compound identity' of being 'both black and British'.[39] Gilroy discusses Turner's painting *Slave Ship* as an 'illustration both of the extent to which race has been tacitly erased from discussion of English culture and how a "racial" theme, relocated at the heart of national self-understanding, can contribute to a new, more pluralistic conceptualisation' of Britain. According to Gilroy, 'one source of Turner's inspiration may have been Thomas Clarkson's account of "barbaric events" [the drowning of some 130 African slaves] aboard the slave ship *Zong*', Clarkson's source, in turn, being Olaudah Equiano.[40] In any event, Gilroy says, 'the picture and its strange history pose a challenge to the black English today. It demands that we strive to integrate the difficult dimensions of our hybrid cultural heritage more effectively'.[41]

In Dabydeen's *Turner*, the awakened slave 'invents a body, a biography, and peoples an imagined landscape. Most of the names of the birds, animals and fruit are made up' (*Turner* IX). The slave is Adamic, calling a world into being by naming it; and yet as we know from Wallace Stevens, 'There was a myth before the myth began' even for 'Adam / In Eden': the medium of poetry, and language itself, denies us access to the primary, the originary, and our condition is one of belatedness.[42] This is the recognition of Section X of *Turner*:

> What sleep will leave me restless when I wake?
> What mindfulness that nothing has remained
> Original? (15)

In the first Section of *Turner* the slave-speaker insists that 'I have given fresh names', and yet names the 'part-born' baby 'Turner', leaving it for the reader to decide whether in so doing the speaker is designating Dabydeen's poem (of which the baby, Turner, is metonymic), as redemptive, as a source of hope and new life, or as hopelessly secondary, accessory. The allusion to Eliot in Section XXI of *Turner*, even if revisionary, tells us that Manu and this (imagined) Africa are not originary, or original, and Manu himself, elaborating on the oxymoron of emptiness-and-surfeit in 'Coolie Odyssey', tells the children of his African village who are scattered in foreign lands, 'Each / Will be barren of ancestral memory /

But each endowed richly with such emptiness / From which to dream, surmise, invent, immortalise' (33).

Where *Coolie Odyssey*, Dabydeen's previous sequence of poems, had been dedicated to the poet's grandmother, *Turner*, a poem steeped in maternal imagery, is dedicated to Dabydeen's mother, but this is a mother whom Dabydeen construes as an absent presence in his life. Dabydeen has said that 'I grew up without a mother, so that the absent mother is probably what moves me very deeply and creates writing. *Turner* is really about the absent mother, too'; and he has identified himself with the 'part born' progeny of his poem's slave mother – 'I feel like the stillborn child in *Turner*'.[43]

Elsewhere, Dabydeen places the absent mother in a wider context when he suggests that West Indian emigration to Britain is 'complicated by the assumption of a shared heritage with the mother country' which is an illusion, since 'West Indian immigrants faced the reality of rejection by the Motherland', a reality more starkly expressed in Dabydeen's first novel *The Intended*: 'Just because you ain't got a mother don't mean that England will mother you'.[44] Dabydeen's poem begins with the word 'Stillborn', in which death and life are merged: a stillborn baby is a dead baby, but in the poem the 'still birth' is also the still, the calm after the storm (of childbirth). Throughout the poem Dabydeen weaves his extended metaphor of birthing as maritime activity, birth passage as sea passage; the baby 'broke the waters' (11); the child is something we 'cannot fathom'.[45]

Turner conducts a search for an origin which is itself known to be an 'illusion', a fiction, something 'fabricated' (15). In Section XIX of *Turner*, Dabydeen discusses African culture and its destruction at the hands of the West: when he asks 'Shall I summon up such a pageant of fruit, / Peopling a country with musicians, dancers, / Poets' (30), Dabydeen's slave-speaker echoes Olaudah Equiano's defence of Africa as 'a nation of dancers, musicians, and poets', but with the difference that the Africa of Dabydeen's speaker is a projection, another imaginative fabrication.[46] Dabydeen's novel *A Harlot's Progress*, a prose rewriting and elaboration of aspects of *Turner*, is similarly focalised through the trickster-like fabulations of a slave whose myriad imaginative scenarios take the place of an originary narrative demanded by a white abolitionist patron but which the slave himself withholds and perhaps knows to be unavailable.[47] At the end of *Turner*, the slave-speaker cannot go 'In search of another image of himself' (40), this signalling, perhaps, Dabydeen's subsequent and one hopes temporary turning away from poetry to fiction. *Turner*, then, is a poem, to quote from *The Waste Land*, of 'the deep sea swell / And the profit and loss'.[48] About the beginnings of life (the sea), it is also a poem about death; and it is, if only potentially in Sections XX and XXV, a redemption song in which 'the dead / Survive catastrophe to speak in one / Redemptive and prophetic voice' (31), a representation in which Turner's drowned slave is redeemed from anteriority and subordination.[49] Yet the poem ends with a list of negatives, the last of which, ending the poem, is 'No mother' (40).

Turner is, in one register, an urgent act of historical reclamation or rememory – the poem's occasion is a maritime atrocity which is metonymic of the atrocity of the Atlantic slave trade as a whole – for Dabydeen, as for Walcott, 'The Sea is History'.[50] In another register, however, (as Stevens writes, 'The sea is so many written words'), the poem is a self-reflexive allegory of Dabydeen's own complex relationship, as son and heir and as disinherited orphan, with Western literary tradition.[51] It is not the intention of this essay either to submerge the individual talent of David Dabydeen in that tradition, or to deny the textuality of his Caribbean inheritance; but it may be that Dabydeen's achievement as a poet is inseparable from his own recognition that 'the connections', although 'difficult', are unavoidable.[52]

Dabydeen, despite his caveats in 'Coolie Odyssey' about the poetic company he will keep, has been co-opted by some as a member of the British New Generation, and indeed he fits uneasily at best into most of the available critical paradigms. Dabydeen's interest in troping, or signifying, upon other texts doesn't answer satisfactorily to Bhabha's analysis of 'the *ambivalence* of mimicry', where postcolonial writing inhabits an 'area between mimicry and mockery'.[53] Dabydeen's own background derives from 'the importation of indentured labour from India' into the West Indies, which 'introduced a new racial element, complicating the white

/ black dichotomy', and so JanMohammed's Manichean allegory doesn't apply here either.[54] A poet who has not chosen Brathwaite's 'model of Creolisation' or Nation Language writing, but who is concerned with intertexts, is perhaps open to the kind of criticism levelled seventy years ago at the poet of *The Waste Land*, for speaking in the voices of others as he had no authentic voice of his own.[55] And yet, if Eliot is, indeed, the 'parent of Caribbean poetry', all Dabydeen's work indicates that the parent is absent.

In his 1993 novel *Disappearance*, Dabydeen's Guyanese narrator says of the sea, 'I was seduced by its endless transformations, which promised me freedom from being fixed as an African, a West-Indian, a member of a particular nationality of a particular epoch'.[56] And although the speaker goes on to resist the dissolution of his identity, it is such a sense of 'the intercultural and transnational formation', which Paul Gilroy has called the black Atlantic, which may most appropriately describe Dabydeen:[57] as his speaker tells us in Section XII of *Turner*, 'the sea has brought me tribute from many lands', including 'scrolls in different letterings' (17).

Notes to Chapter Five

1. Kwame Dawes, 'Interview with David Dabydeen: 1994', in *The Art of David Dabydeen*, ed. by Kevin Grant (Leeds: Peepal Tree, 1997), pp. 199-221 (p. 211). Further references included in the main text of the essay.
2. The focus of this essay is Dabydeen's relation to the European and Anglo-American literary traditions, but this is not to deny the equal significance of his Caribbean literary parentage, the troping on Caribbean forefathers which discloses Dabydeen's debt to and dialogue with, among others, Claude McKay, Derek Walcott, Kamau Brathwaite, and fellow Guyanese writer Wilson Harris, upon whose formulation of the 'limbo imagination' of the Caribbean, 'in which nothing is ultimately alien', the methodology of this essay is premised,

see; 'History, Fable and Myth in The Caribbean and Guianas', *Caribbean Quarterly,* 16.2 (1970), 11-32 (p. 9-10).

3. David Dabydeen, *Slave Song* (Aarhaus: Dangaroo, 1984). Further references are included in the main text of the essay.

4. Wolfgang Binder, 'Interview with David Dabydeen: 1989', in *The Art of David Dabydeen*, ed. by Kevin Grant (Leeds: Peepal Tree, 1997), pp. 159-176 (p. 170-1).

5. David Dabydeen and Nana Wilson-Tagoe, *A Reader's Guide to West Indian and Black British Literature* (London: Hansib, 1997), p. 85.

6. 'Interview: 1989', pp. 159-176 (p. 170).

7. Sarah Lawson Welsh, 'Experiments in Brokenness: The Creative Use of Creole in David Dabydeen's *Slave Song*', in *The Art of David Dabydeen*, ed. by Kevin Grant (Leeds: Peepal Tree, 1997), pp. 47-66 (p. 55); David Dabydeen, *Coolie Odyssey* (London: Hansib/Dangaroo, 1988). Further references included in the main text of the essay.

8. Benita Parry, 'Between Creole and Cambridge English: The Poetry of David Dabydeen', in *The Art of David Dabydeen*, ed. by Kevin Grant (Leeds: Peepal Tree, 1997), pp. 47-66 (p. 55).

9. Tony Harrison, *From The School of Eloquence and other poems* (London: Rex Collings, 1978). Further references included in the main text of the essay; and David Dabydeen, 'On Not Being Milton: Nigger Talk in England Today', in *The State of the Language*, ed. by Christopher Ricks and Leonard Michaels (London: Faber and Faber, 1990), pp. 3-14 (p. 4). Further references included in the main text of the essay.

10. *A Reader's Guide*, p. 164.

11. 'Interview: 1989', pp. 159-176 (p. 170).

12. Fred D'Aguiar suggests that the poem 'Coolie Odyssey' projects the creation of a 'possible world' of 'the unifying poetic mind' out of the 'complex dualities' Dabydeen explores, see; *The Scope of the Possible: New British Poetries*, ed. by Robert Hampson and Peter Barry (Manchester: Manchester University Press, 1993), p. 65.

13. Dabydeen is presumably referring to Dunn's *Terry Street* and to Harrison's *School of Eloquence*; much of Heaney's early poetry, of course, 'bubbles up from peat bogs', from 'Bogland' in the 1969 collection *Door into the Dark*, to 'The Tollund Man' and 'Nerthus' in *Wintering Out* (1972), to the majority of poems in the first part of *North* (1975).

14. 'Interview: 1989', pp. 159-176 (p. 170).

123

15. ibid., pp. 159-176 (p. 172).
16. Victor Erlich, *Russian Formalism*, 3rd edn (New Haven: Yale University Press, 1981), p. 260.
    Followed by: Frank Birbalsingh, 'Interview with David Dabydeen: 1991', in *The Art of David Dabydeen*, ed. by Kevin Grant (Leeds: Peepal Tree, 1997), pp. 177-98 (p. 180).
17. Keith Tuma, *Fishing by Obstinate Isles: Modern and Postmodern British Poetry and American Readers* (London: Faber and Faber, 1990), p. 255.
18. Interview: 1991', pp. 177-198 (p. 181-2).
19. Thompson describes 'a ticket which was perhaps one of the last 'covers' for the old L.C.S.: *Admit for the Season to the School of Eloquence*: quoted in *The School of Eloquence*, p. 9.
20. Davidson was in fact one of the leaders of the Cato Street Conspiracy, the plan to blow up the British Cabinet, and as Dabydeen and Edwards note, 'a grim irony of the situation is that Davidson was a cabinet maker by profession'. See *Black Writers in Britain 1760-1820*, ed. by David Dabydeen and Paul Edwards (Edinburgh: Edinburgh University Press, 1991), p. 127.
21. James Walvin, *An African's Life: The Life and Times of Olaudah Equiano* (London: Cassell, 1998), p. 170.
22. *A Reader's Guide*, p. 83.
23. 'Interview: 1989', pp. 159-176 (p. 170).
24. 'Experiments in Brokenness', pp. 27-46 (p. 41).
25. 'Interview: 1991', pp. 177-198 (p. 182).
26. T. S. Eliot, *Collected Poems 1909-1962* (London: Faber and Faber, 1974), p. 25.
27. 'Interview: 1989', pp. 156-176 (p. 169).
28. Experiments in Brokenness', pp. 27-46 (p. 34, 37).
29. David Dabydeen, *Turner: New and Selected Poems* (London: Cape, 1994). Further references included in the main text of the essay.
30. Dabydeen's use of the sea in his poetry, his concern with memory, slavery, the past, and his Homeric themes and dialogue with canonical texts, all suggest an ongoing negotiation with the work of Walcott and with what Walcott calls 'the marine dialect of the Caribbean'; *Omeros* (London: Faber and Faber, 1990), p. 314. The figure of Odysseus appears throughout Walcott's work, and is central to *Another Life* and *Omeros*. The obeah-woman of *Omeros* is likened to Petronius' and Eliot's Sibyl (245), and a version of the Hanged Man of *The Waste Land* appears in 'Mass Man' from *The Gulf*; in *Collected Poems 1948-1984* (New York: Noonday Press, 1986), p. 99.

31. 'Interview: 1994', pp. 199-221 (p. 200).

32. See Elizabeth Butler Cullingford, *Gender and History in Yeats' Love Poetry* (Cambridge: Cambridge University Press, 1993), pp. 140-64.

33. 'Interview: 1994', pp. 199-221 (p. 201). And see section XXII of 'Turner', where the remembered or invented sister of Dabydeen's slave is addressed as 'my beloved' p. 35.

34. Rich's 'Snapshots', like Dabydeen's 'Turner' also deploys Yeats' 'Leda and the Swan' as one of the poem's many intertexts.

35. Karen McIntyre, 'Necrophilia or Stillbirth? David Dabydeen's 'Turner' as the Embodiment of Postcolonial Creative Decolonisation', in *The Art of David Dabydeen* ed. by Kevin Grant (Leeds: Peepal Tree, 1997), pp. 141-158 (p. 147).

36. 'She seems to have been something of an afterthought, since several years after the picture was acquired, its owner [Ruskin] found to his dismay, that she was coming away from the canvas, having been hastily painted on paper and then simply stuck to the surface. When Turner heard of it he rushed round and painted her in again.': James George Frazer, *The Golden Bough: A New Abridgement*, ed. by Robert Fraser (London: Oxford University Press, 1994), p. xvi-xvii.

37. *The Golden Bough*, p. 9. As Dabydeen among many others has noted, Eliot 'ransacks' Frazer 'for pre-classical fertility images'; *A Reader's Guide*, p. 168. According to Wittgenstein, Frazer's *Golden Bough* is an enlightenment narrative, whereby primitive tribal practises have to be translated into terms both plausible and 'backward'. See Margerie Perloff, *Wittgenstein's Ladder: Poetic Language and the Strangeness of the Ordinary* (Chicago: Chicago University Press, 1996). However, Frazer gives primitive and mythic materials to modernism, and modernists use his sources to invert what Frazer does.

38. Bill Ashcroft, Gareth Griffiths, Helen Tiffin, *The Empire Writes Back: Theory and Practise in Post-Colonial Literature* (London: Routledge, 1989), p. 148.

39. Paul Gilroy, 'Art and Darkness: Black Art and the Problem of Belonging to England', *Third Text*, 10 (1990), 45-52 (p. 46).

40. *An African's Life*, p. 62, p. 152-3.

41. 'Art and Darkness', 45-52 (pp. 49-51).

42. Wallace Stevens, *The Collected Poems of Wallace Stevens* (New York: Knopf, 1954), p. 383.

43. 'Interview: 1994', pp. 199-221 (p. 220).

44. *A Reader's Guide*, p. 49. And see David Dabydeen, *The Intended* (London: Secker and Warburg, 1991), p. 246.

45. Walcott notes that '*mer* was both mother and sea' in Antillean patios, *Omeros*, p. 231.
46. *An African's Life*, p. 6.
47. The magician Manu reappears in the novel, while the violation of the slave child by Thomas Thistlewood complements Dabydeen's investigation of the sexual psychopathology of slavery in 'Turner'; *A Harlot's Progress* (London: Cape, 1999).
48. *Collected Poems 1909-1962*, p. 75.
49. The proximity of the words 'Turner' and 'slave' may suggest insurrection as well as resurrection: Nat Turner may be one of the latent personae of Dabydeen's slave. In correspondence with the author, Dabydeen has corroborated this suggestion, stating that 'In 1987, I visited a statue put up for him [Nat Turner], in Jamaica.' E-mail to Lee Jenkins, 17 August 1999.
50. Walcott, *Collected Poems*, p. 364.
51. Stevens, *Collected Poems*, p. 252.
52. Answers to Naipaul's charge that the Caribbean man is a mimic man include Walcott's essay 'The Caribbean: Culture or Mimicry', a reply to Naipaul's position that 'No gesture, according to this philosophy, is authentic, every sentence is a quotation.' For an extended discussion of Walcott and 'mimicry' see Rei Tereda, *Derek Walcott's Poetry: American Mimicry* (Boston: Northeastern University Press, 1992). For Wilson Harris, the 'limbo imagination' of the Caribbean and the Guianas invalidates Naipaul's diagnosis, in that such an imagination accommodates 'an original reconstitution of variables of myth and legend' (and literature), a reconfiguration which Harris links to Eliot's essay on the Metaphysical poets because of a shared 'range and potency of association in which nothing is ultimately alien', Harris, 'History and Myth', 11-32 (p. 9-10). Harris' notion of a Caribbean 'reconstitution' suggests that a dichotomy of Western literary tradition and a vernacular Caribbean tradition won't hold. Michael North points to the use of metatextual notes in the first Caribbean dialect poems to be published in book form, Claude McKay's *Songs of Jamaica* (1912) in *The Dialect of Modernism: Race, Language and Twentieth-Century Literature* (New York: Oxford University Press, 1994). As Lloyd Brown notes, Brathwaite 'can be as sensitive as Walcott to the nuances and literary significance of the Western dimension in Afro-Caribbean culture': *West Indian Poetry* (London, Kingston: Heinemann, 1984), p. 147. According to Brown, Brathwaite's *Islands*, the second book of the 'New World

126

Trilogy' *The Arrivants*, echoes *The Waste Land*, from its 'mythic method' to its versions of the one-eyed merchant and Fisher King, p. 147. Brathwaite's *X/Self* has its own textual apparatus in the form of notes, to which the author refers in a self-deprecating way (these notes 'which I provide with great reluctance'), with a knowing irony that in so doing, Brathwaite comes closer still to the Eliot who referred to the notes to *The Waste Land* as bogus scholarship. 'Song Charlemagne' in *X/Self* (Oxford: Oxford University Press, 1987) tropes on Eliot in what the poem 'Aachen' calls 'the dialect of the tribes', as 'london bridge is fall / in down' p. 113, 29 and 23. Such signifying on Eliotic Tradition in no sense detracts from Brathwaite's assertion in the notes that 'there is a black Caliban Maroon world with its own aesthetics' p. 130.

53. Homi K Bhabha, *The Location of Culture* (London: Routledge, 1994), p. 86.
54. *A Reader's Guide*, p. 31.
55. And yet Brathwaite, who, as Breiner says, is 'often reductively regarded as an Afro-centrist', has noted that '[Caribbean] poets who were moving from standard English to nation language were influenced basically [...] by T. S. Eliot'. See Laurence Breiner, *An Introduction to West Indian Poetry* (Cambridge: Cambridge University Press, 1998), p. xiii.
56. David Dabydeen, *Disappearance* (London: Vintage, 1999; repr. 1999), p. 132.
57. Paul Gilroy, *The Black Atlantic: Modernity and Double Consciousness* (London: Verso, 1993), p. xi.

CHAPTER SIX

SINGING SONGS OF DESIRE: HUMOUR, MASCULINITY AND LANGUAGE IN DAVID DABYDEEN'S *SLAVE SONG*

PUMLA DINEO GQOLA

This sexual myth – the quest for white flesh – perpetuated by alienated psyches, must no longer be allowed to impede active understanding.

> Franz Fanon, *Black Skin, White Masks*

To counter the fixation on a rhetoric of victimhood, black folks must engage in a discourse of self-determination.

> bell hooks, *Killing rage: ending racism*

The poems of Dabydeen's *Slave Song* are [...] first and foremost songs: songs of resistance.

> Sarah Lawson Welsh, 'Experiments in Brokenness: The Creative Use of Creole in David Dabydeen's *Slave Song*'

Black male sexual desire for white female bodies is a much theorised terrain, documented by writers participating in scholarly and popular writing alike. That such discussions continue to permeate various strata of debate testifies to the complexity of the phenomenon and the difficulty of effectively addressing its dynamics. David Dabydeen's *Slave Song* focuses on historical aspects of this 'desire', engaging with discourses concerning the body and sexuality during the period of slavery.[1] *Slave Song*'s preoccupation with the construction of the rhetoric of black desire is reflected in the structure of the text where, in addition to the 'poetic' text, the processes of interpretation are foregrounded. In the play between poem, translation and commentary, Dabydeen experiments with the boundaries of expression, interpretation and (re)presentation. Working counter to George Lamming's metaphor of skin as seemingly impermeable and fixed (*In The Castle of my Skin*), Dabydeen stresses the importance of the pliability of boundaries, speaking of skin as 'amoeboid' where the shape changes without necessarily bursting the walls encircling the nucleus.[2] As Sarah Lawson Welsh has put it:

> Dabydeen assumes different roles and modes of discourse – historian, polemicist, poet and critic among them, not through necessity but deliberately, *in order to subvert conventional generic boundaries and to problematize definitions of social documentation and imaginative reconstruction*, primarily text and secondary text, testimony and artefact in relation to *Slave Song*.[3] (my emphasis)

In this essay I argue that Dabydeen juxtaposes several representational forms to construct new meanings, and in particular to subvert the manner in which the black male presence is constructed in the discourse of a white supremacist patriarchy. Unsurprisingly, when faced, in interviews, with questions about *Slave Song*, Dabydeen has been circumspect, providing ambiguous answers in keeping with the plurality of meanings in the text. He constantly draws attention to the text's complexities, without resorting to explanation. Within *Slave Song* itself, the diverse registers, the creative conversation between the various forms of expression and the hybrid range of intertextual reference together draw attention to the constructed, contested nature of knowledge.

Throughout the text we can glimpse 'David Dabydeen, the scholar of Africa and of eighteenth and nineteenth-century England, having mischievous fun at the expense of reader, critic and linguist'.[4] Indeed, Dabydeen's text and his discussions of it both within the text and subsequent to its publication warn us not to be too reliant on information gleaned at first glance. Part of the text's sophistication lies in the way in which some 'connections' prove to be misleading. For instance, the poems often go by titles which suggest kinship with established poetic genres.

However, as Benita Parry has demonstrated, using 'Guyana Pastoral' as one example, the particular formal conventions used in this poem resist the tradition flagged in the title. Parry notes that:

> The harshly accented metre violates pastoral poesy; the convention of the moon, sun and wind as benign images in this convention is subverted by recitation of their absence, and another order of naming indigenous to the Guyanese landscape erases the mystique of nature's sublimity.[5]

It is not only in the use of Creole, and the flouting of poetic conventions that Dabydeen's artistic project can be read as one of demystification. With this awareness, critics have questioned the apparent relationship between the poems, notes, and pictures, in which the poems appear central, and the pictures and notes illustratative, or explanatory. Sarah Lawson Welsh asserts that the notes are a 'tease', deliberately fashioned to 'displace our search for authoritative source materials', while Mario Relich points to the manner in which the notes and the poem do not correlate.[6] He suggests, for example, that the commentary in the notes to 'The Canecutters' Song' is misleading, especially in so far as it pretends to explain matter which in actuality does not form part of the poem. The notes to the poem read similarly to Dabydeen's response to Hogarth's *Tempest* and *Marriage à la mode* paintings. For Dabydeen, the poem, which is his response to these paintings, captures the 'moral ambivalence in [Hogarth's paintings] by presenting the Mistress of the plantation as being simultaneously virginal and voracious'.[7] These observations

> about the white woman's desires read like an unwarranted interpolation, a highly ironic one because the fantasies are now those of the poet rather than those of the canecutters.[8]

Mark McWatt's reading is complementary to those of Parry, Welsh and Relich. He argues that the accompanying illustration to 'The Canecutters' Song' is labelled in a manner not to be trusted, and warns against taking the relationship between the illustrations and the poems at surface value. Analysing Dabydeen's usage of the caption, 'A piece of sugar cane', he discusses the context of its depiction and draws attention to the cane:

cut in longitudinal section to reveal infestation by some kind of worm or parasite; it is a horribly phallic image of pestilence and decay, and it is juxtaposed with the poem 'The Canecutters' Song', where the canecutter is again dreaming of illicit sex with the white woman. Again, the picture 'reads' like a sternly negative and minatory image, not only of the consequences of the dream but of the whole life and livelihood of the canecutter.[9]

What follows from McWatt's point here is the presence of an invitation by Dabydeen to re-examine the relevance of naming not only for the captions, but for the poems as well. If the distorted caption in reality points to decay and disease, its juxtaposition with the song of the canecutters draws attention to how deceptive the equally benign title 'The Canecutters' Song' is for what it seeks to name.

This poem is one of two which have additional commentary in the form of stage directions,[10] indicating the metre, the kind of instrumental accompaniment, and the movements made by the *dramatis personae*. This simultaneously frames the reader as one who is eavesdropping on a performance, as well as drawing attention to the orality and immediacy of the performance. This series of frames and lenses through which the reader watches 'the men' watching a canecutter perform is extended when the canecutters become aware that the white 'hooman' walking through the field is there 'for watch we' (25).

The disease and degeneration signified in the accompanying picture of sugar cane is, in one kind of reading, in line with the way in which the canecutters express their desire. Their desire for the white woman is a transgressive one, and there is no attempt on their part to hide this. The singing canecutter, a representative figure since the song is collectively owned, relishes the transgression since his fantasy draws equally from explicit ejaculative imaginings of his body defiling hers ('Me too black fo come deh' (25)) at the same time as visualising her as a deity of some kind. Seeing the woman in this 'divine' manner and singing of his copulatory fantasies in the context of prayer ('O Shanti! Shanti! Shanti!) of course makes the desire even more dangerous and transgressive – so that he speaks of their copulation in terms of snakes and cutlasses, dangerous phallic objects. The lust is not only sexual, indeed it is arguable that the sexual aspect of it is merely secondary since he seems to appreciate her imagined violation more intensely than his actual carnal desire for her. One can also read the song as being about both the right to dream and desire, the only apects of the singer's humanity the estate cannot control, and about collective connection, as the chorus from the other canecutters voices its support, and lust is celebrated through the metaphor of food and feasting.

How are we to see the apparent perversity in the canecutters' desire? How are we to read the accompanying picture of the corruption of the sugar cane. Is Dabydeen drawing parallels between the worms infesting the cane and the desire expressed in the corresponding poem? Clearly the cane is phallic and diseased, and the juxtaposition with the poem suggests that we are to read the desire as similarly diseased, as detrimental to the health of the canecutters as the infestation crippling the cane. In this reading one would see the desire as artificial, constructed in the abnormal relations of slavery and informed by the discourse of sexual violence as a form of policing the body of the slave. We are aware throughout the text that the desire is a fantasy of power denied, even more than sexual lust. In the suggestion that the white woman in some sense shares the sexual fascination ('Lang lace frack loose on she bady like bamboo-flag'(25)), the canecutters' fantasy can be read as implicated in the white slavemasters' projection of desire onto the body of the male slave, which becomes a manifestation of the Other's 'animal sexuality'. Indeed:

By seeking to ideologically distance the white woman from the black man as a principal objective of race discourse, and at the same time socially exposing the black woman to all men, free born children from the black race would always be a very small minority.[11]

This fantasy is connected to the manner in which rape was used to police the body of the slave woman, and to the accompanying paradoxical fear of miscegenation. 'Slave Song' takes this point further by voicing the male slave's challenge to the plantation owner and the discourses (and actual instruments of force) that keep him in power. The rhythm in the first stanza is rigid and tight, reflecting the constant attempts to control the slave's body. The word 'Juk' (28) in the second line and the preponderance of hard sounds in the poem suggest a suddenness in the violence, while pointing to the accompanying picture which depicts the breaking of the slave's body. The third stanza, although different in focus and metre, has a similarly regimented rhythm. In it the challenge started in stanza one develops ironically, as the slave argues that whilst he is labelled as an animal, an orang-utan by the likes of Edward Long, actual brutish behaviour emanates from the ranks of the slavemasters.[12] In these two stanzas the slave challenges the slaveowner's ability to control and police the slave body. They contrast quite sharply with the remaining stanzas which focus on the slave's actions and imagination, rather than the barbarous order of the slavemaster. It is presented as ironic that all the attempts to control and restrict slave bodies cannot restrain the imagination and the slave can thus be seen to have access to 'de goldmine', 'de sunshine', and 'de honeypot' (28). It becomes clear later that these sites are all mapped on the body of the white woman. The slave, then, mocks the slavemaster's inability to control the slave's desire for white women. According to the logic of this interpretation, as the black male addresses the white male planter, all the contempt that the former has for the latter is imaginatively directed at the body of the white woman. She is objectified and the fantasy of counter-violence played out over her body. Or is it?

This reading would be plausible enough were it not directly undermined by the instability paradoxically created by the apparatus of translation and notes where the 'critic' Dabydeen appears to intrude on the space created for his 'poetic' persona. As Mark McWatt observes:

the reader is forced in the end, to be aware of the distractingly manipulative intelligence behind the work. When one reflects, for instance, that the simile 'happy as a hottentot' particularly when applied to a dripping penis, does not seem an image that would be native or natural to the slave in Guyana or to the aloof translator, one is forced to glimpse a different persona, fleshed out perhaps by one's knowledge of David Dabydeen.[13]

Dabydeen's presence as scholar is hinted at earlier through the evocation and mocking of Edward Long's charge that African slaves were not humans but akin to orang-utans. When the happy 'hottentot' enters the poem, Dabydeen seems merely to be ensuring that the reader has glimpsed the scholar interrupting the poetic persona. As the slave mocks the master's fear of the rape of white women, Dabydeen derides the stereotypical representation of the mammoth, violent, ravenous black male body culminating in the black phallus. While the discursive practices that objectify the slave are fortified by the manner in which they become naturalised, Dabydeen forbids his reader from ever forgetting the existence of a creative and deconstructive presence behind the images. The construction of his slave personae, in particular his slave men, is premised on forms of representation which subvert the objectification of the Other in colonialist discourse:

> In colonial representation, exclusion or suppression can often literally be seen as 'embodied'. From the point of view of the coloniser specifically, fears and curiosities, sublimated fascinations with the strange or the 'primitive' are expressed in concrete physical and anatomical images. The seductive and/or repulsive qualities of the wild or Other, and the punishment of the same, are figured on the body, and as body.[14]

Similarly, Angela Y. Davis has argued that the 'myth of the Black rapist has been methodically conjured up whenever recurrent waves of violence and terror against the Black community have required convincing justifications'.[15]

Dabydeen draws links between the myth of the black rapist and the continued widespread rape of female slaves by slave masters. (See 'Slave Woman's Song' – 'belly big with massa') The rape of black women is an integral dimension to the deconstruction of the myth of black rapist because, as Angela Davis argues:

> The fictional image of the Black man as rapist has always strengthened its inseparable companion: the image of the Black woman as chronically promiscuous. For once the notion is accepted that Black men harbour irresistible and animal-like sexual urges, the entire race is invested with bestiality. If Black men have their eyes on white women as sexual objects, then Black women must certainly

welcome the sexual attentions of white men. Viewed as 'loose women' and whores, Black women's cries of rape would necessarily lack legitimacy.[16]

Having shown the connections between the projected personality/ abounding sexuality of male slaves and that of the brutalisation of black women, Dabydeen's speakers (male and female) underline not only the constructedness of racist ideas about black masculinity, but also points to the asymmetrical nature of the power relations between slavemasters and black women on the one hand, and black men and slavemistresses on the other.

The discourses of slavery and imperialism are filled with such moments. While this fear is expressed clearly in terms of embodiment, and is therefore seen to occupy a physical space in the white male psyche, Dabydeen subverts it in two ways. He challenges its very existence by paralleling it to the discursive construction of the 'happy hottentot[s]'. The stereotype of the complicit, passive 'hottentot', is as much a product of the European racist imagination as the image of black desire for the white woman. Dabydeen shows that they are similarly constructed and though equally widespread, false. Again, even without the notes to the poem, the level of hyperbole would lead most readers to see the slave's song as humorous, and not wholly serious, and here I suggest that we give credence to *part* of the notes to this poem, at least: to Dabydeen's insistence that '[t]here is an element of comic, mischievous laughter in the slave's celebration of his cock', and to his note that this amusement 'undermines the surface obscenity of his fantasy' (55). What becomes evident, then, is the poem's laughter as it exposes the absurdity of the white male stereotype/fear of white female violation by black men. This laughter then creates the space for other readings of the poem. Whilst having a white object of desire does appear to reflect negatively on the singer's self-image (and the image of him cowering – 'peep out at yu tween cane-stalk – reinforces this sense), one can read the poem as celebrating the unquenchability of dreaming and desire in one whose body is scarcely his own. One can also read the poem as being about the free play of writing, where it is the pen rather than the penis (cack), '[d]rippin at de tip' (28).

135

But however we read, it is undeniable that the images in the poem are articulated in masculine terms, though we need to read the voice in the poem as both 'in character' and as part of a collection. How else could one whose sexuality is denied speak his desire? As a scholar Dabydeen would know that one of the abnormalities of indenture as an institution was created by the failure of the shippers and the planters to ensure roughly equal numbers of men and women were recruited. And if one can read 'Slave Song' as celebrating masculinity in a patriarchal society, the same masculinity is critiqued and rejected in 'Men and Women'. Here the power dynamics between men and women within the Indian labour force remains hierarchical and abusive. Hence, in the context of the collection as a whole, the celebration cannot be of masculinity but of the liberty to represent black male bodies intricately.

This more intricate represention of black male desire is present in 'Love Song' where the white female figure is represented as located in the chasm *between* the binaries of cool and hot, lover and mother. The male slave escapes imaginatively into her arms. She comforts him willingly with her body both sexually and maternally as she allows him distance from his daily reality. Though one can read the frames adopted here to characterise the white female body as echoing those used by slaveowners to relate to black women's bodies, what stands out are the images of male vulnerability. The poetic persona dwells on how different the white woman, who is the object of his attention, is from him ('Other'); projects that she desires him sexually (though with a cool 'purity' of desire – 'Moon-eye/Blue like blue-saki wing'), and that she has the ability to mother him ('Leh yuh come wid milk in yuh breast').

These poems which foreground black male desire for the body of slavemistresses instead of 'inscribing [their] own inversion only to reinscribe the old hegemonies', subvert these hegemonies in creative ways, for as Dabydeen himself has argued:[17]

In responding to [myths], you rewrite English literature. You are being iconoclastic in a real sense, because you know who the icons are, and you know what the mythic structures are. And by shattering them in your personal way, you not only shatter them, you can also alter them profoundly. [...] I don't think it is sufficient to curse the master with his own tongue; it would mean that you are not progressing beyond retaliation, reaction. *I think what you have to do is revise the myths in a creative way, and in so doing perhaps reveal hidden or original layers of meaning.*[18] (my emphasis)

The poems are subversive because they move beyond refuting the myth of the black rapist and ascribe to a particular kind of deconstruction, much like carnival, which resists and mocks even whilst maintaining the facade of mimicking. This carnivalesque quality is impeccably captured in 'the virtue of Creole and its resourcefulness in conveying certain experiences'.[19] In this instance Creole becomes a 'home' in the manner conceptualised by bell hooks, for whom 'home' signifies 'that place which enables and promotes varied and everchanging perspectives, a place where one discovers new ways of seeing reality, frontiers of difference'.[20] This sense of flux and renewal can be seen in the multiple meanings of the labels and masks contained within the text. Thus the language, Creole, becomes one of the modes through which Dabydeen inverts signification, fashioning new and composite sites of definition.

Slave experience is redefined and begins to be narrated in terms of the psychological rather than the physical. While this shift displaces the slave body as the primary site from which slavery can be re-memoried, it certainly doesn't trivialise the physically and psychologically brutal conditions under which slaves laboured. However, by enlarging the slave experience to encompass the mentally creative and exploratory experience, it becomes possible to view the various masks of the slave and the enslaver as well as those of the institution itself. The slaves for whom Dabydeen sings include African chattel slaves and Indian indentured labourers. *Slave Song* also encompasses some of the concerns of their descendants, caught in the brutality of working the land to produce cane sugar. This connection between African and Indian is crucial because:

To describe the Indian experience you really have to start with the parent experience if you like, or you have to acknowledge it, or fix it. In other words, what I was trying to do in *Slave Song* was to see a continuum of slave and indenture experience.[21]

The songs become a celebration by Dabydeen, poet, literary critic, and art historian, of the diversity of slave experience as he emphasises the resistance that could have gone on in the minds of the slaves. They become songs sung by the slaves themselves as they work, but also acts of carnival which free the slaves to examine the ways in which their bodies are both literally and metaphorically written on. As songs of resistance they inscribe new ways of examining male slave subjectivity. Dabydeen's text invites readings which do not prioritise inflexible meanings. Rather, in its playful contradictions, it draws attention to the manner in which this and all other texts are constructed. In his presentation and 'concern with language and its power to redeem':[22]

> David Dabydeen is unique in being the only poet to employ rural English in his work. Control of the language is a dominant feature of imperial oppression, and only the creation of a postcolonial voice can overthrow such power.[23]

Whilst this claim for Dabydeen's uniqueness with respect to the use of rural English can be challenged, Denise deCaires Narain's more pertinent point is that the Creole speaking voice does not on its own have 'an inflated subversive potential, operating *automatically* as a radically destabilising discourse'.[24] It is when it is placed alongside the other subversive devices within the text, that the Creole becomes an insurgent poetic expression. Maria Lugones has stressed the suitability of creolised utterance to express certain conditions thus:

> I speak them because I want to point to the possibility of becoming playful in the use of different voices and because I want to point to the possibility of coming to appreciate this playfulness. [...] *The more fully this playfulness is appreciated, the less broken I am to you, the more dimensional I am to you. But I want to exercise my multidimensionality even if you do not appreciate it.* To do otherwise would be to engage in self-mutilation, to come to be just the person you see. To play in this way is then an act of resistance as well as an act of self-affirmation.[25] (my emphasis)

This position seems contrary to much of the criticism of Dabydeen's *Slave Song*, in which Creole figures as, and can only represent, fracture and brokenness. Within the paradigm set up by Lugones, however, creolised language is able to capture the consciousness of the speaker, thus contributing towards a language which is readily available for a representation of the complexities of slave life. Dabydeen has articulated a similar stance by arguing against the representation of West Indian identity in language as fracture or crisis:

> I have a multiple identity. There is no crisis. There is a kind of delight as well as anguish in jumping from one identity to the next. It's like electrons which have their own energization circles. Sometimes they jump from one to the next and release an enormous amount of energy; then they jump to another circle: little electrons jumping. That is not a crisis. That is delight and poignancy, and hopefully a release of energy. To see it as a crisis would be to invest in historical grievances.[26]

The charting of multiple and complex identity is a hopeful process, dynamic in its ability to contain both 'delight and poignancy'. This is the space in which Dabydeen locates his slave characters. While his pen frees up his male slaves from the shackles of mental violence, however, his female slaves occupy the margins.

It is clear that the female slave is not the focus of Dabydeen's project here, and in his defence it may be argued that as a poet publishing in 1984 he would have been aware that fellow Guyanese poet Grace Nichols had the year before published a collection which reconfigures female slave identity. If the two texts are read together, (both won the Commonwealth Poetry Prize in successive years) it becomes possible to view Dabydeen's project as supplementing Nichols's, revealing the manner in which slave masculinity is constructed, which differs from the female slave experience, even while they are linked. For although Dabydeen's female slaves are not the focus of the project overall, they are not marginal in a manner which silences them. They speak provocatively in Creole in the poems where they do feature and are therefore not denied language and (self) representation. In these poems their relationships are with the slave men and slavemistresses. However, in choosing to explore the generic meaning of 'slave' as male, the female slave speaks as a slave*woman*. In spite of the number of songs exploring female slave experience or relationships between male and female slaves, the slave experience remains principally male gendered. The slave women's experiences are qualified, so that the poem 'Slave Song' is in actuality the 'Slaveman's Song', even if the collection *Slave Song* encompasses both male and female experiences of slavery.

While the language frees up male slave subjectivity, it becomes precisely the terrain on which slave women remain ambiguous. They remain for us, the reader, like the raped and murdered body in 'Guyana Pastoral', about whom we have been told, 'dem hide she from deh mine' (21). She is unseen having been buried, hidden, and although her parents have searched for her, nine months later with the eggs unhatched she still lies, with '[o]nly de cush-cush ants dat lay dem white eggs in she mout' (21). When she surfaces in Dabydeen's text she is bloated like Mala in the poem of the same name; or crying and refusing to explain the source of her pain as in 'Slave Woman's Song'; or yearning for soothing love in the stanza of the 4th woman in 'Song of the Creole Gang Women'; and being saddled instead with inadequate apologies in 'Men and Women'. An alternative characterisation is present, most noticeably in 'The Servant's Song' where, although not fully fledged elsewhere, female slaves claim the ability to use language, Creole specifically, in the same manner as the male characters in Dabydeen's poetry do. Though the power dynamics in the household are in favour of the mistress, the poem suggests that all terrains have subversive potential and the mistress, far from being venerated, is mocked by the black woman whose behaviour runs counter to any image of subjection. In this poem, the mistress's ring humorously provides the message that small acts of subversion permeate the everyday relationship between mistress and servant.

All relationships between slave and slaveowner are expressed through the mouths of the slaves in language which is 'foul-mouthed, aggressively obscene', and yet the slaves 'aspire to and arrive at lyrical words, their final emancipation from Prospero's definition of them as grunting brutes and people without a literature'.[27] By leaving the reader with his own body in the poem 'Two Cultures', Dabydeen locates himself within the terrain of representation and makes connections between himself and Caribbean politics of representation. Because his subject matter is slavery and his characters are slaves, the issues of giving them voice and his role in this process is explored but not resolved, for resolution would obscure the continued power of the tropes that represent the body of the Other in dominant systems of knowledge production.

Notes to Chapter Six

Epigraphs:

Frantz Fanon, *Black Skin, White Masks* (London: Pluto, 1986 [1952]), p. 81.
bell hooks, *Killing rage: ending racism* (London: Penguin, 1995), p. 61.
Sarah Lawson Welsh, 'Experiments in Brokennness: The Creative Use of Creole in David Dabydeen's *Slave Song*', in *The Art of David Dabydeen*, ed. by Kevin Grant (Leeds: Peepal Tree, 1997), pp. 27-46 (p. 30).

1. David Dabydeen, *Slave Song* (Denmark: Dangaroo Press, 1984), further references are included in the main text of the essay.
2. Frank Birbalsingh, 'Interview with David Dabydeen: 1991', in *The Art of David Dabydeen*, ed. by Kevin Grant (Leeds: Peepal Tree, 1997) pp. 177-198 (p. 198).
3. 'Experiments in Brokenness', pp. 27-46 (p. 36).
4. Mark McWatt, 'His True-True face: Masking and Revelation in David Dabydeen's *Slave Song*', in *The Art of David Dabydeen*, ed. by Kevin Grant (Leeds: Peepal Tree, 1997), pp. 15-26 (p. 21).
5. See her 'Between Creole and Cambridge English: The Poetry of David Dabydeen', in *The Art of David Dabydeen*, ed. by Kevin Grant (Leeds: Peepal Tree, 1997), pp. 47-66 (p. 50).
6. 'Experiments in Brokenness', pp. 27-46 (p. 38).

7. David Dabydeen, 'Hogarth and the Canecutter', in *'The Tempest' and its Travels*, ed. by Peter Hulme and William H. Sharm (London: Reaktion Books, 2000).

8. Mario Relich, 'A Labyrinthine Odyssey: Psychic Division in the Writings of David Dabydeen', in *The Art of David Dabydeen*, ed. by Kevin Grant (Leeds: Peepal Tree, 1997), pp. 123-140 (p. 125).

9. 'His True-True Face', pp. 15-26 (p. 23).

10 . 'The Song of the Creole Gang Women' had additional notes which can be seen to function in a similar manner at the end of the poem.

11. Hilary McD Beckles, 'Centreing Woman: The Political Economy of Gender in West African and Caribbean Slavery', in *Caribbean Portraits: Essays on Gender Ideologies and Identities*, ed. by Christine Barrow (Kingston: Ian Randle, 1998), pp. 93-114 (p. 100).

12. Although Edward Long's is the oft-quoted reference to Africans as orang-utan, Michelle Cliff, in her essay, 'Object Into Subject: Some Thoughts on the Work of Black Women Artists', in *Making Face, Making Soul, Haciendo Caras*, ed. by Gloria Anzaldua (San Francisco: Aunt Lute, 1990), pp. 271-290 (p. 273), asks; 'Did you know that, for example, Thomas Jefferson held the popular view that the Black race was created when Black women mated with orang-utans? (I do not know where the original Black women were supposed to have come from.)'.

13. 'His True-True Face', pp. 15-26 (p. 21).

14. Elleke Boehmer, 'Transfiguring: Colonial Body as Postcolonial Narrative', *Novel: A Forum for Fiction*, 26.1 (Fall 1992) 268-277 (p. 269).

15. Angela Y. Davis, *Women, Race and Class* (London: Women's Press, 1982), p. 173.

16. ibid., p. 182.

17. 'Experiments in Brokenness', pp. 27-46 (p. 42).

18. Wolfgang Binder, 'Interview with David Dabydeen: 1989', in *The Art of David Dabydeen*, ed. by Kevin Grant (Leeds: Peepal Tree, 1997), pp. 159-166 (p. 173).

19. ibid., p.170.

20. bell hooks, *Yearning: race, gender and cultural politics* (London: Turnaround, 1991), p. 148.

21. 'Interview with David Dabydeen: 1991', pp. 177-198 (p. 187).

22. Kevin Grant, 'Preface', in *The Art of David Dabydeen*, ed. by Kevin Grant (Leeds: Peepal Tree, 1997), pp. 9-14 (p. 13).

23. ibid., p. 10.

24. Denise deCaires Narain, 'Body Talk: Writing and Speaking the Body in the Texts of Caribbean Writers', in *Caribbean Portraits: Essays on Gender Ideologies and Identities*, ed. by Christine Barrow (Kingston: Ian Randle, 1998), p. 255-275 (p. 258).

25. See her 'Hablando cara a cara/ Speaking Face to Face: An Exploration of Ethnocentric Racism', in *Making Face, Making Soul, Haciendo Caras*, ed. by Gloria Anzaldua (San Francisco: Aunt Lute, 1990), pp. 46-54 (46).

26. 'Interview with David Dabydeen: 1991', pp. 177-198 (p. 195).

27. 'Hogarth and the Cane Cutter' in *'The Tempest' and its Travels*, ed. by Peter Hulme and William H. Sharm (London: Reaktion Books, 2000).

CHAPTER SEVEN

ONE-HAND CLAPPING: *DISAPPEARANCE*

MICHAEL MITCHELL

For whatever we lose (like a you or a me)
it's always ourselves we find in the sea

> E. E. Cummings

Among the newsreel footage of the arrival of the *Empire Windrush* at Tilbury there is a bizarre interview with the legendary Trinidad calypsonian Lord Kitchener. Concurring with the rather supercilious interviewer that he is indeed the 'king' of calypso, the singer, dressed in a suit and trilby hat, when encouraged to give an example of his art, breaks into:

London is the place for me,
London, this lovely city;
You can go to France or America,
India, Asia or Australia
But you must come back to London city [1]

The song from the margin about a Londoner's return to the metropolis has a number of ironies, not least in the performance. The rhythm is perfect, but the bemused audience is not given the essential steel band accompaniment, apart from the singer's half-suppressed percussive hums. The effect is of one hand clapping, of presence and absence, the disappearance compensated and completed by the potential knowledge or intuition and empathy of the listener. It is a weird dialogue with the self, setting up unforgettable resonances in which the apparent certainties of the status quo can be interrogated. As the new Londoners came down the gangway, an urban population from cities which resembled rural English market towns, their illusions of a warm welcome to the rich metropolitan centre would soon be shattered. The new Dick Whittingtons seeking the streets paved with gold would relive, ironically, the myth which had set off the commercial expansion creating the very Empire which had shaped the circumstances of their lives.

The condition of the immigrant to London is an experience shared by David Dabydeen. It informs the setting of his first novel, *The Intended*, and has been referred to by him as 'not linear, because immigrants are liable to appear and disappear. This is what immigrant life is: you appear in one society, then you disappear'.[2] It was a theme he was to take up in his second novel, *Disappearance*, where one of the characters claims: 'I does stray about in circles. I does curl and disappear like smoke ring and reappear somewhere else. I already done convolute and circumnavigate the world before I come to this spot.'[3] Migration thus becomes far more than simple geographical displacement, and this in turn affects traditional immigrant concerns like 'return', whether return to an immediate point of departure ('home' in the Caribbean) or the more remote mythical return to Africa or India. *Disappearance* initially appears to be a novel about immigrant sensibilities. However, as the more perceptive critics immediately appreciated, the apparently realistic narrative of *Disappearance* uses every conceivable strategy to conceal and reveal an essentially lyrical exploration of a far more subtle web of significance, unsurprising in a poet, but which upsets expectations founded on mimetic realism.[4] The apparent smoothness of the narrative is fissured, allowing access to other worlds, and continually frustrating attempts to fix and contain experience within preconceived parameters.

Paradoxically, many of the strategies used by the author appear at first sight to be clichés of postcolonial and postmodern sensibility. The basic plot situation itself is an ironic reversal. The Afro-Guyanese engineer is sent by his revered mentor, an English professor employed by the regime in post-independence Guyana, to shore up the crumbling cliffs of squabbling Albion, where beneath the pastoral surface of rural life a horror of darkness lies buried. His landlady, a white ex-colonial expat who has returned from Africa, urges him to find pride and identity in his black African otherness. There is a writing back, not only to imperial master-narratives, but to an older generation of postcolonial writers who themselves wrote back to those master narratives, which gives the impression of an endlessly self-referential story with a narrative 'disappearing, as it were, up its own aporia', according to Mark McWatt.[5] All this has led McWatt to suggest that the work is merely an attempt to put academic theory into practice, in which case 'if there is no "truth" in the novel (except the endless restatement of the political correctness of postcolonial theory) then the reader is at least as diminished as the fiction'.[6]

Is it narrative overkill or mischievous fun, for example, when 'the obvious disappearance of the book is its narrator, who remains unnamed throughout', constantly enquiring and seeking after a 'truth' which also disappears before it can be grasped?[7] The author is at great pains to point out that all apparent reality shifts into its opposite as you try to observe it. Not only is nothing what it seems:

> Mrs. Rutherford herself, on one of our trips to Hastings, had pointed me to a splendid mansion in the Georgian style. "To think that West-Indian slave money built that," she said, "but the crowds who go to gape at the fine furniture and fine paintings think it the best of English heritage". (178)

Things themselves alter before one's eyes:

> From a safe distance his cottage had the appearance of a picturesque shambles [...]. It was the kind of dwelling you'd imagine a hermit to be inhabiting, in an English fairy tale from one of my story-books. When I looked again I could see it for what it was – woodwormed, crippled with hatred, wanting to crash to the ground more catastrophically than the cliff's fall. (168)

This description of the Irish labourer Christie's house follows a meeting in which he tells the narrator that all his assumptions are false, that his English mentor is a crook and the whole of his project bogged in corruption:

> It's all stories. Everything is stories. If you want certainty take

up a shell from the beach, put your ears to it and listen to what the ghost of the flesh that lived in it is telling you. What you hear might as well be the truth, the whole truth and nothing but the truth. Today I've been your shell, tomorrow you'll find another. Mr. Curtis is blooming, Professor Fenwick is an honest priest, Rushton is the kind of manager that martyrs are made of. (167)

Mrs. Rutherford warns the narrator: 'Don't be taken in by him' (74), but it is just as dangerous to be misled into thinking that what Mrs. Rutherford says can be taken at face value. In view of the author's repeated stress on the unreliability of any report, this would be ingenuous. So what Mrs. Rutherford has to say about her vanished husband Jack and his perverted sexual excesses, or about the mysterious Mr. Curtis and his contribution to saving the crumbling cliff, must also be taken with a grain of salt. As personalities in a traditional realistic sense, all these characters simply vanish in explicit or implied contradictions:

Take Jack. There's not a trace of him here, yet we keep mentioning his name. Take Curtis. He's a photograph in a newspaper and a lot of descriptions, that's all. As to the villagers, I've rarely seen any of them in real life. They might as well be Christie's ghosts. (157)

Truth in the novel centres less on a search for the essence of Dunsmere, the English village, or even the essence of Englishness behind the collection of enigmatic personalities, but rather on the narrator himself and the central question to which Mrs. Rutherford, and the book, return again and again: 'Why, Mrs. Rutherford wanted to know, did I become an engineer?' (3). As an engineer, the narrator never ceases to probe the apparent nature of reality and to find it as elusive and shifting as ocean water, to find that everything has two names, or disappears in ambivalence and ambiguity. Even the English flowers with their pretty names have ugly counterparts with names suggesting cruelty or obscenity.[8]

An engineer attempts to order. As the schoolmaster in the narrator's Guyanese village points out: 'an engineer is a man who builds a dam against the wild sea. An engineer makes things spick and span, he straightens out whatever is lopsided' (60). Yet the narrator's dams in Guyana and, it is suggested, his English project, do not achieve permanence. The sea eventually returns and washes them away. This is the basic polarity between a view of the world founded on Newtonian principles of order, a universe of 'single vision', and a Blakean world in constant visionary flux where definitions, always merging with their opposites, merely disappear.

So who is the narrator? Does the key to the book lie in discovering his identity and ethnic affiliations? Mrs. Rutherford constantly tries to force on him an African past, wanting him to relate to her collection of masks. It is hard to avoid reading this as a criticism of academic theory which seeks to press writers into a preordained scheme; whereas the recognition of Otherness is initially liberating, the attempt to define what Otherness must mean and only allow it validity within set, formal structures becomes its own kind of hegemonic colonization, and the writer is expected to conform to a historical past which is as much of a construction as the old imperial narratives had been. This is reflected in the fact that even Mrs. Rutherford's African masks and pots hint at discrepancies and mysteries in their origins and distribution, destabilizing conceptions of tradition and history. The narrator, by contrast, shares Derek Walcott's wariness about the determinism of the past.[9] He insists that as a West Indian he is not driven by a sense of the past: 'As a West-Indian I had no cause to anticipate the future nor to fear death because I had cultivated no sense of the past. I was always present, always new' (10). Yet the narrator never ceases to be preoccupied by the past, the past of the characters, of the land, of his own past. But it is a past which remains in flux, ambiguous, beyond classification, reaching up to interact with the present and retreating into inscrutability like the half-heard calypso accompaniment to an asymmetrical melody.

Neither is the narrator a mask for the author. Though they share biographical similarities, which invite the reader to search for what is 'real' in the fiction, this soon turns into a game of hide-and-seek in which the author becomes just as fictional as the character. David Dabydeen is a highly accessible writer who readily gives interviews and talks about his work, but it should be borne in mind that, as with the notes which accompany the poetry in *Slave*

Song, Dabydeen uses authorial comments as part of the work of literature itself, and not privileged above it. They are an additional indication that, as Mario Relich puts it, 'David Dabydeen [is] a writer who is particularly intent on finding objective equivalents for dramatizing a conflict which is essentially *inner*.'[10] The apparently concrete borderline between 'reality' and 'fiction', the heard and the unheard, disappears like the contours of flooded land.

Though Mrs. Rutherford urges the narrator to find an inner identity in her collection of masks, he is more interested in the collection of books in her house. These are texts which do not limit their forms to words on the printed page, but are concerned with the physical presence of the book medium, their texture or smell, and with the readers of the books in *ex libris* or dedicatory inscriptions. The whole process of production and reception of texts, as well as their subsistence through time and their social and political nexus become part of the narrator's vision, which is filtered through the same authorial destabilization and ambiguity:

Books which when opened creaked at the spine and gave off a pleasurably damp smell and the fine dust of another age. Books with raised holes made by insects in their pages, resembling Braille, as if even the blind could have access to the knowledge contained therein. Books that bore curious inscriptions in faded ink, in handwriting shaped by quill or ancient nib. *Ex libris Joseph Countryman Esq. Dominus Illuminatio Mea.* Others were more personal, making me feel intrusive and uncomfortable when I read them because I was from the future they could not envisage, a future which could well have brought terrors and disappointments to their evolving lives, a future which ruptured the innocence of the moment. *For Albert, on being sixteen. May God keep you steadfast in your studies and prosper in His Grace and Wisdom. Your Loving Father; Dearest Annie, each word in this book tells your life and mine. Love John.* How was the father to know that Albert would indeed go on to become Professor of Classics at Oxford, Jack the Ripper's pimp or a leader of the Cato Street Conspiracy? And Annie, Dearest Annie, with apple-juice breasts that men gurgled and choked on, marble thighs that made men slip and break their necks; Annie who may have married John, lived in a farmhouse and produced six healthy children (brown and speckled like farmhouse eggs) who worked on the land and cared for their parents in their old age; Annie who, burdened with John's molestations and fetishes, perhaps absconded with an early feminist and wrote treatises against Royalty, Episcopacy, the Judiciary and other phallocentric institutions. (9)

Joseph Countryman, it will be recalled, is the name given to the illiterate black British Rasta in *The Intended*, whose unconventional intensity of vision ends in tragic suicide. Commenting on this passage, in which the Latin motto of the Oxford University Press and the archaic Esq. are juxtaposed playfully with the ignorant genius and, who knows, with a whole biography from his own experience for the author to draw on, Mark McWatt says:

> Manipulated by the postcolonial awareness of the author, the narrator is made to stand counter to text, insinuating into its narrative fastnesses the chaos of possibility, of counter-discourse.[11]

Intertextuality is thus less a device than a mode in which *Disappearance* is written, and it emerges that the texts the author has used are just as significant as the repertoire of a conventional novel, because this complex metonymic process is employed in a way normally associated with the poetic image, to set up resonances which may reach deep into the reader's imagination. These texts are presences which have 'disappeared', and yet which haunt the book with their uncanny absence.

I intend to concentrate here on three types of intertextuality: book, character and land. Through them it is possible to reach an awareness of the 'inner conflict' referred to earlier and indicate what needs to be interpolated in order to hear the full calypso, the clapping of both hands.

Dabydeen offers his readers a starting point for their trail in his epigraphs: from Wilson Harris, V. S. Naipaul, T. S. Eliot, Jacques Derrida and Margaret Thatcher. Eliot's 'Mistah Kurtz – he dead' is a further quip of intertextuality indicating the absent presence of Conrad. Although other texts echo within the novel – Jean Popeau has pointed to *Prester John* – these are the defining ones, like a constellation of main characters.[12]

From Mrs. Thatcher Dabydeen draws a political context, a fixed point in time for the narration. The words 'Rejoice! Rejoice!', the Conservative Prime Minister's reaction to the news that the

Argentine forces in the Falkland Islands had surrendered and that this small piece of the former Empire had been shored up against assault, serve to define a particular self-image of Britain in the 1980s. As part of a discourse of invasion and settlement it is, of course, one of a number of self-images which the novel refracts and undermines as part of its project of ambivalence.

With Derrida, we encounter the title of the novel. Derrida argues that the traditional value put on speech as anterior to writing and somehow nearer to the 'reality' to which both refer cannot be justified. 'Natural presence', which is a condition of ontological certainty, cannot be achieved. All speech, and writing, differ from that reality and defer it, because they cannot be simultaneous in time. The result is a constant 'play' between the sign and what it is believed to refer to, which continually recedes. Taking Rousseau as a model, he mischievously points out that Rousseau's masturbatory substitute for what he believes to be the reality of the object of his desire is in fact all there is: 'il n'y a pas de hors-texte'.[13] This allows the old tyranny of the mimetic relationship to be broken; instead of a stable reality within fixed frontiers accessible to single vision, it suggests that the play of resonances between the reality of absence in the artistic image and the fiction of presence in the objective correlative of 'reality' is the only truth that can be counted on.

Naipaul provides the setting and tone of the narration. It is a skilful, if ironic tribute by the younger writer that Dabydeen so deftly catches the exact cadences of Naipaul's prose. The unemotional, autobiographical voice, the sharpness of detail, probing outside and within the narrative personality, the peripatetic excursions round an enigmatic point are all techniques used in *The Enigma of Arrival*, which also sees a West Indian in a rural setting of central historical significance (with Naipaul it is Stonehenge) seeking the nature of his relationship with England and finding it in relation to a character called Jack, or more particularly Jack's garden:

> My ideas about Jack were wrong. He was not exactly a remnant; he had created his own life, his own world, almost his own continent. But the world about him, which he so enjoyed and used, was too precious not to be used by others. And it was only when he had

151

gone, it was only then that I saw how tenuous, really, the hold of all these people had been on the land they worked or lived in.[14]

By 'writing back' to Naipaul in this way, Dabydeen points out that West Indian fiction has 'come of age' and is able to relate to and distance itself from its first generation, treating it as part of a seamless tradition of writing in English. It also addresses the whole issue of immigration and settlement, releasing it from its ghetto-like context of late twentieth-century sensibility, and making it clear that migration and change are part of the human condition and not the exception to it, and that seemingly immovable and static imperial conditions are in fact subject to constant fluctuation, like the changing outlines of seacoasts.

With the Eliot quotation we move towards one of the central texts of postcolonial intertextuality, Conrad's *Heart of Darkness*. But this text, too, is seen through the filter of Eliot's poetry, not just 'The Hollow Men' with its flavour of disillusion, but the mysterious presence in the rose garden of the *Four Quartets*: 'the unheard music hidden in the shrubbery, And the unseen eyebeam crossed' which is 'England and nowhere. Never and always'.[15]

The Intended, Kurtz's fiancée in *Heart of Darkness*, has 'a soul as translucently pure as a cliff of pure crystal'.[16] It is tempting to associate this figure with the cliff at Dunsmere, which takes on the role of the engineer's perilous muse. The illustration on the cover of the first edition showing the faces of a man and woman etched in relief on the cliff strengthens this impression. The Intended is a shadowy presence first encountered at the end of Conrad's novel, when the narrator Marlow, on his return to Brussels to report Kurtz's final days, finds himself unable to tell her his last words were 'the horror, the horror!' and substitutes 'Your name'. Kurtz, like Marlow, had left with high ideals from the Brussels office where the three ominous women, like the Norns of Norse mythology, supervise the signing of a Faustian pact. In Africa he discovers his 'heart of darkness' and the price of his bargain. The Intended and her dark counterpart, the magnificent African woman at Kurtz's station, are the vague female anima figures presiding over Kurtz's heroic dreams and brutal hubris. They highlight the fact that there is no equivalent female figure in Dabydeen's novel. She is another casualty of disappearance.

Apart from the acknowledged debt to Wilson Harris for the name of the narrator's mentor,[17] Fenwick, which is the name of the surveyor / engineer in Harris's *The Secret Ladder*, Dabydeen has clearly employed a technique which can be observed in most of Harris's novels, from *Palace of the Peacock* to *Jonestown*: the multiplication of single characters, while other separate characters turn out to be the same. At the beginning of *Palace* it becomes clear that Donne is both narrator, a 'seeing eye', and protagonist, a 'blind eye'. The two crews, on the other hand, are one and the same, and in their multi-ethnic composition turn out to be multiple aspects of the same identity. This process is a function of psyche, in which language, by transcending realism, enables that which does not exist to come into existence, and the resultant reality to achieve the richness of both itself and its opposite.[18]

Here, in *Disappearance*, characters disappear in order to reappear under other names and with fresh identities, but remain recognisably discreet as an inner entity; they reflect a quality Dabydeen recognizes in *Heart of Darkness* when he says it 'ceased being an exploration of a different geography and landscape and became a Freudian exploration of the energies that people exchange'.[19] The use of character in this case might find a musical parallel in the way the same note is recognizable although it is played by different instruments. Another approach might be through the Jungian archetype.[20]

Among the archetypes which are fractured and refracted through the book we can distinguish the Mother. The narrator's real mother in Guyana, the black woman who believes that only whites can create order out of chaos ('"Why everything black people handle become ruination and ash?" she asked, looking directly at me as I swung in the hammock. "Is like King Midas in reverse. What he touch turn gold but we convert things to bush and blackness like we own skin"' (63)) is associated with Mrs Rutherford, the motherly landlady who denigrates everything English and urges the narrator to adopt an African identity. He feels attracted to her with a kind of repulsion suggestive of incestuous desire: 'I looked away, faintly nauseated by the possibility of her embrace, the closing of her fulsome creased flesh about mine' (76). His attraction to Annette, the canteen waitress in Guyana, is based on the size of her breasts and the fact that 'I saw my mother in her' (86). When Swami, the Indian-descended labourer on the Guyanese dam, complains that he spends all his time with books instead of women, the narrator reacts furiously when he picks up a picture of his mother, asking if she 'is wife or is sweet-woman?' (29). This is something Mrs. Rutherford recognizes: 'you were never in love. The only person you've ever cared for is your mother' (140).[21]

Jack and Curtis, similarly, share with the narrator's real father the fact of absence. Jack is the magician who disappeared one day in a 'puff of smoke' (5). Absconded, dead or reclusive, they have withdrawn, leaving a new set of father figures: Mr. Leroy, the brutal schoolmaster, or Professor Fenwick, perhaps even the 'quietly efficient' Mr. Rushton, the site manager. They represent, in their various ways, the magician's quest for power over things, the attempt to use technology to control nature, the belief that the flux of time can be controlled in straight lines, a Newtonian linear physics as compared to the turbulence of apparent chaos. The phallically-named Wally Pearce, the engineer on the Guyana sea wall, is said by Swami to be planning 'one straight clean-cut fuck'. He links technology with phallocentric post-imperialism:

> [...] like how your bulldozer blade does slice a line in the land. All-you people is straight-line folk, all-you does live along ruler's edge. The white man who used to rule you so fulsomely left you with a plastic ruler to rule you. (36)

As for Swami himself, the messenger of the 'spirits of this land': he is the trickster, the alchemical spirit Mercurius, the shape-shifter, catalyst and bringer of wisdom, replicated in Christie, but also in the enigmatic Alfred, Mr. Roosevelt, the alcoholic sage of the narrator's boyhood, who shares with Swami the honour of being elevated to the status of a god; the god of chance. It is mere chance that allows him, as 'Freddo', to score the first goal at the village's new American-built basketball pitch signalling another of the book's characteristic sets of appearance and disappearance; he temporarily

154

rises from drunken penury to a kind of respectability before reverting to his old ways, as the basketball pitch reverts to bush, or the drained land is once again swamped by the sea.[22]

It is Mr. Roosevelt, Alfred, who activates the narrator's imagination, telling him that 'real life is abroad and big-big stories' (51) and sending him to the sea wall to watch for three days with the promise of a gift if he can report on three things in detail.[23] The boy returns, having seen only the sea, and makes up elaborate lies from his own imagination. Alfred comments that the boy 'must have the clearest eyesight in the village' before asking if he did not see God: 'You got to close your eyes if you want to see God, like you praying' (52). But the narrator is unable to appreciate the paradoxical significance of the sea as infinite matrix of the imagination from which all images can be born, seeing only emptiness without pattern.[24] He scorns the crooked lines Alfred sews with his sewing machine, the amorphous sea, and chooses instead the engineer's straight lines and the dam.

The association of numbers based on three with the sea is significant. In alchemical and Jungian literature three is an imperfect and feminine number. It reminds the reader that Newtonian physics, on which Western technology is based, found its limits in the study of turbulence, which has now led through so-called chaos theory to a revelation that underlying patterns based on bifurcations leave islands of order in seas of apparent chaos.[25] Newton himself famously said that he felt all his life had been spent like a child playing with stones by the sea, and Blake, whose vision of the imagination so radically opposed Newton's, formulated his ideas about 'Newton's sleep' when he observed the sun on the sand of the Sussex coast. The engineer is Faust, choosing the path of knowledge and control, even at the cost of his own soul. In Goethe's play, Faust is given jurisdiction over the shore 'between the salt-water and the sea-strand', as the folk-song puts it. There he drains a vast territory, oppressing the inhabitants in his search for profit. In *Disappearance*, the narrator is urged to 'Rejoice!' for having carved his name on English history, but he is filled only with resentment. He feels again the desire to smash things, as he had smashed the lights on the basketball pitch as a boy, putting out

155

the four eyes, before blaming it on his *alter ego* Jamal. The project is completed, but at the cost of the anima or soul.

In this context Christie's words about seashells take on new meaning. In a shell the sound of the sea is supposedly heard. Christie points out that along with all the contradictory stories the narrator may hear around the village, in the shell he can hear the 'ghost of the flesh that lived in it' (168). One can read, too, the analogy between the shape of the seashell and the snail-like shape of the cochlea – the inner ear within the skull – and the implication that what is heard as external reality derives from inner human imagination. On the beach below the cliffs at Hastings shells can be found interspersed with fossils many millions of years old. One is reminded forcibly of Wilson Harris's influential essay 'Fossil and Psyche' in which he points out that time can be manifested as pregnant with possibilities of birth and otherness, or as merely inflated with its own identity, which is a kind of death wish.[26] Harris observes this phenomenon in the 'cliché of conquest' which makes of Conrad's Kurtz an abortion or 'ghost-child'. He goes on to trace the similarities and dissimilarities fifty years later in Patrick White's story of Voss and his relationship with Laura. Whereas, as Harris points out, Marlow suffers from 'an eclipse of the word' when he is unable to tell the Intended the truth about Kurtz, I would argue that Dabydeen, (behind a narrator who recognizes the inability of his chosen craft to make sense of the multiplicity of voices that the sea symbolizes), is seeking 'that de-escalating factor or irony [which] may paradoxically enrich the range and content of experience in that it exposes given targets as involuntary animations in a new dress, and triggers off afresh a long and endless quest for motifs of relief from implacable polarizations within history'.[27]

So the essential polarity of the book becomes that of sea and land, the unconscious and consciousness. The narrator recognizes that there are mutualities between the sea in England and the sea in Guyana:

> It was the same sea that I had done battle with for years, but the English end of it. I could not wait to discover how the rogue and

monster behaved itself on the English coast: whether it was more mannered and restrained, as I imagined the English to be, or whether it charged and brawled in our creole ways. (20)

He also discovers mutualities on the land; Hastings is chosen as the site of historical invasions and depredations which determined the whole pattern of the land as well as the lives of the people. The Norman Conquest with its imposition of feudal hierarchies was just as traumatic for the people who suffered it as was the experience of colonialism in Guyana.[28] The horrors of witch-hunts on nearby Romney Marsh are historically documented events which mean 'Dunsmere might as well be a village in the Congo' (117). Through this identification the other resonances and intertextualities employed by the author become all the more powerful, as they echo not only through books and history, but in and out of reality itself: Alfred, the Guyanese peasant, and King Alfred the Great, who recognized the importance of the sea to his kingdom; or Cnut, who knew it could not be conquered; Curtis and Kurtz; Swami the Indian priest and Christie the Christian; the date of Jack's disappearance corresponding with the date of Guyana's independence (which is then altered in the fiction) and the narrator's sexual maturity; Mrs. Rutherford's name perhaps a mischievous reference to the editor of the postcolonial journal, *Kunapipi*, as well as the great physicist and successor to Newton, Ernest Rutherford; Dunsmere an echo of the drowned medieval city of Dunwich.[29] Undoubtedly, the author's acquaintance with Fairlight, a Sussex village threatened by coastal erosion, relates to this novel with its missing female polarity, but a search to read one only in terms of the other is misguided. The more fruitful approach is in discovering the resonances between what appears and what seems to have disappeared. Such resonances are best described by Jung in his term synchronicity. They result from an acausal connecting principle which makes connections by meaning, though the link is invisible to the scientific eye. It is a link which works through metonymy, in the realm of the imagination, but which manifests itself in the real world. Only fiction and poetry are capable of charting or measuring the numinous forces which operate there.

It is the kind of link which sees Lord Kitchener (of the poster 'Your Country Needs You') disappearing on a warship heading for the Arctic Sea and reappearing from the Caribbean as a calypso singer on the *Empire Windrush* answering the call for labour from the 'Mother Country'.

Disappearance is one hand clapping, a song whose elements, when they are supplied by the imagination, begin to resonate fully in the realization that the best hope for a society threatened by the massive forces of the unconscious in the shape of human brutality, greed and blindness does not lie exclusively in the ruling tools of technology but in the fragile survival of an ambiguously named flower, the blue flower of the imagination which the writer finds in his pocket as he leaves on the train, a story 'dried and grown flat' like the leaves of a book, but which has not yet disappeared.[30]

Notes to Chapter Seven

1. *Pathé* News, 22 June 1948.
2. Frank Birbalsingh, 'Interview with David Dabydeen: 1991', in *The Art of David Dabydeen*, ed. by Kevin Grant (Leeds: Peepal Tree, 1997), pp. 177-198 (p. 195).
3. David Dabydeen, *Disappearance* (London: Martin Secker & Warburg, 1993), p.36. All subsequent references included in the main text of the essay.
4. For example, Sean French in *The Times*, 18 March 1993, concludes that Dabydeen 'is not yet fired with the unifying energy of a storyteller', or James Walton in *The Daily Telegraph*, 20 February 1993, finds the novel's chief quality in 'the deft gentleness of the reminiscing and the strangely touching central relationship'. By contrast, Maya Jaggi, writing in *The Times Literary Supplement*, 2 March 1993, or Rosemary Sorensen in the *Australian Book Review* [February/March] 1993, have far more perceptive insights.
5. Mark McWatt, ' "Self-Consciously Post-Colonial": The Fiction of David Dabydeen', in *The Art of David Dabydeen* (Leeds: Peepal Tree, 1997), pp. 111-222 (p. 122).

6. ibid., p. 122.
7. Brendan deCaires, A Review, *Stabroek News*, 2 April 1993, p. 13.
8. Mrs Rutherford scoffs at the narrator's naïve enthusiasm for lyrical names like Lady's tresses or Queen Anne's lace, pointing to others such as Devil's-bit scabious or Dane's-blood (p. 70).
9. As expressed, for instance, in his essay 'The Muse of History', where he describes history as 'that Medusa of the New World': Derek Walcott, *What the Twilight Says:Essays* (London: Faber & Faber, 1998).
10. Mario Relich, 'A Labyrinthine Odyssey: Psychic Division in the Writings of David Dabydeen', in *The Art of David Dabydeen*, ed. by Kevin Grant (Leeds: Peepal Tree, 1997), pp. 123-140 (p. 124).
11. '"Self-Consciously Post-Colonial"', pp. 111-222 (p. 118).
12. Jean Popeau, *'Disappearance'* , in *The Art of David Dabydeen*, ed. by Kevin Grant (Leeds: Peepal Tree, 1997), pp. 99-109 (p. 102).
13. Jacques Derrida, *De la Grammatologie* (Paris: Éditions de Minuit, 1967), p. 227. The epigraph is drawn from later in the same passage, p. 228.
14. V. S. Naipaul, *The Enigma of Arrival* (Harmondsworth: Penguin, 1987), p. 87.
15. T. S. Eliot, *Four Quartets*, 'Burnt Norton', in *The Complete Poems and Plays* (London: Faber & Faber, 1969), p.172: the following quotation is from the same edition, *Four Quartets*, 'Little Gidding', p. 192.
16. Joseph Conrad, *Heart of Darkness* (London: Penguin, 1995), p. 114.
17. See Dabydeen's hilariously 'calypsoed' version of how Harris gave him permission for this borrowing in the interview given to Kwame Dawes in 1994, in *The Art of David Dabydeen*, pp. 199-221 (p. 210), for a good illustration of Dabydeen's playful fictionalisation of autobiographical details.
18. Harris has written of the 'adversarial twinship of Merlin and Parsifal'. Merlin has been trapped and eclipsed, while Parsifal has framed and enshrined a 'seemingly invincible core-bias of communication. Harris refers to Jung in pointing out that a new conceptual language is needed to breach that core-bias if a deeper hidden rapport is to come into play between Parsifal (and all that Parsifal entails as a vessel of sovereign power) and apparently trapped Merlin (and all that Merlin entails as a vessel of shamanic lore and a visionary, stranger, self-confessional, self-judgmental orbit slumbering in the iron-clad but deceptive logic of ruthless materialism).' Wilson Harris,

'Merlin and Parsifal: Adversarial Twins', in *Selected Essays*, ed. by Andrew Bundy (London: Routledge, 1999), pp. 58-74 (p. 59).

19. 'Interview: 1991', pp. 177-198 (p. 185).
20. It should be noted that Jung regards archetypes not as essences, not 'unconscious ideas', but processes, pathways of symbolic connections and possibilities of representation. Jung himself compares them with the matrix of crystalline growth, allowing endless variation and play: 'The only thing that remains constant is the axial system, or rather, the invariable geometric proportions underlying it.' C. G. Jung, *The Archetypes and the Collective Unconscious*, in *The Collected Works*, 9 vols (London: Routledge & Kegan Paul, 1968), I, 80.
21. Note also in this context the exchange between the narrator and Mrs Rutherford in which her remark: 'Perhaps that's why you are driven, because you're always on edge, either between your mother and a lover or [...]' prompts the narrator to recall Swami: 'He told me I lived at the edge of a ruler, afraid to venture off in case I collapsed in a heap of madness' p. 158.
22. Among these rises and falls we may note the school career of Jamal pp. 58 – 62, or the campaigning popularity of Curtis.
23. According to Dabydeen, one important influence on him as a child was his primary school headmaster, 'an old black man called Mr Spencer [...] He had been abroad and he would tell us stories of how things were done abroad'; 'Interview: 1991', pp. 177-198 (p. 180).
24. It is significant that Dabydeen stresses the role of the sea in his poem *Turner*; 'I deliberately set the poem in the sea. Most of it takes place in the actuality of the sea, and the sea is actual, not just as the location of the drowned man, but in the rhythms of the poem.' In Kwame Dawe's 'Interview with David Dabydeen: 1994', in *The Art of David Dabydeen*, ed. by Kevin Grant (Leeds: Peepal Tree, 1997), pp. 199-221 (p. 205).
25. It goes beyond the scope of this essay to discuss the full significance of the discoveries of so-called 'chaos' science, as summarized in James Gleick, *Chaos: Making a New Science* (London: Heinemann, 1988) or the 'dissipative structures' and their self-organization which are the subject of Prigogine and Stengers, *Order Out of Chaos* (London: Heinemann, 1984); it will suffice to note that their critique of Newtonian 'single vision' and the technology which springs from it runs parallel with the discomfort of Dabydeen's engineer.
26. In Wilson Harris, 'Fossil and Psyche', in *Explorations: A Selection*

of Talks and Articles 1966-1981, ed. by Hena Maes-Jelinek (Denmark: Dangaroo, 1981), pp. 68-82. The sense in which Harris understands 'fossil' becomes clear in the following remarks: 'Mental phenomena – the visualizations in which one is involved within the language of fiction – possess their authenticity in a series of fossilizations of identity as musical / architectonic spaces sprung from a rhythm of pressures to revise limits – to revise a canvas of existence – to re-sense other buried / renascent horizons *within* and *without* given appearances, *within* and *without* a given field of experience' (77).

27. ibid., p. 78.

28. It involves the realization, central to Walcott's poem 'The Ruins of a Great House' and a premise of *Omeros*; 'That Albion too was once / A Colony like ours'; Derek Walcott, *Collected Poems 1948-1984* (New York: Farrar, Straus & Giroux, 1986), p. 19.

29. Where, according to Roland Parker in *Men of Dunwich* (London: Collins, 1978), the dissension and petty squabbles among the inhabitants in the 13th to 16th centuries closely matched the description of the course of the campaign to save Dunsmere cliff which the narrator finds in Mrs Rutherford's press clippings file. Indeed, the disputes seem to have contributed to the fate of the East Anglian port.

30. Introduced by Novalis, the blue flower was the symbol of the poetic truth of the imagination which linked the inanimate, animate and divine worlds for the German Romantic Movement.

CHAPTER EIGHT

WRITING PLACE: THE PERCEPTION OF LANGUAGE AND ARCHITECTURE IN V. S. NAIPAUL'S *THE ENIGMA OF ARRIVAL* AND DAVID DABYDEEN'S *DISAPPEARANCE*

MARK STEIN

There is not much wilderness in this anciently worked island, and most of it is a man-made facsimile of the real thing.
Raymond Williams, 'Between Country and City'

This essay will investigate the perception of landscape and architecture in V. S. Naipaul's *The Enigma of Arrival* and David Dabydeen's *Disappearance*.[1] Both texts map out the responses of their protagonists to landscape, architecture, and fellow human beings, and raise questions as to how these responses are generated and what they mean in view of the protagonists' specific backgrounds. I will first lay out the basis for this comparison, indicating the relevant similarities and differences between the two texts.

Disappearance, published six years after Naipaul's text, is related to *The Enigma of Arrival* in several ways. Both authors, born in the Caribbean of Indian-Caribbean parentage, British educated and living in England, have their narrators journey from the Caribbean to Britain, where both feel that they have come to England too late in its history:

England had long ceased to matter. To smash up England would be no more than going berserk in a waxwork museum. (*Disappearance*, 179)

So I grew to feel that the grandeur belonged to the past; that I had come to England at the wrong time; that I had come too late to find the England, the heart of the empire, which (like a provincial, from a far corner of the empire) I had created in my fantasy. (*Enigma*, 120)

Both narrators spend time living in rural areas of England – Dunsmere and Salisbury Plains, respectively – where they have difficulty in feeling part of their new environment, and try to familiarize themselves with the alien yet familiar landscape by learning the names of flowers and trees. Their perception of their surroundings is influenced by their previous knowledge, their expectations, and by their childhoods in Guyana and Trinidad. In *Disappearance*, the narrator is reminded of a 'brightly coloured drawing in my colonial story-book' (92) when scrutinising Dunsmere, while Naipaul's narrator notes: 'Of literature and antiquity and the landscape Jack and his garden and his geese and cottage and his father-in-law seemed emanations' (25).

Disappearance is preambled by five quotations, important pointers towards the reading of the text, one of which, taken from Naipaul's work, acknowledges the novel's relationship with *Enigma*: 'Was it Jack? I didn't take the person in; I was more concerned with the strangeness of the walk, my own strangeness, and the absurdity of my inquiry.'[2] In their proper context, these lines are part of a self-critical passage in which Naipaul's narrator begins to understand the unfolding nature of his perceptual processes. He reconstructs how he initially saw and responded to his environment, determining what caused him to notice Jack. As a quotation, the passage stresses the introspective, subjective nature of perception and signals the speculative, unstable nature of any thematic enquiry that *Disappearance* might make.[3]

In view of its thematic links and the explicit textual reference, *Disappearance* can be read as a rejoinder to *The Enigma of Arrival*, 'writing back' to Naipaul's earlier text. The following extended citation will take us further into the discussion:

Cottages were sprinkled here and there, each seeded in its own private bed and curtained off by trees, the meagre remains of the woodland that once flourished for miles around. Axes, then chain saws, had reduced the forest to arable plots and, while men were hacking the land behind, the sea was equally intent on the cliff before. Still there was a certain beauty in the sparseness of the landscape, a settled order such as follows inevitably from centuries of plunder. The generations [...] settled down, multiplied and prospered within the boundaries they had marked in the land, marks enshrined in law, protecting neighbour from neighbour. Fields of barley and wheat, hedges that defined territory, a stabilised woodland, secluded cottages and a sense of the Law of the land – this was Dunsmere. Nothing, it seemed had happened to the village in living memory. Other places had apparently suffered from an influx of young city people [who] disturbed the character of village life [...] Dunsmere though was preserved from the world outside its boundaries; the perilous state of the cliff meant that no one wanted to invest in property. From afar it looked like waxwork, colourful and still. (*Disappearance*, 92, 130, 170)

In time, Dabydeen's narrator overcomes the distance from which Dunsmere looks like 'waxwork', like a fragile work of art. The very fact that it is 'preserved' reflects that it was once built, and reveals the effort of maintaining it. The 'order' perceived is a 'settled' one. Legal definitions of boundaries and privacy become tropes for capital and private property. Through the eyes of the narrator who unveils England's 'drift into a deliberate unconsciousness' (178), the village betrays that it *has* changed 'in living memory'. Unlike Naipaul's Salisbury Plains, Dabydeen's Dunsmere has been 'preserved from the world outside its boundaries', rather than 'suffer[ing] from an influx of young city people' as lamented in *Enigma*. Ironically, 'the perilous state of the cliff', which threatens the very existence of the community, helps to sustain the air of an unchanging *hortus conclusus* by fending off property investors.

But the Dunsmere of *Disappearance* not merely makes connections to Naipaul's version of Englishness, but also to Guyana, birthplace both of Dabydeen and his narrator, the Afro-Guyanese engineer who brings his skills to the enterprise of shoring up the Kentish cliffs. Both places are threatened by the sea. Guyana, which lies below sea-level, requires the protection of a sea-wall, as well as a system of canals, dams and sluices (kokers) to protect it from torrents of water from the interior.[4] Given that the country owes its survival to Dutch engineers and African labour in the 18th and 19th centuries, there is a double irony in that the Guyanese narrator, educated by the British Professor Fenwick (and apparently Anglicised in the process) contributes to the construction of a sea wall in Britain[5] and that both Dunsmere (heart of Empire) and Guyana (colonial outpost) are threatened by untamable forces. But though the engineer comes to the aid of Dunsmere and is thus incorporated in 'preserving' its 'settled order', has 'carved [his] name in [English] history' (177), he still feels like a 'transient worker' (178), a replication of the way Africans and Indians were brought as an expendable labour force to Guyana's sugar estates. Again, in much the same way that the work of Dutch engineers has enabled the commodification and capital exploitation of land and labour, so too the construction of Dunsmere's sea defences may have the (unintended) consequence of opening up the village to those investors that the 'perilous state of the cliff' had fended off, a threat to its mythical Englishness. Invisible from the village, the wall serves the purpose of upholding Dunsmere's pretence of invulnerability and continuity. Only from below, from the beach, does it become visible. And this view from below suggests a sense of subversion, 'overturning from below', particularly because the engineer himself doubts the wall's stability and wonders whether he has thus unintentionally undermined the foundations of Dunsmere. The very rot and decay that the narrator perceives and finds frustrating in Britain has metaphorical expression in the flawed and treacherous foundations of the sea wall. The appearance of the village's intactness is maintained but concurrently exposed as an illusion; however, the psychic disposition of the engineer does not allow him to acknowledge this.

V. S. Naipaul inhabits a curious position in the field of black British literature; while he is one of the most widely recognized writers in Britain, arguably second only to Salman Rushdie, he is a highly controversial figure and both his fiction and his non-fictional work have met with as much negative criticism as praise. He is considered by some as a traitor to his community, as an intellectual snob, and has been charged with neo-colonialism, racism, and misogyny.[6] However, though the narrator of *Enigma* is drawn to the 'seat of power' (his cottage at the manor mimicking that of his aristocratic landlord), no less than Dabydeen's novel, Naipaul's text can be read as a critique of 'Englishness'. In *Enigma*, Naipaul has already made the connections between England and the Caribbean that have been noted in *Disappearance*. The label on a tin of milk becomes iconic both for the English countryside and for Trinidadian memory. Naipaul notes, 'I was in the original of that condensed-milk label drawing' (297); 'this was something like the design on the condensed-milk label I knew as a child in Trinidad, where cows as handsome as those were not to be seen' (38). However, the image of the cows leads to a perception that undermines any sense of rural idyll. This is in the two accounts of mutated cattle which are 'healthy, big [,...] beauti[ful]' but numbered, and without 'sanctity' (81). They are 'reminders of assisted insemination or gestation going wrong [...] with that extra bit of flesh and hair (with the black and white Friesian pattern) hanging down their middle, as of cow-material that had leaked through the two halves of the cow-mould' (81). The mutated cattle become counter icons for a soulless, industrialised process and the alienation of people from the land.

Indeed, one reviewer of *Enigma* maintains that the novel constitutes a work of religious prose.[7] The novel does have a focus on spirituality and its absence, noting that 'relics of recent Christianity dotted the region. So many kinds of religion here, so many relics.'[8] The designation 'relic' is ambiguous. It can denote something which has survived from the past, but more commonly it suggests a melancholic regret for fragments treasured as keepsakes of something expired.

But beyond the note of regret for something once virtuous, now a relic, Naipaul's gaze is more abrasive. He describes a church as standing next to 'a building that *pretended* to be a rough old farmhouse' and realizes that the church, too, has been restored and [is] as *artificial* as the farmhouse'. He sees 'the church not as "church", but as part of the wealth and security of Victorian-Edwardian times'. This secular view of the church leads him to speculate that 'perhaps not even the faith was old'. 'Play farmhouse, renovated church. Had that been a kind of play, too, the religion of the renovated church?' (50). Not only is religion depicted as being as 'artificial' as the building that it inhabits, but in its very function as 'a kind of play' it has lost touch with the sacred. This absence seems also to characterise human relations. Thus, after one character, Brenda, has been murdered by her husband, the narrator observes that 'collecting the dead person's things [...] seemed to call for some kind of ritual. But there was none' (72). Implied in all this is the idea that Naipaul once held the view of England as a place of cultural continuity and human pieties that actual involvement reveals as a hollow myth. This is reinforced by the contrast with Naipaul's description of the Hindu rituals carried out for his recently deceased sister in Trinidad, described in 'The Ceremony of Arrival'.

The weight of English history is demystified yet not utterly rejected, but it is seeing his lugubrious aristocratic landlord through the prism of a Trinidadian Hindu consciousness that makes the narrator feel close to him, see him as his psychological double, both in temperament and in view of their mutual relationship to empire – be it from different ends.[9] Naipaul observes, too, the same decay of knowledge in both the imperial centre and the colonial periphery, despite which that knowledge serves to shore up a necessary sense of identity. He records that the Hindu rituals for his sister's death are 'incorrect' and secularized, but as Robert Hamner notes '[Naipaul] arrives at a positive conclusion, seeing value in Hindu ritual and clearly granting ordinary citizens of Trinidad due regard'.[10] In much the same way he observes of his landlord:

History! He had run together the events of 1498 [...] 1784 [...] and 1845 [...]. He had created a composite history. But it was enough for him. Men need history, it helps them to have an idea of who they are. (318)

Most importantly, Naipaul's narrator, in a movement which compares interestingly with Edward Said's notion of 'migration as a universal condition', comes to realize that his 'raw sense of the unaccommodating world' as a migrant from a former colony is shared by the English people surrounding him, whom he had initially only superficially noticed[11] and whom he had supposed to be as rooted in England as he had felt out of place.

> I had thought that because of this I had been given an especially tender or raw sense of an accommodating world. [...But] it was only then that I saw how tenuous, really, the hold of all these people had been on the *land* they worked or lived in. (87, my emphasis)

In opposition to Naipaul's apparent reconciliation of former coloniser and postcolonial Trinidad in *Enigma*, Dabydeen's narrator, who unlike Naipaul's narrator's oppressed sense of colonial 'rawness', emphasises not his difference but his common humanity ('I'm not black, I'm an engineer' (102)), significantly comes to realize that he is 'invisible to the village', and has no more than the status of a 'transient worker' (177). He departs, presumably for Guyana, at the close of the novel. If Naipaul's theme is reconciliation, the narrative movement of *Disappearance* points to the impossibility of reconciliation between erstwhile coloniser and colonized. By leaving his mentor and landlord, Mrs. Rutherford, and vanishing,[12] the engineer implies that he prefers *historical amnesia* to the constant struggle of working through the legacy of empire.

II

In the following section, the emphasis on the processes of perception that negotiate both narrators' relationship to England and Englishness will be analysed through a comparison of their descriptions of the iconic English cottage. Both narrators come to question the 'naturalness' of what they perceive. They sense that what they at first saw as simple, or in some sense 'natural', has either been created in order to achieve a specific effect which serves the interests of those who created it, or is the complex result of a combination of factors.

When Dabydeen's narrator visits the Irishman Christie, one of his workers, he reports that he finds Christie's habitation in a desolate state, which accords with Christie's account of his life.

Christie has told him that though his circumstances have now deteriorated, he once knew 'about pâté in an ornamental dish or scoops of foie gras' (161). But Christie himself constantly undermines his own credibility by insisting on one story and then twisting it around, or revoking it altogether. The narrator comes to wonder, as he looks round the room, 'whether its desolation was not designed' (164), and but a part of the complexities of Christie's construction of appearances. Echoing the accounts of how slaves constructed a naive persona to fool 'massa', Christie confesses that 'playing Paddy is our national pastime: I joke, I grin, I talk in a bog accent, I get drunk and slur my grammar, I plot, I wave my shovel against the English, I believe in fairies' (164). The distinct and conflicting *inscenations*[13] or versions of Christie are confusing and unsettling, not only for his visitor, (and through him for the reader) but for Christie himself as well: 'After a while you crawl into your own entrails and disappear up your own disguise' (165).

Whereas the scepticism of Naipaul's narrator is a result of a long process from migration to 'Arrival', the scepticism of Dabydeen's narrator is invited by Christie's behaviour. He has long been sceptical of Christie's inscenation of himself as a cliché-Irishman. Nevertheless, Dabydeen's narrator, as befitting a rationalist engineer, is tenacious about the concept of 'the real truth' (160), and goes to Christie to find out the history of Mr. Curtis and his relationship to Mrs. Rutherford. By contrast, Naipaul's narrator expresses his reservations towards his own perception in a more nuanced manner:

> The manor grounds grew on me. Unused to the seasons (in the way I have described) and, so far as architecture went, still perhaps tending to take things too much for granted, seeing 'ordinary' buildings too much as natural expressions of a particular place, it took me time to understand what I was seeing. It took me time to understand that this was no country 'naturalness', that the cottage had been designed to create just that effect [...]. And once I saw the design and the intention, I also saw that the masonry was craftsman's work. (*Enigma*, 175)

Being unfamiliar with the landscape and the architecture, the narrator has no experience to which to relate the images he perceives.

Nevertheless, 'like the design on the condensed milk label' (38) he feels 'that [he] had always known them'. But he, too, is misled by the term 'cottage', associating this term with a simple structure. Initially he cannot but see his abode in these terms until he realizes 'that the cottage had been designed to create just that effect'. This accords with Naipaul's perception of semantic instability:

> The point that worried me was one of vocabulary, of the differing meanings or associations of words. *Garden, house, plantation, gardener, estate*: these words mean one thing in England and mean something quite different to the man from Trinidad, an agricultural colony, a colony settled for the purpose of plantation agriculture. [14]

Displacement from one linguistic community to another has heightened the narrator's awareness of the unstable relationship between the signifier and signified.[15]

Dabydeen's narrator, newly arrived from Guyana, problematizes the process of perception more superficially than Naipaul's. He seems to believe that perception is essentially dependent on the correct perspective. The quotation cited above continues as follows:

> From a safe distance his cottage had the appearance of a picturesque shambles, leaning to one side, tiles missing from the roof and gutters overhanging with moss. It was the kind of dwelling you'd imagine a hermit to be inhabiting, in an English fairy tale from one of my story-books. When I looked again I could see it for what it was – woodwormed, crippled with hatred, wanting to crash to the ground more catastrophically than the cliff's fall. (169)

In this passage the engineer distinguishes between a mere 'appearance' and 'what it was', between 'illusion' and 'reality'. By putting the right distance between himself and the cottage, and by looking twice, he feels capable of truly perceiving Christie's dwelling without the interference of cultural patterns or 'fairy tale[s]'. This focus on illusion and reality underlies, of course, the contrast built into both novels between the imperial metropole and the (post) colonial periphery. For Naipaul's narrator's younger self, although the England of his childhood was in reality imaginary, it nevertheless seemed more 'real' than colonial Trinidad. Looking back, the narrator comments that an aerial view of Trinidad endowed the landscape with 'logic and larger pattern' (97). But it is *'like* a landscape in a book, *like* the landscape of a real country' (97, my emphases): the repeated use of the preposition 'like' inscribing doubt as to the 'truth value' of the perception.

Now, though, the England of the mature observer appears as no less a constructed illusion. But if the *inscenation* of 'naturalness' (176) may be called fraudulent, yet that does not render it futile or ineffective. The quotation cited above continues:

> And yet it made a whole. It worked. You could take it for granted, as I had done at the beginning, and see it as something that went with an Edwardian big house in this part of the country. Or you could enter the fantasy, a child's vision made concrete, child's play by an adult or adults: extraordinary, this gratuitous expression of great wealth and security in this corner of an estate that once was so much bigger [...]. And yet it was this element of play – the child's play of the toy settlement around the manor 'green' or lawn – which, when I recognized, I yielded to. (177)

More importantly, the mature narrator no longer dichotomises the contract between illusion and reality as something somehow residing in the object of perception itself. Rather, perception becomes an intellectual and emotional activity which dialectically establishes a connection between the subject and his or her world. As in the appreciation of a theatrical production, the narrator engages in full knowledge of the 'artificiality' of what he discerns; his appreciation is not vitiated but heightened by the knowledge. Using the metaphor of a child playing, the narrator compares the arrangement, the inscenation of the manor, to a child's 'toy settlement'. The family of the dying landlord had the financial resources, 'created in part by the wealth of the empire' (52) as the narrative acknowledges repeatedly, to allow 'play' on this scale. It is understandable that the narrator's 'yielding' to this kind of 'play' is interpreted as an act of neo-colonial betrayal by some postcolonial critics.

The unnamed first person narrator of *Enigma* experiences an 'awakening' (91) on a large estate that was founded during the Industrial Revolution and expanded considerably 'with the spread of the empire in the nineteenth century' (174). In the beginning he is comforted by the estate's soothing pace. Observing Jack, his wife, his father-in-law, other employees, and his landlord, induces in him a feeling of participation in a larger process and provides a measure of accommodation. He 'considered [Jack] to be part of the view. [He] saw his life as genuine, rooted, fitting: man fitting the landscape.' He finds comfort in this perception that seems to counter his feeling of 'out-of-placeness [...] [as] a man from another hemisphere' (19). Yet this is no sentimentalising vision, since he also sees Jack as 'a remnant of the past.'

And at the same time, the decay of the estate, the result of the landlord's financial incapacity and his illness, does not irritate the narrator. On the contrary; 'I liked the decay, such as it was. It gave me no wish to prune or weed or set right or remake. It couldn't last, clearly. But while it lasted, it was perfection' (52). The process of decay enhances his feeling of accommodation. The trajectories of flux and decay seem indicative of larger processes that encompass both former coloniser and colonised. It is a consoling view, but not one that dissolves the nature of the former relationship. Instead, a more nuanced reading of 'England' generates a more nuanced reading of 'Trinidad', in which perceptions once raw, once overwhelmed by a sense of deracination, historyless and ancestral decay, can be seen as falsely dichotomised.

Now the narrator sees his perceptions as much shaped by temperament as circumstance. It was his 'temperament' to 'see the possibility, the certainty, of ruin, even at the moment of creation' (52) and that 'the decadence [...] was in [his] eye' (77).

It takes him time, but Naipaul's narrator comes to shed his romanticist notion of finding a landscape and a population in tune with its history, landscape, and architecture. As he comes to historicize landscape and architecture, he questions their 'naturalness' and perceives them as determined by human influence and design, concluding that 'nothing was natural here; everything was considered. Grass and trees concealed as much engineering as a Roman forum' (199). Here is Naipaul reading back to Empire and uncovering its aesthetics and cultural construction.

The foregoing discussion has shown that *Enigma* and *Disappearance* question the notion of referentiality and both can be read as post-structuralist texts in which signifiers can only point to other signifiers, ad infinitum, reducing reality to a construction conjured up textually.

One example of how *Enigma* deals with this question is the following bare three-word sentence from the opening page: 'It was winter' (11). This seemingly unproblematic and straightforward statement is expounded in six consecutive paragraphs; we learn that 'it was hard for [the narrator] to distinguish one section *or* one season from the other' (11, my emphasis). The very idea of giving alternative terms, 'section *or* season', accentuates the conventionality of our terminology.[16] We learn of the different associations 'winter' has for the narrator, and through which he perceives it. If he recalls, 'if I say it was winter [...] it was because I remembered the mist', he also concludes: 'it was winter, too, *because* I was worried about the cost of heating' (11, my emphasis). Winter ceases to be an external phenomenon but a signifier constituted by the observer's preoccupations. Winter can be related to other concepts, words, and signifiers, but not directly to the real thing.

However, Naipaul's narrator does not revoke the notion of referentiality altogether; instead he seems to inhabit the margin between denial and acceptance. Thus when the novel draws to a close, and the narrator 'arrives', he understands that:

> We had become self-aware. [...] We had made ourselves anew. The world we had found ourselves in [...] was one we had partly made ourselves; we couldn't go back. There was no ship of antique shape to take us back. We had come out of the nightmare; and there was nowhere else to go. (316)

No longer just a victim of history (a world 'one found oneself in'), because the world was 'one we had partially made ourselves', Naipaul brings his sense of active perception and the possibility of arriving at some kind of truth into alignment. As he records in the following comment on his novel:

I felt that truly to render what I saw, I had to define myself as writer or narrator; I had to reinterpret things. [...] My aim was truth, truth to a particular experience, containing a definition of the writing self.[17]

The efforts of Dabydeen's and Naipaul's narrators to map their position in an English context is explored through the walks that both undertake. Naipaul's narrator finds the country curiously marked by 'those oddly-placed rolled-up plastic sacks' (28) left by Jack's father-in-law, 'creating stiles and steps and padded passing-places over and through the barbed wire' (27). The old man has thus left visible traces of his daily walk, which counter the new pattern etched on the land with barbed wire. As the narrator encounters one 'order' superimposed on another, he realizes that a 'whole life, a whole enduring personality, was expressed in that "run"' (28). This kind of 'mapping' mediates between imposing one's own marks and reading/utilizing those that others have left. The late father-in-law's actions provide the narrator with a model for accommodating himself to his new environment and the awareness that: 'My own presence [was] another kind of change' (34).

But if Naipaul's narrator finds a point of arrival in his perceptual reconstruction of England and its landscape, Dabydeen's narrator never feels other than excluded. If he comes to a point of scepticism about what at first, with its boundaries and protecting hedges appeared a 'settled order', if he too comes to see the artificiality, the decay, the play-acting (the heart of 'venerable England' (8) as a 'waxwork museum' (179), there is for him no point of arrival or proper sense of exit. He remains invisible in Dunsmere, and leaves in a state of confusion. His experience is akin to that described in Frederic Jameson's metaphorical search for an exit from the relativity of postmodernism (the confusions of a Los Angeles hotel, part of 'the great global multinational and decentred communicational network in which we find ourselves caught as individual subjects'[18])

If Naipaul's narrator embraces the system of signification he encounters despite his scepticism, Dabydeen's engineer is overpowered by his misgivings. And unlike Jameson's (and one suspects Dabydeen's) attempt to find an exit from the maze of postmodernism that involves neither facile repudiation or acceptance (as Jameson writes: 'The point is that we are *within* the culture of postmodernism to the point where its facile repudiation is as impossible as any equally facile celebration of it is complacent and corrupt'[19]), Dabydeen's narrator retreats baffled from England's self-referential maze of signification to escape to his 'vast and empty' Guyana, a world as if without signifiers. In England he has wandered around trying to find an exit to 'some reality or other [...] I don't care. So long as it exists. I'm beginning to think nothing exists in England. Everything is a reported story. You can't know anything for certain' (156). He searches for something concrete and real, but cannot find it. He will look instead for escape to the unmarked, uninhabited, the virgin, the empty, the amnesiac.[20] He will escape to Guyana, hoping that the land will be 'vast and empty enough to encourage new beginnings in obscure corners' (179). We are back with Sir Walter Raliegh's dreams of an Eldorado awaiting discovery. So it is one of the ironies of the text that it has its narrator disappear, presumably into the fantasy of a 'vast and empty' Guyana where he will be neither disturbed nor reassured in his notion of reality. The subsequent sentence ('I had to believe this, otherwise there would have been nowhere to go and nothing to do') discloses his fundamental 'doubt of a concrete existence'. This distrust is also expressed in the novel's beautiful last sentences as the narrator vanishes with his 'lover's memento' (108):

> I eased it out: the head of the flower I had picked by the wayside on my first day at work. [...] I held it carefully in the cup of my hand, appalled that the slightest movement could cause it to flake and disappear. (180)

As the novel ends, the narrative, its narrator, and the flower are carefully arrested. We retain a sense of an unreal Guyana, where possibly only Swami's gold teeth, evoking the myth of El Dorado, the gilded man and the gilded land, remain; and an equally unreal Dunsmere, both of which are destined to disappear.

If an earlier generation of Caribbean novels explore the movement from periphery to centre and record the disillusionment found there, in even the most radically nationalist of these works there is a tendency to employ such tropes as carrying resistance into the heart of empire, in that very movement reinforcing the construct of centre and periphery. Both Naipaul's and Dabydeen's novels, in deconstructing the idea of Englishness, also deconstruct the idea of centre. What they find is a withdrawal from the centre, a withdrawal that is imaged, for instance, in both novels by the prevalence of descriptions of nervous illnesses and madness in the characters closest to the narrators.

Both narrators find reluctant workers, withdrawn individuals, narrow-minded patriots, decomposition, death, and decay. The Guyanese engineer is 'more than ever convinced that [Mrs. Rutherford] was mad' (107), there is 'an intensity in her eyes bordering on disorder' (118). Her neighbour, Mrs. Goldsmith, is described as 'totally gone in the head' (118). In *Enigma* the narrator similarly encounters Alan the suicidal writer, the landlord's accidia which 'had turned him into a recluse' (53), and Ray's inexplicable tears that can only be stopped by psychopharmacology.

In this decentred world, both narrators reject the role of the 'colonial subject', 'black man', immigrant, while also resisting assimilation into white England. In the case of *Disappearance*, which does not have the patience of the filigree inquiry of *Enigma*, but is propelled by the angrier, more passionate energy of the narrator who asserts 'I just want to build my sea-dam' (103), and explicitly articulates his project in terms of the construction of identity that has nothing to do with race: 'Deep down I knew a dam was my identity, an obstacle to put between shore and sea to assert my substantialness, my indissoluble presence, without reference to colour, culture or age' (133).

In *Enigma*, Naipaul's narrator traverses the disruption of the displaced émigré (in relation to place and identity) to become, despite his withdrawn life-style in the countryside, a 'citoyen metropolitain' who feels the force of globalization, new technologies and the resulting time-space-compression as he bounces between different parts of the world.[21]

The most manifest difference between the two texts lies in their different construction of the narrative voice and consciousness. The narrator of *Enigma* has a writer's fascination that embraces a world that he knows he may not fully comprehend while Dabydeen's engineer is appalled by the incomprehensible. Naipaul's narrator 'arrives' as *Enigma* comes full circle, his new sense of compassion allowing him to live with the distortions he perceives. He is consoled by relics and fragments, even fraudulent ones. Witnessing decay provides him with the fiction of being part of a larger process, even a transcendent one of decay and change. Dabydeen's narrator follows a different path: his engineer's desire for factuality, corporeality, certainty, which is unconsummated by the construction of the sea wall, triggers in him the wish to retreat, to disappear. Disgusted with the inscenations that he has encountered, with transience, he paradoxically decides to have faith in a permanent void, hoping that on his return to Guyana he will at least not be so unsettled. The protagonist seeks to exchange a stage brimming with disjointed histories for an apparently empty one. By mapping out their readings of Dunsmere and the Manor, the protagonists, as postcolonial figures gravitating towards the former imperial centre and inhabiting positions that they could scarcely have held during the empire, appropriate public space and inscribe their critique. In relativizing their perceptions of the very ground on which they stand, of the villages in which they reside, they reveal the constructed foundations of 'Englishness'.

Epigraph:

Raymond Williams, 'Between Country and City', in *Reading Landscape: Country-City-Capital*, ed. by Simon Pugh (Manchester: Manchester University Press, 1990), pp. 7-18.

1. V. S. Naipaul, *The Enigma of Arrival* (London: Penguin, 1987) and David Dabydeen, *Disappearance* (London: Secker & Warburg, 1993). Page references to these texts are included parenthetically in the main body of the text and supplemented by a title word if necessary.
2. *Enigma*, p. 15. The narratives are also connected through a character called Jack who, despite his absence, is frequently referred to in both texts. The second Jack in *Disappearance*, Mrs. Rutherford's Jack Russell, replaces her husband and is his namesake.
3. This explicit link to Naipaul's *Enigma* suggests an affinity beyond the intertextual reference; it would be interesting to analyse the filial relationships between Caryl Phillips and James Baldwin, Fred D'Aguiar and George Lamming, and David Dabydeen and V. S. Naipaul, respectively.
4. Note that Dunsmere, in the same way as Guyana, is assaulted from two sides, thus further heightening their affinity: 'While men were hacking the land behind, the sea was equally intent on the cliff before'. (*Disappearance*, 92).
5. The name of the British professor is of course that of the government surveyor, Fenwick, who is the protagonist of Wilson Harris's *The Secret Ladder*.
6. Naipaul has been awarded many prestigious prizes, was knighted in 1990, and received the Nobel Prize in 2001; yet his work is frequently under heavy attack. Considering the statements which Naipaul has made, and in the light of particular works, some of the accusations are arguably pertinent. Nevertheless, I will look at *Enigma* in isolation rather than in conjunction with Naipaul's authorial persona and his other writings. Cf. the comments made by Selwyn R Cudjoe, *V. S. Naipaul: A Materialist Reading* (Amherst: University of Massachusetts Press, 1988) pp. 191, 245n31, 255n2; Chris Searle, 'Naipaulacity: A Form of Cultural Imperialism', *Race*

and Class, 26, 2 (1984), 45-62 (p. 61); and Ambalavaner Sivanandan, 'The Enigma of the Colonised: Reflections on Naipaul's Arrival', *Race and Class*, 31,1 (1990), 33-43 (p. 33).

7. Andreas Isenschmidt, 'Im Wendekreis des Nebels', *Die Zeit*, [Hamburg], 11 Mar. 1994, p. 73.

8. *Enigma*, p. 78: Asa Briggs argues that this topic is a typical feature of anatomies of England; he quotes the historian G. M. Trevelyan (1941) saying: 'The Modern Englishman [...] is fed and clothed better than his ancestor, but his spiritual side, in all that connects him with the beauty of the world, is utterly starved as no people have been starved in the history of the world.' Trevelyan's position accords with my reading of *Enigma*. See Asa Briggs, 'The English: How the Nation Sees Itself', *Literature in the Modern World*, ed. by Dennis Walder (Oxford: Oxford University Press, 191), pp. 189-94 (p. 194).

9. The narrator's view that the 'perfection such as [his] landlord looked out on contained its own corruption' (185) seems to echo the narrator's phrase, the 'decadence [...] was in my eye' (77).

10. Robert D. Hamner, 'A Review of *The Enigma of Arrival* by V. S. Naipaul', *World Literature Written in English*, 27, 2 (1987), 289-290 (p. 290).

11. Edward Said, *Culture and Imperialism* (London: Chatto & Windus, 1994), pp. 395-408.

12. The following quotation suggests a desire for *historical amnesia*, (Fredric Jameson's phrase) which is echoed in *Turner*: 'Guyana had its own legacy of deceit and cruelty, but there was space to forget' (179).

13. The term 'inscenation' probably derives from the Latinate German theatrical word 'Inszenierung' which denotes 'theatrical representation', 'mise en scène'. According to the OED it entered English in the late nineteenth century: uses between the 1890s and 1970s are recorded. It is used here to describe the intentional and unintentional formation of scenes, images, and atmospheres through architecture, landscape, and masquerade. These are constructed, fabricated and thus fictive formations – which is not to suggest that they could be disassembled to retrieve a less fictive or fraudulent meaning. To claim the constructedness of an inscenation is not to assert its illusoriness or artificiality, where those terms are understood to reside within a polarity that counterpoises the 'authentic' or the 'real' as oppositional terms. The term is used here because it links the concept of multiple identities (generated and assumed as in a

masquerade) to the production of meaning by architecture and landscape, all the while implying an observer, an audience.

14. V. S. Naipaul, 'On Being a Writer', *New York Review of Books*, 34, 7 (1987), p. 7.

15. See also the anecdote about the flower related at the end of Naipaul's essay 'Jasmine', *TLS*, 4 June 1964, rpt. in *The Overcrowded Barracoon* (Harmondsworth: Penguin, 1976), pp. 24-31.

16. This is a commonplace insight, and one that springs from a particular geographical location, i.e. Trinidad's closeness to the equator and the resulting absence of four seasons.

17. 'On Being a Writer', p. 7.

18. Fredric Jameson, *Postmodernism or, the Cultural Logic of Late Capitalism* (London and New York: Verso, 1991), pp. 39-42. For a powerful critique of Jameson's article see Robert Young's 'The Jameson Raid', in *White Mythologies* (London: Routledge, 1990).

19. Ibid., p. 62.

20. The engineer's endeavour ties in with the epigraph from Wilson Harris's *The Secret Ladder* inserted into *Disappearance*: 'All at once he leaned down and splashed the liquid extravagantly on his face *to clear away all doubt of a concrete existence*' (my emphasis). Here the reflection on the water's surface is obliterated and exchanged for a directly tactile sense impression. *Disappearance* does not, however, seem to accord with its fourth epigraph: 'What opens meaning and language is writing as the disappearance of natural presence' from Jacques Derrida's *Of Grammatology*; it is ridiculed by its juxtaposition with a quote from Margaret Thatcher.

21. In just two pages, at the beginning of 'The Ceremony of Farewell', we learn of journeys between Wiltshire, the narrator's London flat, Dallas, Berlin, and Trinidad all made within a very brief period of time.

CHAPTER NINE

A HARLOT'S PROGRESS: MEMORIES IN KNOTS AND STAYS

CHRISTINE PAGNOULLE

> I remember nothing, but I pity Mr. Pringle's solicitousness, and I am in need of his charity, so I must create characters, endow them with traits and peculiarities, and sow dialogue between us to make luxuriant plots of the pages of his notebook.
>
> David Dabydeen, *A Harlot's Progress* [1]

In Dabydeen's fourth novel, memory is something of a Sternean game: 'I can change memory, like I can change my posture' (2), 'I had many beginnings' (27). The protagonist's memories are as skilfully trussed up in knots and stays as harlot Moll's clients (55). The uncertainties relate to all stages of the narrator's life: to what happened in Africa and on the ship with Captain Thistlewood, and to his later experience in London at Lady Montague's, with the Jew and with the prostitutes. As a result of the traumatic experiences of enslavement and transportation, the protagonist's origins are irretrievably lost, along with his name and the ability to enter into any love relationship. The blurred voices that haunt and taunt him from the past are mixed, he knows, with tales derived from what he has read in European travel books. But if, in part, the uncertainty and unreliability of memory arises from the violent disruptions of the slave trade (and the wilful amnesia of those who profited from it), the novel also plays with postmodern scepticism about the possibility of any kind of reliable reconstruction of the past. For example, the truth about what happens to Lady Montague's lace handkerchief, or the actual circumstances in which she meets the Jew, are hidden under competing narrative versions. One might argue, indeed, that there is an unwitting complicity between postmodern scepticism about historical reconstruction and certain versions of the eighteenth-century European enlightenment that have tended to conceal its darker underside, such as the period's prevalent anti-Semitism and the oppressed condition of the servant class.

If only commonsense reasons were advanced for the narrative uncertainty, and if the indecisiveness about what actually happened could be accounted for and explained away, *A Harlot's Progress* might have been another sentimental exposure of the slave trade, its causes and consequences. But because of the playful dimension in the telling, Dabydeen sidesteps the pitfalls of self-righteousness just as he escapes the vice of a simplifying polarity between victimisers and victims.

Framing the narrative, and undermining it, is the relationship between Mr. Pringle, the young secretary to the Committee for the Abolition of Slavery, and an aged African whom he calls Mungo, a name commonly given to black characters in the literature of the time. Pringle tries to tap Mungo's apparently faulty memory before he dies, whilst the latter plays around with Pringle's need and eagerness to own his story.

Pringle may be paying the piper, (although his attitude as patron is throughout one of a constipated retentiveness) but it is the old African, though occasionally pandering to Pringle's prejudices, who calls the tune: Mungo is 'master of the situation' and Pringle looks at him 'with a dog's imploring eyes' (1). In reality, Mungo's manipulativeness is his only real weapon in a context where he knows his story will always be turned into a commodity.

At some points, indeed, as in Part VI, Chapter V, Pringle takes over and recasts an episode in the protagonist's life. As Mungo grumbles:

> I don't know nothing, so let Mr. Pringle tell it as he want to, of Lord and Lady Montague, and I will shut my rambling mouth while he properize and give them pedigree, and make me present, and make of me a present to you, grateful reader. (186)

The ironic implication is that only in the standard grammar of

182

the educated English writer can a black man's story be made present, and turned into a present to the reader – just as Lord Montague buys Mungo as a wedding anniversary present for his wife. But most of the time, the piecing together, or dismembering, of the scattered parts of an exploded life occurs in the protagonist's own voice, or voices, for he fluctuates between various registers. There is the 'ungrammatical' English he knows is expected of him, but there are also sustained passages of educated diction. He refers to his 'classical breeding', which he betrays in moments of unwariness, and the origin of which is one of the mysteries of the book:[2]

> No I am not uncouth, I can write the story myself, for I have imbibed many of your mannerisms of language, and the King James Bible is at hand to furnish me with such expressions as could set your soul aglow with compassion for the plight of the Negro. Bah! I could sting you for a bounty of reparations, but keep your money and let me talk like dis and dat. (5)

With Pringle he plays the part of the savage, the missing link between ape and man:

> nigger does munch and crunch English, nigger does jape and jackass with the language, for he is of low brow and ape resemblances. (5)

Thus, part of the time he acts the uneducated slave whose 'heathen grammar' has to be 'properized' (11). In the first account of his early childhood he slips in and out of this 'improper' grammar, which is mainly signposted by a simplified syntax and the absence of -s in the third person singular; he 'bongobongoes'.[3] In Part VI, when he is bought by Lord Montague and enters the household as a house-slave who has to know how to behave, the language shifts along the continuum towards standard, with examples of hyper-correction and mixed standard/Creole forms, for example the addition of past forms with 'done': 'the Lady's handkerchief I done steal', (246), 'I already done forget', (247). By contrast, except for the odd sentence, the intensity of the last part is sustained by a polished diction worthy of a European classical tragedy.

Embedded in the eighteenth century characterisation, one can read a late 20th century postcolonial metatext about the limited spaces allowed for the Black/Third World writer in the commoditised world of corporate publishing.

The sentence quoted as an epigraph to this essay illustrates the tone of the novel. The diction is reminiscent of eighteenth century writing, though not with absolute consistency, but through markers such as direct address to the reader, or the use of words that are now rare or no longer used in quite the same way (for example, 'solicitousness' for anxious concern). I have already pointed to the major eighteenth century intertextual reference – Sterne's *Tristram Shandy* – and the reference to 'character', 'dialogue', and 'plot' signals the metafictional dimension of a novel that keeps reminding readers of its fictional status (a Sternean device, earlier used by Fielding). Yet next to this rather abstract dimension, words such as 'sow' and 'luxuriant' present Pringle's pages as pieces of land to be cultivated; a waste land that will only prove fertile if Mungo relents and co-operates in this frequently vexed collaboration.

The impetus behind Pringle's inquiry (and presumably the starting point of the novel, knowing Dabydeen's long-standing interest in Hogarth) is the representation of a black servant carrying a kettle in one of the prints in the series called 'A Harlot's Progress'.[4] However, the precariously merry circumstances of plate 2, which shows a laughing young woman kicking over a tea table to divert the attention of her keeper, a rich Jewish merchant, as her lover slips out of the door while two servants (a boy slave in the foreground to the right and a maid in the background to the left) look on, are not to be found in Mungo's narrative.

Hogarth's 'harlot' is present in several figures within the novel. Betty's dimwitted friend Mary is said to have '[come] to town in a York wagon, with other country girls, looking for work' (128). This repeats the situation of Mary/Moll, the girl in Plate 1. Betty tells Mungo how she stepped in and took on Mary as servant to Lady Montague 'before pimps could get hold of her' (129). When Mungo leaves Betty for good when he is taken off to be auctioned ('I go into the smoke and disappear from her love of me' (168)), he commends her to the reader with the worried concern that she may meet with the same dismal fate as the girl in Hogarth's plates.

Other figures common to Hogarth's plates and the novel are the handsome Jew and Magistrate Gonson. The latter leads the party that comes to arrest Moll Hackabout in Plate 3. While the real life Sir John Gonson, on whom the magistrate in the engravings is supposedly modelled, is recorded as having expressed humane views against the slave trade, (as in the novel when, in his cups, he expresses his indignation at the actions of a Captain Thistlewood who has thrown slaves overboard in order to claim their insurance value[5]), he was also notorious for his harshness in the defence of property and for sentencing prostitutes to transportation to the New World colonies.[6] At one point in the novel he is even referred to as having raped a woman prisoner:

> Nightly they bled her of virtue. Their chief was one called Magistrate Gonson. He had the choicest meat of her. When she was plundered and vandalized beyond remembrance of her origin, they let her go. (266)

The passage recalls the prison scene in Plate 4 (although the only 'raping' actually shown is Moll's finery being taken away), and echoes Betty's words to Mary when she warns her about Bridewell jail: 'and such a pretty virgin girl, the turnkey and the lice will take turn in blooding you' (128).

The figure of the Jew Gideon occurs in four different contexts in the novel, but never as the affluent protector of a prostitute as in Hogarth's plate 2, except in Pringle's prejudiced references to 'the notorious Jewish trickster Mr. Gideon, and his mistress, Mary ('Moll') Hackabout' (3). He is first mentioned by Betty as Lady Montague's lover: 'So the Jew came. Dark, fine-boned, exotic in manner. He spoke with a musical lilt. The bitch lapped him up' (145); he also proceeds to seduce Mary, the maid. There is also the occasion when Mungo is serving Lady Montague and she falls ill because of the 'terror' (223) he embodies as a representative of the inhumane but all too human system of slavery. In this episode the Jew is both a quack promoting his miraculous potion or 'Amazing Eastern Cordial' (227), and a devoted doctor who tries to diagnose the reason for her distemper and find a cure. Gideon's indeterminacy as a character is also created in the play between the anti-semitic stereotypes of the period and the person Perseus (aka Mungo) is surprised to open the door to:

> Perseus opens the door expecting to find a crooked-back and bearded Jew, hook-nosed, darkly complexioned, his hands worn by a lifetime of counting money [...]. Instead he is confronted by a fresh-faced man, dark-haired, handsome, in his mid-twenties. (227)

Later, perhaps as a consequence of his meeting Perseus (*Me it is who change his life and without a word from my mouth speak to him of Godliness*' (258)), Gideon gives up 'all his worldly ambition so as to wait upon the most despised of women' (259), retreating to a stable where he looks after the dying prostitutes, and poisons them as an act of 'mercy'. In the fourth part of the novel he may also be the young doctor who massages the slaves in the hold of the slave ship, whom the slaves recall for his gentleness and decency. 'He was so gentle, he must have been of a different tribe from the sailors. Perhaps not even human' (140). The 'young ship surgeon' is mentioned in the clippings on the Thistlewood case as 'a Jew named Gideon, Gildeon, Gillian, Galton or Lillington', who 'had fallen prey to the disease and was also tossed overboard' (197).

Hogarth's prints are present in two other ways. Firstly, they are repeatedly mentioned in the text as being the starting point for Mr. Pringle's report: 'Hogarth's portrait of Mungo as a boy slave to Moll Hackabout' (4). On another occasion, Mungo comes upon an advertisement in Johnson's Coffee House for Mr. Hogarth's latest prints in the same newspaper announcing his sale, and the same prints are described as providing Lord Montague with a glimpse of 'crudeness and bawdy' (195). Finally, a fictive Hogarth comes to visit Gideon's stable and paint the prostitutes: he is portrayed as prying into their lives and misrepresenting them all: the Jew, the dying women, and the black man.[7]

The prints are also present in the illustrations on the title pages of each part of the novel, significantly reduced to isolated details. Most of them (Parts I, II, III, IV, VI, VII) belong to the second plate in the series, when Moll is deceivingly in command. The connections between the plates and the novel are not literal but work by analogy. The first illustration shows the little black boy bringing fresh boiling water for the tea: he is both the origin and focus of the whole book. Part II, which tells of the various wailings at the protagonist's birth and of the end of the African village, is prefaced by a close-up of the falling cup and teapot. The flaccid, round-faced lover stealing away unnoticed – except by the maid who opens the door and the entering slave boy – is reproduced on the title page of Part III in which the protagonist is both raped and introduced to the figure of crucified Christ. Part IV, (which takes place on the ship, which is invaded by the ghosts of his fellow villagers), has the carnival mask on its title page. This no doubt illustrates the hypocrisy of the traders, and of the European society that thrived on the profits of slavery, but also reflects the complex relationship between truth and lies to be found in the story of Kaka's truthful lie and its dire consequences. For Part V, in which Mungo is cleaned and fattened by Betty, we have a detail of the print in which the soldiers led by Magistrate Gonson enter the room in which Mary/Moll is breakfasting. The little monkey scampering away from the tea table is used for Part VI, in which Lord Montague buys Mungo/ Noah as a pet for his wife. Like the monkey on the plate, Lady Montague's Medusa is a reminder that for all their scorn of merchants, the Montagues' affluence depended on colonial trade. For Part VII, in which the Jewish physician is called upon to cure Lady Montague's mysterious disease, Dabydeen uses the wigged tea-drinking Jew of the second plate. The last two parts, which tell of Mungo leaving the Montagues' place, joining the Jew and caring for Mary, have respectively the *pietà* figure of the dying toothless Mary/Moll, and an even more terrible close-up which comes from the prison plate showing her being disrobed by a winking vicious female warder at Bridewell jail.

This signifier of a fragmented narrative connects to the protean nature of 'characterisation' in the novel. Not only do characters appear in a variety of guises, but different characters blend in the same archetypal forms.

Thus, the harlot of the novel's title is as much the male narrator as Mary or any of the other whores mentioned in the text. In one account of his early life Mungo says that the painted women who initiated him into sex 'made [him] their slave, not to flesh but to their ways of suffering' (18), thus fating him to serve Mary/Moll. Although he says there that 'no man [. . .] will bewoman me', he is turned into a woman by Thistlewood, who sodomises him, thus making him his 'catamite' (75). Manu (who also appears in Dabydeen's narrative poem, *Turner*) tells Mungo that he has 'become a woman's ache and guile' (64), and misshapen Ellar prophetically 'challenges [the villagers'] adoration of the child' on similar grounds:

> He is a strumpet and a thief. He walked in the katran bush and found a white man and led him to us to steal our lives. Afterwards he lay on his belly for the white man and cackled. (139)

The word 'strumpet' is used later in the context of his telling tales for Mr. Pringle's grudging coins: 'he makes me feel like a strumpet whose performance is undeserving of his coin' (78). Dabydeen does several things here. He deconstructs the usual gender-specific usage of the word and in making a connection between the status of women and blacks he uncovers the essential dimension of the word as being not about gender or morality, but about the lack of power. Further, Dabydeen expands the connotations and equivalences of the term. Mungo is a survivor because he is a harlot.

The novel's protagonist is given several names, inducing a floating sense of identity. The first page seems to establish that his name is Mungo, and the name is repeated no less than eight times in twenty-five lines, both in Mr. Pringle's mouth and in parts that read like stage directions. But this is deceptive. The protagonist answers to at least three different names, all of them imposed on him by white people. He is known first and last as Mungo; he is Mungo to Mr. Pringle, and he is Mungo to Betty the washerwoman. The fact that the word is used as a proper name does not become clear to him until another one is used in the advertisement for his sale – Noah, which he finds 'a queer name'

(164); until then he had thought that 'Mungo' was a generic name, 'what white people call our folk, like "Negur" and "blackamoor", and "Boy" and other words the sailors used on us' (164). He is not Noah for very long, since almost as soon as Lady Montague sets eyes on him she decides that he will be called Perseus, or Percy 'when he has become familiar' (204). In Greek mythology Perseus is the hero who slew the Gorgon Medusa. The pet monkey that the protagonist replaces was called Medusa, and Mungo/Perseus can be said to have killed her insofar as he cancels Lady Montague's grief. Retrieving his lost 'true name' (184, 186) would be a clue to his 'lost true identity' (217-218), but is an impossible endeavour.

What stays with him for life is a sign branded on his forehead which looks like the Greek letter pi, or like two TTs, or two crosses without their top parts. But even for this fixed signifier, a variety of interpretations are put forward as the narration unfolds. He may have been 'a blighted seed' (36), 'a harbinger of a new darkness, a new sterility' (33), and his father, endowed with prophetic gift, as Rima says he was, may have known this and yet proceeded to procreate him, either out of lust or in order to contribute to the course of history: 'for although the miracle of such birth would bring destruction to the tribe, it would also loose them into a necessary future' (36). In this version, because of some previous transgression, either on the part of the procreating father or the first mythical woman who enjoyed being penetrated by a bushrat, the protagonist is born as 'a male child bearing on his forehead *peia*, the sign of evil reserved only for women' (45), the sign that was branded into the palms of sterile women who were expelled into the wilderness to starve.[8] The association with Mungo's later fate as Thistlewood's 'catamite' is clear. But then the very first mention of the sign refers to his being branded with a 'hot stone [...] for I had trespassed in the spaces of the dead' (19) by entering the katran bush. This association with punishment is repeated later: 'the headman carved my forehead with the sign of evil.' However, Manu, the wise man and soothsayer of the tribe, gives a completely different explanation: 'do you not remember how we shaved your head and marked your forehead in preparation for your manhood' (65). Because of its connection with the Greek letter and with

189

the mathematical sign, the mark is repeatedly interpreted as 'a sign of Greek learning'.[9] The most likely explanation, but also the least satisfying to his self-respect, is that the sign consists of Captain Thomas Thistlewood's initials and serves as a label; he is 'Thomas Thistlewood's creature' (107) who has been 'tamed and trained'.[10] The advertisement for his sale mentions 'some slight tribal scarring on his forehead' (164). Sign of evil, tribal scarring, sign of learning testifying to his belonging to the descendants of strayed Greek ancestors, or Thistlewood's mark, the various explanations are repeatedly presented as competing and mutually exclusive versions, as for instance when 'he dares not try to explain his scars as evidence of his Greek ancestry, passing them off instead as Thistlewood's brutal doing' (224). Yet sometimes two versions do coexist as, for example, in the protagonist's lament that the sign is both 'an imprint of a lost tribe of Greeks' and 'the sign of evil' (33). In this instance, we see how the same sign can include the dimension of religious alienation which is integral to the colonizing process, and a stamping (or branding as a mark of ownership) connected with an amnesia about origins wrought by slavery. Rationalists, Mungo says, will follow Pringle's narrative and see the mark as no more than a mark of ownership, but he insists that even in this context it was a sign of his baptism into faith that he received with 'gratitude':

> This iron was a crucifix blinding my eye to my own heathen past. He pressed it twice into my forehead, the first pain so excruciating that it banished desire for Africa from my mind; the second exquisitely timed to stop my mouth from execrations, the final traces of African utterances. (75)

The crucifix becomes a perverse symbol proclaiming that redemption has to be bought in blood. Significantly, when Lord Montague is about to write instructions for Mungo's sale to a West Indian merchant, the black man '[holds his] head high so that he can see the crosses on [his] forehead shining with forgiveness' (215). Dabydeen's treatment of character in *A Harlot's Progress* is as radical as that of Wilson Harris in his abandonment of the construct of the 'self-sufficient individual', of characterisation as a closed system of plausible traits.

This play with fragmentation – in the deconstruction of the plates, in naming and in the openness of character – is echoed in the ironic play on the novel's title.

In the eighteenth century the word 'Progress' could be used in three different ways: it could refer to a royal or stately procession; it could simply mean a journey, often with a desirable end as in Bunyan's *Pilgrim's Progress*, or it could be associated with scientific developments such as the Royal Society and would refer to the ongoing improvement of human knowledge and wisdom; as in 'centuries of progress from the Dark Ages' (190), or 'centuries of constant progress' (184). All three meanings are relevant in an ironic way both to Hogarth's prints and the novel. Although there is a 'progress' (in the second sense) of sorts in the novel, in that we move from an uncertain Africa to a London underworld which is in some respects surreal, but portrayed with a plausibly solid reality, after an almost allegorical evocation of the Middle Passage, the application of the word (in its first or third sense) to Mungo's life passage is clearly ironical, and the irony is nowhere more obvious than when he refers to his role as the helper towards death of the sick prostitutes: 'Men had started them on the path to their death. I had brought such Progress to completion' (261). Both at the macro-level of disrupting the linearity and trajectory of the conventional novel that is signalled here, and at micro-level of the deliberate uncertainty, confusion, and even contradiction in textual detail, *A Harlot's Progress* is a celebration of the storyteller's freedom. Just as Mungo can at will keep silent or tell a tale, stay prostrate in bed or dance a jig, so too he can apparently choose among different versions of the same events. The further back he goes in his memories, the less definite he is. One can read this in a conventional realist way, but one can also say that the further back Mungo goes, the more freedom he has to invent.

For instance, does Mungo imagine the episode in which Betty nearly drowns him, out of spite? Her anger at his boasting, and afterwards, at having been provoked to almost commit an act that would have been her undoing seems real enough. But in Chapter VIII (Part V) she seems just as genuinely surprised at his fear, and 'he decides he must have been dreaming after all'

(127). The narrating Mungo puzzles about how and why Betty betrayed Mary, if she betrayed her, or if there ever was a Mary:

> Or else there was no Mary except a baby that Betty bore the Jew, and out of shame strangled it, cleansing it first in her washing-tub of sin, and baptizing it Mary, for that is the name of the mother of their Christian god. And was there or was there not a handkerchief? What do these things matter, except her tragedy? (142)

The last words of the quoted paragraph clinch the matter; and in any case, whatever may or may not have happened – saving on soap, stealing a handkerchief – it will be blamed on the servants and slaves.

The affair of the handkerchief and snuffbox is a neat illustration of the kind of baffling confusion in which the narrator (and presumably the writer) delights. The objects are first mentioned in Betty's narrative about Mary as the gifts which the Jew presents to Mary in order to win her favour. By the next page they have been stolen. When two pages later the same objects 'weaken' Mungo, and trigger his memory, they may also 'recall' events which may not yet have happened – his stealing of the same handkerchief, and receiving the snuffbox from Lord Montague, or his taking the two items among other mementoes whose total market value amounts to the price that Montague paid for him.[11] As Mr. Pringle presses him to say more about Lord Montague, Mungo is caught contradicting his own tale when he mentions 'a snuffbox of tortoise-shell mounted with silver', and starts elaborating in the same way 'as a guilty man confused by being discovered volunteers additional crimes he never committed' (178). Another strategy used to destabilize, again concerning the theft of the handkerchief, is when we are presented with two parallel and contradictory accounts of the same event: Pringle's (?) in plain Roman font, and Mungo's in italics.[12] All these elements enact a Sternean freedom in fictional narration.

Even in the case of the apparently factual – as in the file of newspaper clippings on the Thistlewood case, which Lady Montague compiles for her husband – confusion and contradictions abound. Captain Thistlewood is on trial because he 'shackled some forty slaves' and 'ordered them to be thrown overboard' (192). The reports bluntly contradict each other, not only in their evaluation of his decision (was it criminal or exemplary?), but also in the matter of apparently easily verifiable facts, such as the destination of the voyage, the nature of the cargo, and whether or not Thistlewood committed suicide (197-8).

Confusion (or uncertainty) is also evident in the recurring use of widely varied alternatives concerning the protagonist's life in England, (the time he spent in the Montague household, 'months or years' (176, 184)), events in Africa, (the number of widows banished to the wilderness, 'five or thirty' (27)), and the duration of the Middle Passage ('three years or thirty days' (47)).

What we have instead of 'reliable' linear narrative is a thematic patterning or echoing of events. So when Betty wants to sell her meagre belongings, essentially the handkerchief and snuff box, in order to redeem Mungo, and falls pitifully short of the required amount, we are reminded of the child's mother helplessly offering all she has to redeem him – a brass-bangle, an egg, and a wood carving of the god Zain, protector of travellers – all to no avail: 'Her god has no power before the white man's knowledge of science and trade. The child is to be sold for 11 guineas no less' (123-4). In another account of his childhood, Mungo's mother is described as a veiled votary 'sworn to absolute silence' who communicates in sign language, usually with great restraint, but who, when giving birth, suddenly begins 'screaming [...] in a crazed fluttering of her fingers' (37). He later observes the same 'crazed fluttering' in Betty's hands 'as she works the broom and resolves that she will not suffer the fate of his mother' (149). Similarly, as he watches Lady Montague's sewing hands (184) he remembers the movements in his mother's fingers and is reminded of the common fate of women as victims of a patriarchal order. Moll too, his beautiful dying Ceres, attempts to use her hands for communication: 'a sudden commotion of hands', 'broken signatures she made in the air' (268).

Then there is the common fairy-tale motif of the finger pricked by a needle which recurs in the novel. Lady Montague 'makes a wrong stitch, and in attempting to unpick it, pricks her finger'

(204); Betty 'takes up needle and thread to repair the rags that are her wardrobe. A careless stitch awakens her, the needle lodging in the flesh of her thumb' (135). Blood binds servant and mistress, and binds them to Mungo through Rima, his substitute mother, the woman who nurtured and cradled him, by the same device of the needle prick: 'it is an inconsequential hurt but given her state of mind it takes on the magnitude of a fatal wound, as if gunshot has exploded in her lap' (135).

These parallels can, of course, be read in different ways. Do they suggest some germ of 'true' memory that Mungo returns to? Does he project backwards or forwards? But though these parallels point again to the narrative's unreliability, they also give the narrative poetic coherence, like the rhetorical device of parallelism in the Biblical narratives on medieval stained-glass windows.

The uncertainty also covers what would, in a conventional novel, be regarded as its most significant events. How did the white man come to Mungo's village? Were he and his fellow villagers taken into slavery or slaughtered? The book does not offer any single answer. The child may be the sole survivor taking, as survivors will, the guilt for what happened upon himself. What his actual responsibility may have been we are not to know.

Memories of his childhood in Africa almost all include a visit to the katran bush, the forbidden wood set aside for the ancestors. Entering it amounts to a major transgression and brings about not just terrible punishment but the end of a world:

> In a moment, in the space of a gunshot, all that they owned and were ceased, all the efforts over all the ages that made them a tribe with its own scars. (59)

The first reference occurs very early when Mungo delivers snatches of incoherent narrative in 'Bongobongo' gibberish: 'Hot hot place. Fire! Fire! The katran bush burn down. White. The world turn white white smoke, thick like Manu beard' (3). The most elaborate version of this transgressive intrusion conveyed by the narrator occurs in Part I. The bush is a place of inhospitable sterility, 'thick with mist and white liquid which bleed from the face of rock' (123), the 'white slick on the face of Africa's land' (12), it 'leaks a white mucus' (16). In this version Mungo's father is newly dead and needs fresh blood, or again perhaps not. Perhaps it is sheer perversity that makes Mungo drive his friend/slave, Saba, into the whiteness.[13] The sick whiteness of the place goes together with the cosmic undoing represented by the arrival of Europeans. In the wake of his trespassing the ancestors depart, 'the white hunter [...] comes with gun [...] and torch and chain and cup and cross' (22) and the whole village is turned into katran bush. Another version tells how he strayed into the white bush and met white people there, whom he first took for ghosts, and against his better judgement led to the village, which is what Ellar seems to refer to when she sneers: 'He walked in the katran bush and found a white man and led him to us to steal our lives' (139). Other passages implicate the village community in responsibility for the catastrophe. Ellar wrings the neck of one of her hens and draws 'all the houses of the village' with the spurting blood, cursing, *'Now we'll all go to the wilderness [...] barren or not'* (83-84). In the last paragraph of the novel, Ellar sets the katran bush on fire; the bush burns here as it does in the broken utterance at the beginning, but now it burns with the purifying flames of kindly remembrance (280). Another fanciful explanation for the 'fall' is Kaka's lie, or rather the consequences of his telling the truth about Ellar's barrenness. Since his function in the village is to spread unfounded rumours, he is credited with announcing that she is with child, the father being good-natured Tanda. When Kaka comes to believe the lies he has helped spread, he kills Tanda with a stone. His multiple transgression is offered as another reason why the whole village is enslaved or killed.[14] All these versions compound the narrative instability, but they also point to a coherent perception: the vision of slavery as a 'fall', an expulsion from the garden, and the need to invent both a myth of prior perfection and an explanation of guilt. This despair is focused on Manu, once their prophet and spiritual guide (whose name also belongs to Hindu mythology as the ancestor of mankind who was rescued from the Flood by a big fish), but who is now helpless and cannot restore them to a prelapsarian state of innocence:

We want him to prophesy, but backwards, into the past, into a time when we were still whole, a time before Kaka's lies, or Ellar's blood-curse or my sinning with Saba, or whatever it was that caused us to be murdered by the whiteman. (98)

Manu can do little to counter the villagers' common human need to rationalise the end of their world as a punishment for some guilty action; all he can do is assert (when charged with having failed them):

Perhaps the white man could not be foretold [...]. He is neither storm nor drought. He is not the will of sky nor earth. An iron needle guides him across water. He points an iron stick at us from afar and kills. (63-64)

There are many other unanswered riddles about the protagonist's birth and early childhood. Who wailed at his birth? Was his mother a normal anxious mother or a silent and jealous votary who banished Rima to the wilderness? Did she die 'in bearing [him]'(65), leaving a distracted widower who no longer knew how to till or kill? Did she have a hand in his punishment, digging the hole into which he was lowered? Was she raped and murdered 'at the lip of the pit', her 'blood and bone' (63) sticking on everyone's skin after the explosion? Was she eaten by Captain Thistlewood (whose identity merges with that of the white intruder)? Was she on the slave ship with him, manacled in the hold and gradually freed in the most horrible manner?[15] When and how did his father die? Was he 'the most fleetfooted of hunters', endowed with 'powers of prophesy' (35)? Was he forever absent 'tilling field or fighting war' (11), or was he a devoted husband who was so thoroughly destroyed by grief at his wife's death that he could not even support himself?

We are reminded more than once that nothing of what he claims to remember may be true, that his memories may actually have been absorbed from some popular reports published at the time either by a former slave like Equiano or by European explorers. He tells at length of the tribulations of widows who were proved barren, but he acknowledges that he may have 'dreamt them out of self loathing' (28) or 'absorbed [them] from books' (33); and when Mungo tells Manu about 'widows scavenging in the wilderness', Manu says, 'There were no such women, only in your imagining' (65). Another recurring memory that may be directly inspired by some travelogue is his initiation into sexuality by naked, painted women at the death of his father.

While the identity of his parents is beset by question marks, some figures among his fellow villagers emerge as more recognisable: embittered Ellar, good-hearted Tanda, victimised Saba, wily and distrusted Kaka, wise Manu. They first crowd in on him with curses after they have died and he is about to be killed. They besiege him again on the slaveship, in Betty's cellar, and, in a last burst of compassionate understanding, in the novel's final pages.[16] They entrust him with the task of memory, though he cannot provide any accurate record about what may or may not have happened. Europeans have trampled the place to mud; Thistlewood has branded oblivion into his mind.[17] All that is left are disembodied, bitter voices. This enforced forgetting is contrasted with the call to remember, not only at Pringle's interested insistence, but in his kin's expectation voiced by Manu: 'Remember us as we are, not as the white man will make you' (62), and again:

So remember us as we are, and the earth that not only suckled us but after the rains, it ran with colours, and gave astonishment and even in a season of drought, dust masked our faces in the richest dyes. (66)

The duty to remember is all the more urgent because all that the record amounts to is 'two or three fish-boxes, such is the scantiness of our history' (243), and these contain mainly newspapers, ballads and broadsheets full of denigrating references to niggers, with headings which are 'like stubborn stains' on all their wrongdoings. Most Europeans (including some abolitionists who wanted to send Africans back to Africa) saw blacks as 'the undoing of Europe, darkening its bright historic fabric; black moth, black adder, black beetle, blackfly, black bryony, infecting and strangling and poisoning and blighting England's heritage' (242). But though Europe wants to protect its 'purity of race and lineage', the truth is like Lady Montague's body, a compendium of colonial wares: her 'skin of bleached sugar, bales of cotton her breasts, veins of gold running through her arms, her lap a mine of inexhaustible ores' (184). Such abundance, based on exploitation, has to be fenced and stockaded:

> Her mothers were ovoviviparous, securing their inheritance from the foul and the foreign by Law and Religion and Language and Title, and Moat and Castle Wall and the King's Militia. (185)

Mungo's testimony, which may help to end the slave trade (and separate white and black) is thus urgently needed. Why does he equivocate?

Why is the record we receive as thickly veiled in uncertainty as the katran bush in a viscous white mist? No single answer is enough. Confusion and contradiction obviously give Dabydeen's novel a texture, a complexity it would otherwise have lacked. Again, as indicated in the opening quotation, Mungo's inability to remember leads to complete freedom to invent. But even those episodes that he does appear to remember, we suspect that he distorts or blurs in order to resist and thwart the prying of well-intentioned but prejudiced people like Pringle and Hogarth (whom he does not trust any more than he trusts himself).

Pringle insists on Mungo producing a story with 'a beginning, a middle, an end', and in that insistence is bent on chaining him 'to the old firmament of stars':

> Making me familiar in my Christian hatred of the Jew, my Christian distress at the sexual sin he financed and made me slave to. (275)

This attempt to align Mungo's infinitely branching story to the known and therefore easily accessible, 'the old firmament', parallels Pringle's reduction of Betty's 'anguished and complicated' (145) tale to an 'ordinary tale' (142).

But why the charge against Hogarth whom in his critical works Dabydeen praises for his insight into the moral corruption of his time, his attention to common people and his perception of the tight connection between the slave trade and the various luxuries the European upper class could afford, such as collecting art?[18]

One reason can be seen as relating to the perception that though

Hogarth condemned the immorality of commercialism, he was unaware of the anti-Semitism he unwittingly fuelled. Mungo writes of how Hogarth presented him as 'servant to Moll and to the oldest profession. And servant too to the Jew who was the oldest Jew in the book, in terms of cunning, his hoarding of coin, his purchase of Christian women' (273).[19]

In a way that reflects reflexively on the novel itself, Hogarth is also charged with misrepresenting those he wants to immortalise in art. He betrays them, we are told, but just as much as Mungo betrays the members of his tribe who had looked to him 'to resurrect them in happy stories':

> Did he betray their faith out of malice? Or for money, an account of sensationalism being more marketable than the sacred in our age of Commerce? Or was he not gifted enough to portray the sacred, as words were beyond my own grasp? Whatever the reason or reasons, he broadcast their lives as everyday and bleak, evoking nothing more worthy than pity in the viewer. (272)

Few would question the useful role played first by the Society for the Abolition of the Slave Trade, and later by the Anti-Slavery Society. Yet the novel does more than expose the underlying self-interest that lurks in those forms of activism that arise out of a need to assuage a sense of guilt; and it shows the persistence of blind spots in even the most alert of minds.[20]

Thus Pringle sees the evil of slavery as essentially related to the three arch representatives of public evil in the 18th century: 'the Jews, the Papists and the Jacobites' (144) – a neat cluster of ingrained prejudices, besides which he wishes to whitewash negroes, as though the colour of their skin was a result of their condition:

> He will wash the Aethiop white, scrubbing off the colours of sin and greed that stained Mungo's skin as a result of slavery. (6)

Added to this may be the author's (and readers') awareness that by the end of the eighteenth century slavery was not only 'sinful' and thus morally undermining the worthiness of Britain's imperial enterprise, but was increasingly recognised as far more wasteful in terms of production and profit than wage labour.[21]

In different ways and to various degrees, Hogarth, Pringle, and Montague condemn the slave trade while being caught within its all-embracing web. The issue is fraught with paradoxes at a time of transition between an economy that still depended on slavery and one based on wage labour. Montague is indignant about merchants' undermining the greatness of the nation, not perceiving that his buying of a work of art and a boy slave is part of the same commercial logic (188-191)[22]. As a patriot, Pringle can only approve of commerce since 'mercantilism underpins the welfare of the people, giving occupation to thousands and prestige to the nation' (143). Uneducated Betty dramatically sums up the matter when she explains:

> In England all is money [...] and if you don't deal in it then the whole world will come tumbling down, plague and starvation will overcome us. (132)

I see three major reasons for Dabydeen's fourth novel being the success it is. The first is his nuanced approach to slavery, where he escapes from black and white dichotomies. Next, in spite of the juxtaposition of incompatible accounts and the combination of eighteenth century references and lexis with twentieth century literary devices, by virtue of other devices of pattern and parallelism the novel conveys a compelling sense of unity. Finally, it manages to balance a repeatedly reinforced disbelief in the reliability of the narrative with a hugely persuasive adhesion to a plural tale. Just as Hogarth's prints offer a compelling picture of the time, though they stage largely invented situations, so too, through its juxtaposition of uncertain and often contradictory reports and its collage of openly fictitious accounts, the novel presents a comprehensive picture of British society in the eighteenth century, covering the squalid underbelly of life in an upper-class household, the emerging values of mercantile greed, the scruples and prejudices of white British citizens, and the dispossession of a former slave, who is yet granted the power and freedom of saying and unsaying, of knitting and knotting memories.

1. London : Cape, 1999, p. 67. All page references are included in the main text of the essay.
2. In the Prologue the narrator shows he can quote the Ancients. The phrase 'Radix malorum est cupiditas' refers here to Pringle storing his shilling ('his myrrh') until Mungo delivers his story (7). It is used again in the same situation but including a reference to Moll's throwing it as a curse to a mean customer who would not pay for her performance: '"Radix malorum est cupiditas, you piece of shit."' In Part II when he first refers to the 'Alexandrians', the 'Greek marauders' who had somehow lost their way and wandered off their route, he says that his tribe has lost their knowledge and gift for abstraction (30). Apparently, however, these live on in him, or so he claims at different points of his narrative. In the last stage of the story, he associates his beautiful Moll with Ceres, sees in her an image of Grecian 'grace and symmetry' (263, see also 41), calls her 'my fair Alexandrian' (266) and 'my fair Alexandrine' (268), and curses her in Latin in order to prompt some response in her (267-8).
3. The protagonist 'bongobongoes' , see p. 11, 14, 55-6 and 66. The reference is almost certainly to the infamous speech by the one time Conservative Party minister, Alan Clark, who suggested that immigrants be sent back to Bongo-Bongo Land. For usage of 'uneducated' English see pp. 173-5, 183-6, 226, the first Chapter of Part VIII, and more erratically, the second Chapter.
4. 'His only source of information is Hogarth's portrait of Mungo as a boy-slave to the harlot Moll Hackabout', p. 4.
5. 'A veritable rogue and unchristian fellow, ought to hang. What's his name, Larwood, or was it Thistlefield ?'(192).
6. See David Dabydeen, *Hogarth's Blacks: Images of Blacks in Eighteenth Century English Art* (Denmark: Dangaroo, 1985), p. 116; and David Dabydeen, *Hogarth, Walpole and Commercial Britain* (London: Hansib 1987), p. 112-4. Betty refers to Magistrate Gonson several times, always with dread. After she has almost drowned the black boy in her anger, she says: 'If you had died on me I would have got a dozen lashes then swung. Even if I had pleaded belly and Barbados [usually pregnant women were sent to the colonies, not hanged] Magistrate Gonson would have denied me life and made an example of me' (109). She also tries to warn Mary; 'Magistrate Gonson will

punish you. He'll bang down his hammer and away you go in bonds' (127-8). Similarly, the prostitutes' terror of the man is plain when they mistake the visiting artist Hogarth for Magistrate Gonson, thinking that he has come with 'posthumous sentences' (271). In the Montague household he is a frightening figure of retribution, and when Mungo/Perseus charges Lizzie with having cut his ear off, Lady Montague asks whether he wants her to call Magistrate Gonson (239).

7. References to Hogarth's Prints, see p. 164, 195, 271-5.

8. For the treatment of barren widows in the African village, see p. 50.

9. A Greek sign of learning, see p. 63, 75 and 122 for further references.

10. See p. 66 and 153 for further references. The branding is also compared to 'the claw print of an unclean animal' (168).

11. For the handkerchief and snuff box, see p. 145, p. 204, 245 and 246.

12. See the following quotation: '(*It was me who thief the kerchief. Yes me* [...]) Then she replaces the handkerchief carefully in her sleeve (*No. In Truth I swear she let it fall*), for it is a token of Lord Montague's love, especially made in Flanders for her, with her initials in raised gold letters. (*But it never. It was plain, no mark except of blood*)' (204).

13. Saba is one of the figures who haunts him most: 'Where is Saba?' he asks when visited by people from his village in Betty's cellar (114, 118) ; he gathers moisture to wet his lips as Saba must have done in his tomb (158), and thinks he recognizes him in Lady Cardew's black servant (218). Finally, when he digs a grave for Moll he feels that he also digs to free Saba and Rima from where they are entombed (278).

14. See p. 176.

15. 'His mother is pinned to the slaveship's boards, her body rigid as the body of a compass. Then she is freed. Sans legs, sans arms, she spins by her neck like a gentleman strolling happily to his Club twirls his pocket-watch by its chain. Freed from her neck, she lands beside him, but his hands are fastened in iron, he cannot angle them towards her.' (123) This terrible scene parallels one reported earlier of a woman in the hold of the slave ship 'torn from her chains, sans head and feet', who 'landed alongside her son', who recognized her and 'yanked at his chains in a bid to embrace her' (48-9).

16. For the voices of his fellow villagers see also pp. 23-4, 60-4, 79-102, 113-4, 118-22 and 136-42.

17. Branding and oblivion, see p. 75, 152 and 247.
18. See *Hogarth's Blacks* (pp. 87-9) for the juxtaposition of auctions in Johnson's Coffee House: Lord Montague buys both Mantegna's *Pietà* and Captain Thistlewood's boy, p. 189.
19. Anti-Semitism is particularly obvious in Pringle's discourse. When 'recording the Progress of the oldest African inhabitant of London', he mentions 'the notorious Jewish trickster Mr. Gideon' (3). We have seen above how he panders to the prejudices of his time by making Mungo 'familiar in [his] Christian hatred of the Jew' (275) and how he holds Jews responsible for forms of mercantilism he does not approve of ('the Jews manipulating stock prices in the South Sea Scheme [...] made millions' (143). Anti-Semitism is pervasive; 'after a while I too believe: vile Jew, rich Jew, rob-and-cheat Jew, Jew carpenter who shave and plane the wood into Christ's Cross, then charge extra for nails?' (250-1). Gideon is not the least surprised when he is thrown out from the Montague household (232). Even Betty is suspicious; when she tells of Lady Montague's paramour, she adds 'and a Jew at that, for she's fond of that particular breed' (110). She is similarly jealous of a Jew seducing Mary (*O let the Jews do what they want with the rich, rob them blind and wreck their lives, but not my Mary!'* (130)). She says of Captain Thistlewood that he is 'worse than the Jew' (130). It is left to whores and Blacks to appreciate Gideon's kindness.
20. For activism and guilt, see p. 156.
21. Britain's enterprise, see pp. 143-4.
22. See pp. 188-191. For Lord Montague, Thistlewood epitomizes the evil of mercantilism, so that buying the boy from him to be brought up by his wife supposedly weakens a system which he abhors.

CHAPTER TEN

'TO MAKE BOUNTIFUL OUR MINDS IN AN ENGLAND STARVED OF GOLD': READING *THE COUNTING HOUSE*

GAIL LOW

The interrogation of the British involvement in the history of slavery and the slave trade has been the subject of much contemporary Black British fiction as, for example, Caryl Phillips's *Cambridge, Crossing the River* and *The Nature of Blood*, and Fred D'Aguiar's *The Longest Memory* and *Feeding the Ghosts*.[1] The task of reconstructing the lives and stories of slaves from the anonymity of history in *Crossing the River* and *Feeding the Ghosts* can be seen as part of a contemporary ethical and archival project of re-memory: a process of coming to terms with the past in order to move on. In a recent interview, Caryl Phillips, who might be seen as almost obsessive in his focus on slavery in his writing from the nineteen-eighties onwards, defends his focus as an attempt to deal with the repetition of the past in the present. He writes, 'the root of our problem – of all those people, white and non-white, who live in Europe or the Americas – is to do with the forces that were engendered by this "peculiar institution" of slavery'; coming to terms with the past is part of a process of 'understanding where we are or where we might be going.'[2] In his essay 'The Last Essay about Slavery', D'Aguiar writes of imagining 'final acts of creativity', a 'last poem, a last play, a last novel, a last song', which would 'kill slavery off' and 'somehow disqualify any future need to return to it'.[3] Yet he, too, argues that this laying to rest of the past is not possible in the 'conflicts between races', and in the fracturing and scrambling of history, all of which are part and parcel of slavery's legacy. His novel *Feeding the Ghosts* offers an imaginative reconstruction of the tragic deaths of the slaves aboard the ship *Zong*, the individual lives that have been erased from the official documentation that survives from claims and counter-claims for insurance money. If, according to the narrator, 'there is only the fact of the *Zong* and its unending voyage and those deaths that cannot be undone', 'the past is laid to rest when it is told'.[4] Similarly, Phillips's *Crossing the River* represents an ambitious attempt to produce a slave poetics that transcends the trade in bodies and lives; the novel's utopian vision reveals a diasporian chorus of voices that, to adapt Paul Gilroy's words, repeat, mutate, and transform the motif of exile in the original rupture of families under slavery.[5]

Initially, I turned to David Dabydeen's novel, *The Counting House*, as another novel that appeared to be located within this broadly similar genre of remembering.[6] The prologue encourages such an approach, with its references to artifacts and fragments from the lost history of Plantation Albion in Guyana. These objects – a list of Indian names, a cow-skin purse, a child's tooth, an ivory button, a drawing of Rama, a set of iron needles, some kumari seeds and an empty biscuit tin – 'lie like texts' (a phrase Dabydeen uses in 'Coolie Odyssey') and create expectations that the story behind their presence will be forthcoming; one hopes that such tales might offer an educational, redemptive or cathartic vision.[7] The objects are, indeed, woven artfully through the life stories of Rohini, Vidia, Miriam and Kampta, and on one level, *The Counting House* presents an imaginative reconstruction of those who were transported from India to Guyana, and those free slaves who remained to work on the sugar plantations in the aftermath of abolition. The novel offers us not only the individual tragedies of the people involved, but also reminds us of the larger global forces that managed and governed the human traffic from India to the Caribbean. Yet, like the poet narrator of 'Coolie Odyssey' who seeks 'fables' from ancestral graves only to be greeted with the rebuke, '*Got no story to tell*', Dabydeen's novel ultimately frustrates expectations of a redemptive and cathartic delivery.[8] Its epilogue is one of negations, and this essay is offered in an attempt to puzzle out why.

I want to begin with the context of indentured labour. This is because the novel presumes such knowledge and makes no attempt to present a 'representative' picture of the plantation system of labour. From studies by Hugh Tinker (*A New System of Slavery*), Alan Adamson (*Sugar without Slaves*) and Clive Thomas (*Plantations, Peasants and State*) [9], it is clear that the plantation system in Europe's colonies provided the 'highly capitalized [and industrialized] system of agricultural organization' demanded by sugar cultivation for export to the developed world.[10] Its gradual ascendancy as the primary staple crop in Guyana occurred between 1817 and 1825.[11] Sugar cultivation had important advantages over other crops produced for mass consumption in the 18th and 19th centuries; it provided a high yield yet required relatively less skilled and sophisticated farming skills. Sugar cultivation, however, depended on the organization and regimentation of a large labour force for planting and harvesting in order to maximize efficiency. It also needed a large capital outlay for the machinery required to process the cane. In places like Guyana, where coastal cultivation meant that additional capital was needed not only for roads and transport but also for drainage of its coastal regions and irrigation, (and a large enough population to sustain such work), the system of large private plantations seemed best suited to providing these requirements.[12] Slavery, of course, provided the method of obtaining the labour needed to sustain such an enterprise. After the legal abolition of slavery, labour shortages and relative wage rises, planters sought to maintain the plantation system through the importation of indentured labour. Indian indentured labour began with the importation of workers to (the French Island) Reunion in 1826. In 1836, John Gladstone, father to William Ewart Gladstone wrote to his agents Gillanders and Arbuthnot in Calcutta to inquire about the viability of obtaining labour for his sugar plantations in Demerara.[13] In July 1837, Lord Glenelg, the then Colonial Secretary, authorized the movement of indentured labour with an agreed contracted term of five years.[14] In December 1837, the first consignment arrived to work on Gladstone's estates *Vreendenhoop* and *Vreedestein*. While indentured labour also came from Malta, Brazil, China, Madeira, Africa, and other Caribbean islands, between 1835 and 1917, two thirds of all immigrants that came to Guyana were of Indian origin.[15]

Immigrants worked long hours (up to 10 hours in comparison with the standard 7 ½ hour day for free labourers) and were paid less; 16 cents plus food compared with the 32 cents paid to the free labourer.[16] A number of ordinances were established that were designed to keep the indentured labourer impoverished, dependent, 'servile' and bound to the plantation. These include a five year period of industrial residence before leave was granted to the immigrant to return home, and a compulsory assignment period of 12 months for all immigrants whose original contract specified no named estate. Those not under contract were obliged to pay monthly fines and any unpaid fines could result in 14 days imprisonment with hard labour. Labourers contributed towards their lodging and medical expenses; for any day a labourer did not work, not only was his wage forfeited, but he was also fined more than his wages. Labourers were also not allowed to leave their estates without written documentation, and could not leave the colony without a passport; furthermore, they were obliged to contribute towards a fund designed to help with the return passage home.[17] In the words of Herman Merivale, the permanent under-secretary to Lord Grey, 'a free labourer ought to be "by a law of nature dependent on capitalists" and that, where this dependence did not exist, as in [the case of] British Guiana, it "must be created by artificial means"'.[18] In effect, as Tinker and others argue, indentured labour became a new system of slavery.

David Dabydeen's novel begins with the recruitment of Rohini and Vidia to Guyana with promises of a better life. The India that both characters come from is depicted as one of unchanging poverty with its seasonal cycle of drought and flood. To Rohini, their village, like others in the region, is simply a 'group of mudhuts set down in baked or waterlogged earth' (4), characterized by 'shabbiness', 'haphazardness' and a 'population [that] laboured piecemeal with nothing but sticks or hoes in their hands' (118). To Vidia, the village represents his inability to change the condition of his existence and rise in the world; 'I is nothing, worse than grass, I might as well have four foot and bleat' (16). Rohini, Finee (her mother) and Vidia (her husband) are deeply ambitious and want something more than what life allots them. Finee, poor, widowed and low caste, lives on the scraps of what she can cultivate from her small plot of land and remnants from neighbours' cooking pots. She dreams of 'transformations which would make her matriarch of the village, chief-money lender and market gardener' (24). Vidia is tormented by Kumar's words, 'Yes, money. Only money can catch Rohini's pussy proper [...] unless you want to snap and bruk-up all your life' (37). He spends all his waking hours dreaming of schemes that will enable him to accumulate more for him and his wife. Rohini's words, 'Vidia not enough', 'I want more', sum up her personality and the prevalent mood; even minor characters thieve and have little qualms about using others to better their fortunes or to gratify their own desires. In such a world, Rohini's body and Vidia's good looks are counters in a game they and others play to win.

In this world that is marked by great hardship and equally great longing, Guyana is presented as the fabled land of plenty; in the words of the recruiter, it is a place 'that have so much gold that you don't have enough hand and neck and foot to wear bangle' (4). With the entrance of the recruiter in the village, the fantasies of betterment take on specific forms; what he symbolizes (and what he provides them with) is a gradual coalescing of their needs and wants into a more generalised narrative of desire, and (paradoxically) a more specific fantasy of wealth and progress. Rohini remembers that when Vidia first saw Calcutta, his eyes strained 'with greed for the bigness of the buildings, as if he wanted all of them to belong to him' (4). Even Rohini herself mutters 'What I want with bruk-down leaning place like this [... when the] big-big world outside, tall stone houses and courtyards with fountains and carriages rolling down wide streets' (45). The recruiter comes with the full force and narrative of Empire behind him, as he puts to his audience:

> This land here no more belong to Indians, [...] Everything own by British and I am agent of British. [...] I tell you, British coming and all-you will scoot. [...] Law is British now [...] Once you is

brown, is pow! pow! Gunshot bore hole in you and bayonet like plough in your arse. (46-7)

The recruiter's assertions are supported by Kumar's premonition of impending British rule: in his vision, the British come with the promise of delivery, hauling a boar 'enough to feed God mouth' – but they also 'butcher it and build fort and barrack around it to keep you and we from what belong to all-body' (44). In the recruiter's rhetoric, this dark vision is sweetened by his representation of the British as a force of modernity; 'British people them come and clear away all we mud and bamboo huts'; they put up impressive, solid and permanent buildings; 'massive building[s] surrounded by colonnades [...] enriched with white marble and coloured stones' (46).

With the transportation of Rohini and Vidia to Guyana, we see exactly how both husband and wife are interpellated by the rhetoric of British modernity and progress. They see themselves as part of a great enterprise and desire only to rise up within its ranks. Rohini, working in the Great House, senses rightly that the plantation is part of a larger global network of technology, markets and capital. Their history is now integrated with and part of a larger global history: the development of capitalism in Britain, her industrialization and technological innovations, the creation of a mass market for the consumption of commodities and products like sugar, tea and coffee. The transportation of labour, firstly in the traffic of slaves and then in indentured immigration, is an integral part of the production and concentration of surplus wealth, the expansion abroad in search of further wealth-generation. But Rohini does not see such developments as violence and violation; in a curiously detached manner, she condenses such developments into an abstract and aesthetic metaphor. Echoing Conrad's *Heart of Darkness*, she sees the plantation economy as an idea, 'the idea of making structure in the bush':

The whiteman had stitched the world together with beautiful embroidery, differently coloured threads joining different coloured continents to make a priceless tapestry. The ships came and went, ferrying sugar, tobacco, spices, cloth and machinery from all corners of the globe. Even the ships themselves were crafted in Malabar teak, Irish oak, American mahogany, though they wore the flag of one country. Rohini didn't have all such details at hand but [...] she knew she was in the midst of a great enterprise. (118)

Against this vision of capitalist order, she places the shabbiness and unfinished quality of her past life, and the bush and chaos she associates with Miriam and others who rebel against Gladstone their master. For Rohini, their subjection on the estate represents a benevolent gesture: 'they were put to work, but it was work which gave them a place in the progress of the world – the factory and the sugar it made were the future, not cow-milk and handspun cotton' (118). Vidia's estimation of 'making structure in the bush' is put in more forthright terms; in a conversation with Kampta, a rebellious labourer in *The Counting House*, Vidia asserts, 'if you leave Gladstone you become less than man' (147). With rhetoric borrowed from a crude social Darwinism, Vidia knows:

> that to be something you had to be like Gladstone. Gladstone was the science that invented machines, and the world run by machines like the steam turbines and boilers which made molasses, sugar and rum from a simple plant. [...] To be a Gladstone-coolie was the first stage in becoming Gladstone himself. (147)

What was formerly a simple desire to better one's lot in life mutates into a complex desire to be part of a system of capitalist wealth creation and accumulation. Vidia's desire to have more money to change his circumstances turns into a feverish desire to simply accumulate more money. For Vidia, being present on the plantation is a fortunate opportunity: 'so much riches to be got by piecework or day-wage, however buckra boss chose to pay, and for chopping, weeding, manuring, pan-boiling and seven hundred other tasks each giving seven cents or seventy cents' (61). But Vidia cannot see the futility of his ill-paid work; as the seven cents turns into seventy, Vidia is driven by the magical property of money as a commodity: 'money was everywhere, even in fowl-belly and fowl battie, he only had to get at it. And if you lent it out, money could breed money, a miracle – even though metal, each coin could bring forth other coins, like how a man could multiply himself into seven children' (66). Vidia fetishises money, saving his coins in jars buried under the calabash tree only to dig them up furtively at night and count them in the privacy of his hut. Like other coolies, he envies Gladstone's wealth and imagines him in his counting house at night, 'weighing and re-weighing his gold'. In Rohini's lucid moments, she can see the futility of the enterprise and the foolishness of the pursuit. Yet her desires are equally, if differently, tied to the greater enterprise of wealth generation. She is one of the most ambitious characters in the novel, introduced at its beginning as forever 'wanting more, wanting a sack stuffed with coins, or a belly stuffed with child' (3). Pregnant with Gladstone's child towards the end of the novel, she contemplates the roundness of her body, a roundness which matches 'the roundness of the globe which one day it would inherit' (155).

What we have in the characterization of Rohini and Vidia is a bleak picture of how the relentless march of global capitalism restructures and translates not only individual labour, but also individual desires, into a system of exchanges, equivalences that allow the progress and expansion of capital outwards from developed nations. As Robert Young, employing a Deleuzean metaphor argues:

> capitalism is the destroyer of signification, the reducer of everything to a Jakobsonian system of equivalences, to commodification through power of money [...]. Colonialism operated through a forced symbiosis between territorialization as, quite literally, plantation, and the demands for labour which involved the commodification of bodies and their exchange through international trade.[19]

Not only does *The Counting House* revolve around money and the exchange of money for services that enable the accumulation of wealth, it also shows how commodification reformulates, manages and regulates individual desires. In this climate, sexual desire is not exempt from the system of exchanges: Rohini represents her lovemaking with her husband as an exchange for Vidia's labour. Both Rohini and Miriam work in the Great House and gain small rewards and privileges for their services; both compete for the Master's little favours, are granted the left-overs from the kitchen, the pretty biscuit tin, etc. Both also jostle each other for Gladstone's sole attention, sole ownership. In a particularly telling metaphor, Rohini describes her desirability in terms of the very sugar that both she and her husband slave to produce: 'Is you I want to own like tin can', she says in an imaginary conversation with Gladstone, 'I can put in coolie confectionery. I can dip my hand in white-sugar bowl and hold it over your face and circle, like blessings, like bangles of light' (128).

Given such overwhelming territorialization, what are the possibilities for individuation, let alone resistance? The two figures that tease us with their contradictory rebelliousness are Miriam, the black woman who precedes Rohini in the Great House, and Kampta, her coolie lover, who stages minor acts of wilfulness against Gladstone. Both are described as storytellers, and as storytellers, they are gifted with the ability to narrate different endings. Yet both are written out of history at the end of the tale. Part 2 of the novel which is headed 'Kampta' details Kampta's 'vagrancy' which stands in opposition to the orderly workings of the estate. Kampta disappears from the estate on the slightest whim despite punitive laws prohibiting travel outside of the estate without permission; he also quite arbitrarily downs his tools, despite the heavy punishment meted out to those deliberately absent from work. Kampta occasionally joins the Amerindian tribes in the interior because they had 'no care for possessions', 'made no marks of ownership on the land' and 'hunted only for what they needed, not for the sport of killing' (146), but even Kampta is pulled back into the orbit of the estate. He has dreams of killing Gladstone, but in the final analysis they are simply fantasies. When he fails to translate his desires into reality, he loses the source of his influence among his fellow labourers. Kampta realizes that his rebellious acts are essentially spectacles rather than effective actions, and if spectacular it is not because of their grandeur but because of their theatrical quality. His failure to kill Gladstone is put down to an absence of audience; 'there was no one to witness his courage so he remain supine, like some terrified bush-animal' (146). Miriam, Kampta's lover, a Creole woman working in the Great House also dreams of destroying the plantation by poisoning

Gladstone. She roams through the House as if she owns it and steals from Gladstone just because she can; she reasons, 'If I ask him he would give ten coin but I'd rather thief. He thief it from me in the first place, from my Ma and Pa and grandpa and all the niggers who old Gladstone murder, so how he can give what don't belong to him?' (124). Not only does she treat Gladstone's possessions with irreverence, but she also expresses contempt for the memory of previous masters and mistresses.

Yet, by the end of the novel, Miriam's abortion of Rohini's baby by Gladstone is put down to jealousy and her realization that its birth would destroy the cosy world she has set up as a house slave. The end of the novel is particularly bleak. Vidia is driven to madness when his jars of coins under the calabash tree are stolen. He dies on the journey back home to India, lost among the high mortality statistics of the returning coolie at the end of his term. Kampta disappears in ignoble fashion into the bush; when asked what will happen to him, Miriam predicts his death. Rohini loses her sanity and makes up parcels to represent the babies she never produced. Even Miriam is left vulnerable and full of self-doubt; her dependency on Gladstone is complete when she depicts him as the only person who responds to her imaginary calls for help.

The novel's epilogue represents one long list of negations. If Gladstone's estate was sold on his death in 1889 and disappears from the pages of history, Miriam, Rohini, Vidia and Kampta's stories are also lost.[20] The attempt at reconstructing the past through the fragments and objects passed down to the present offers no cathartic relief, for what we witness is not only the negation of various lives as characters lose their minds or die, but also the erasure and loss of lives. What happens to the characters in the novel corresponds to the real life experience of indentured labourers, swept up in the anonymous statistics of capitalism's remorseless expansion across the globe. At best, what the novel offers us is the tragedy of individual lives, the pathos, contradictions and complexities of the various acts of ambition and survival that move all the figures in the text. None are made into heroic figures; there are no altruistic grand acts of rebellion; contradictory forces of self-denial and self-interest motivate all the characters. Yet if they are victims – these people ruthlessly exploited in the production of sugar – one cannot also deny them the messiness of their own lives.

In the closing sections of Dabydeen's poem 'Coolie Odyssey', the poet narrator returns too late for the funeral of his mother. The world he presently lives in, one of aeroplanes, machines and library books is contrasted with a 'coolie's' El Dorado: Guyana with her 'canefields ripening in the sun / Wait to be gathered in armfuls of gold'. The returning poet visits the cemetery, a 'small clearing of scrubland' with 'no headstones, epitaphs, dates', where ancestors 'curl to scrolls of parchment' and 'lie like texts / Waiting to be written by the children / For whom they hacked and ploughed and saved / To send to faraway schools'.[21] The narrator speaks very self-consciously of the expectation that he will 'folk it up', that he will 'hymn' the past from this 'library of graves', that he will be able to recover and reconstruct the past through story. In a climate where the 'peasantry is in vogue', this recovery of the past is the new El Dorado, and the poet the conduit or means by which England, 'starved of gold' plunders the past.[22]

But the question of who consumes these 'memor[ies] in songs/ Fleshed in the emptiness of folk' over wine and dinner will not go away. These expectations and motivations corrupt the act of recovery and imagination. The voice of old Dabydeen's wife comments:

Is foolishness fill your head.
Me dead.
Dog-bone and dry-well
Got no story to tell.
Just how me born stupid is so me gone.[23]

Her reply shows the gap between the poet, his ancestors, the audience, and those 'fleshed' out in 'folk'. And in a sense, *The Counting House* can be seen as a response to this ambivalence about what the past means for the present, how the past is imagined by the present and for what ends. The negations of the epilogue, the depiction of the messiness of characters' lives and motivations, make it difficult for a reader to come away with clear-cut moral certainties; as I've remarked earlier, they frustrate expectations of an unproblematic redemptive and cathartic experience. The very structure of the novel with its oscillation between time past and time present adds to this difficulty; the past is contaminated by the present and future. The novel starts with Rohini and Vidia already having worked for some years on the Plantation Albion: their perceptions and memories have been coloured by the dream of rising up the capitalist ladder. In the sections of the novel where we are transported back in time to the Indian village of their birth, before their migration to Guyana, characters express themselves in a curiously similar manner to when they live in Guyana. Similar syntax, creolised and folk expressions (for example, 'boy-pickni', or 'bruk-down') are used deliberately for both before and after their journey. This has the effect of making the world of the village community echo the world of Plantation Albion, as if the latter has already been prefigured in the former, or the latter has corrupted – against apparent causal logic – even the temporal space of the former. The result is a pessimistic account which frustrates. Yet such frustrations are perhaps salutary in the present climate of reading off, all too easily, lessons from the past. I want to end with a long quotation from an interview with Dabydeen which I chanced upon when finishing this essay:

We live in a world where we are burdened by meaning. In this politically correct world, we are trying to find meaning all the time, and to express that meaning in rational terms. Given the race relations situation in America and the Caribbean or Britain, writers are expected to be very correct, to bear all kinds of responsibilities towards the notion of being 'truthful' and 'moral' and to provide a kind of explanatory system by which people can live. What pisses me off about critics or about community activists [...] is that they expect a consistency from you and they expect a kind of linear development or they expect sense from you all the time; and you have to be 'one of the boys' and you have to be saying the right things on television, defending the race. It's a very sincere expectation but I think it goes against the nature of the very processes of writing, where what you are much more interested in at times is transgression, and abandonment, and the confusion of metaphor, and opaqueness, and multiply-fused yet contradictory perspectives, and revelling in contradictions, muddle, wrong-headedness, hydra-headedness.[24]

I think the quotation from Dabydeen perhaps makes a fitting comment on the initial expectations I had of the novel, which created their own problems of reading and interpretation. In the words of 'Coolie Odyssey', the demand to folk it up, the demand that the story deliver a moral fable is all too easily a demand made by what the narrator ironically describes as 'congregations of the educated / Sipping wine, attentive between courses [...] the applause fluttering from their white hands / Like so many messy table napkins.'[25] The messiness of *The Counting House*, and the difficulties it presents, is perhaps a worthy obstacle in the pathway of the easy transformation of ethical impulse into yet another commodity.

Notes to Chapter Ten

1. Caryl Phillips, *Cambridge* (London: Picador, 1991), *Crossing the River* (London: Picador, 1993); Fred D'Aguiar, *The Longest Memory* (London: Vintage, 1995), *Feeding the Ghosts* (London: Vintage, 1998).
2. Maya Jaggi, 'Crossing the River: Caryl Phillips talks to Maya Jaggi', *Wasafiri* 20 (1994), p. 26.
3. Fred D'Aguiar, 'The Last Essay about Slavery', in *The Age of Anxiety*, ed. by Sarah Dunnant and Roy Porter (London: Virago, 1997), p. 125.
4. 'The Last Essay About Slavery', p. 230.
5. Paul Gilroy, *The Black Atlantic: Modernity and Double Consciousness* (London: Verso, 1993).
6. David Dabydeen, *The Counting House* (London: Vintage, 1996). Following references will be included parenthetically in the main text.
7. David Dabydeen, 'Coolie Odyssey', *Turner: New & Selected Poems* (London: Cape, 1994), p. 73.
8. 'Coolie Odyssey', *Turner*, p. 73.
9. Hugh Tinker, *A New System of Slavery* (Oxford: Oxford University Press, 1974), Alan Adamson, *Sugar without Slaves: the political economy*

of British Guiana, 1838-1904 (New Haven: Princeton University Press, 1972) and C. Thomas, *Plantations, Peasants and State* (California: Centre for Afro-American Studies, University of California Los Angeles and Institute of Social and Economic Research and University of West Indies, Mona, 1984).

10. *Plantations, Peasants and State*, p. 7.
11. *Sugar without Slaves*, p. 26.
12. *Plantations, Peasants and State*, p. 7.
13. *A New System of Slavery*, p. 63.
14. S. G. Checkland, *The Gladstones: A Family Biography* (Cambridge: Cambridge University Press, 1971), p. 321.
15. *Plantations, Peasant and State*, p. 21.
16. *Sugar without Slaves*, p. 42; *Plantations, Peasant and State*, p. 21.
17. *Sugar without Slaves*, p. 50-56.
18. ibid., p. 51.
19. Robert Young, *Colonial Desire* (London: Routledge, 1995), p. 173.
20. While there was a John Gladstone who had estates in Guyana, the Gladstone of the novel, who is linked with the British Prime Minister in the epilogue is a fictional character. This may be a kind of wonderful 'joke' on Dabydeen's part; an inversion of the problem of marginality. For if Rohini's, Vidia's, Miriam's and Kampta's stories are lost to history, if their stories are deemed too minor and insignificant for the official record, there is a rough kind of poetic justice in creating a character who ostensibly attains historical importance (books devoted to him, a statue commemorating him) but whose credentials turns out to be (equally) hollow.
21. 'Coolie Odyssey', p. 73.
22. ibid., p. 70; p. 74.
23. ibid., p. 73.
24. Kwame Dawes, 'Interview with David Dabydeen', in *The Art of David Dabydeen*, ed. by Kevin Grant (Leeds: Peepal Tree Press, 1997), pp. 199-221 (p. 209).
25. 'Coolie Odyssey', *Turner*, p. 74.

Abrams, M. H.: *The Mirror and the Lamp* (New York: Oxford University Press, 1953).

Adamson, Alan: *Sugar without Slaves: the political economy of British Guiana, 1838-1904* (New Haven: Princeton University Press, 1972).

Alvarez, Julia: 'Finding a Home in the Comunidad of Words', *Middlebury Magazine*, Fall (1998).

Anderson, Benedict: *Imagined Communities: Reflections on the Origin and Spread of Nationalism* (London, New York: Verso, 1991).

Arnold, James. (ed.): *A History of Literature in the Caribbean*, Vol. 3, (Amsterdam: John Benjamins, 1997).

Ashcroft, Bill. et al. (eds.): *The Empire Writes Back: Theory and Practise in Post-Colonial Literature* (London: Routledge, 1989).

Bakhtin, Mikhail: *The Dialogic Imagination: Four Essays*, trans. by M. Holquist (Austin: University of Texas, 1981).

bell hooks: *Yearning: race, gender and cultural politics* (London: Turnaround, 1991).

Bhabha, Homi: *The Location of Culture* (London, New York: Routledge, 1994).

Binder, Wolfgang: 'Interview with David Dabydeen: 1989', in *The Art of David Dabydeen*, ed. by Kevin Grant (Leeds: Peepal Tree, 1997).

Birbalsingh, Frank: 'Interview with David Dabydeen: 1991', in *The Art of David Dabydeen*, ed. by Kevin Grant (Leeds: Peepal Tree, 1997).

Boehmer, Elleke: 'Transfiguring: Colonial Body as Postcolonial Narrative', *Novel: A Forum for Fiction*, 26.1 (Fall 1992).

Brantlinger, Patrick: *Rule of Darkness: British Literature and Imperialism, 1830-1914* (Ithaca and London: Cornell University Press, 1988).

Brathwaite, Edward Kamau: *History of the Voice: The Development of Nation Language in Anglophone Caribbean Poetry* (London: New Beacon Books, 1984).

Breiner, Laurence: *An Introduction to West Indian Poetry*, (Cambridge: Cambridge University Press, 1998).

Briggs, Asa: 'The English: How the Nation Sees Itself', *Literature in the Modern World*, ed. by Dennis Walder (Oxford: OUP, 191).

Brown, Lloyd: *West Indian Poetry* (London, Kingston: Heinemann, 1984).

Burnett, Paula: 'Where else to row, but backward? Addressing Caribbean Futures through Re-Visions of the Past', *Ariel*, 30:1 (January 1990).

Checkland, S. G.: *The Gladstones: A Family Biography* (Cambridge: Cambridge University Press, 1971).

Cliff, Michelle: 'Object Into Subject: Some Thoughts on the Work of Black Women Artists', in *Making Face, Making Soul, Haciendo Caras*, ed. by Gloria Anzaldua (San Francisco: Aunt Lute, 1990).

Cudjoe, Selwyn: *V. S. Naipaul: A Materialist Reading* (Amherst: University of Massachusetts Press, 1988).

D'Aguiar, Fred: 'The Last Essay about Slavery', in *The Age of Anxiety*, ed. by Sarah Dunant and Roy Porter (London: Virago, 1997).

Dabydeen, David: *Slave Song* (Aarhus: Dangaroo, 1984).

Dabydeen, David: *Hogarth's Blacks: Images of Blacks in Eighteenth Century English Art* (Denmark: Dangaroo, 1985).

Dabydeen, David: *Hogarth, Walpole and Commercial Britain* (London: Hansib, 1987).

Dabydeen, David: *Coolie Odyssey* (Coventry: Hansib/Dangaroo, 1988).

Dabydeen, David: 'On Not Being Milton: Nigger Talk in England Today', in Ricks Christopher and Leonard Michaels (eds.): *The State of the Language* (London: Faber and Faber, 1990).

Dabydeen, David and Paul Edwards (eds.): *Black Writers in Britain 1760-1820* (Edinburgh: Edinburgh University Press, 1991).

Dabydeen, David: *The Intended* (Secker & Warburg: London, 1991).

Dabydeen, David: *Turner: New and Selected Poems* (London: Cape, 1994).

Dabydeen, David: 'Interview', *Configurations of Exile: South Asian Writers and Their Word*, ed. by Chelva Kanaganayakam, (Toronto: TSAR, 1995).

Dabydeen, David: *The Counting House* (London: Vintage, 1996).

Dabydeen, David and Nana Wilson-Tagoe: *A Reader's Guide to West Indian and Black British Literature* (London: Hansib, 1997).

Dabydeen, David: *Disappearance* (London: Vintage, 1999).

Dabydeen, David: *A Harlot's Progress* (London: Cape, 1999).

Davis, Angela: *Women, Race and Class* (London: Women's Press, 1982).

Dawes, Kwame: 'Interview with David Dabydeen: 1994', in *The Art of David Dabydeen*, ed. by Kevin Grant (Leeds: Peepal Tree, 1997).

De Bolla, Peter: *The Discourse of the Sublime: Readings in History, Aesthetics, and the Subject* (Oxford: Blackwell, 1989).

deCaires Narain, Denise: 'Body Talk: Writing and Speaking the Body in the Texts of Caribbean Writers', in *Caribbean Portraits: Essays on Gender Ideologies and Identities*, ed. by Christine Barrow (Kingston: Ian Randle, 1998).

Döring, Tobias and Heike Härting: 'Amphibian Hermaphrodites: Marina Warner and David Dabydeen in Dialogue', *Third Text*, 30 (Spring 1995).

Fanon, Frantz: *Black Skin, White Masks* (London: Pluto Press, 1986).

Fanon, Frantz: *The Wretched of the Earth* (London: MacGibbon & Kee, 1986).

Foucault, Michel: *The History of Sexuality*, trans. by Robert Hurley, 3 vols. (New York: Vintage, 1978).

Frazer, James George: *The Golden Bough: A New Abridgement*, ed. by Robert Fraser (London: Oxford University Press, 1994).

Gikandi, Simon: *Maps of Englishness: Writing Identity in the Culture of Colonialism* (New York: Columbia University Press, 1996).

Gilroy, Paul: 'Art and Darkness: Black Art and the Problem of Belonging to England', *Third Text*, 10 (1990).

Gilroy, Paul: *The Black Atlantic: Modernity and Double Consciousness* (London: Verso, 1993).

Glissant, Édouard: *Caribbean Discourses: Selected Essays*, trans. by J. Michael Dash (Ithaca and London: Cornell University Press, 1988).

Grant, Kevin: 'Preface', in *The Art of David Dabydeen*, ed. by Kevin Grant (Leeds: Peepal Tree, 1997).

Hamner, Robert: 'A Review of The Enigma of Arrival by V. S. Naipaul', *World Literature Written in English*, 27, 2 (1987).

Harris, Wilson: 'An Interview with Wilson Harris', *Kunapipi*, 2:1 (1980).

Harris, Wilson: 'Metaphor and Myth', in *Myth and Metaphor*, ed. by Robert Sellick (Adelaide: Centre for Research in the Literatures in English, 1982).

Harrison, Tony: *The School of Eloquence and other poems* (London: Rex Collings, 1978).

Hezekiah, Randolph: 'Martinique and Guadeloupe: Time and Space', in *A History of Literature in the Caribbean*, Vol. 1. (1994)

Hutcheon, Linda: 'Crypto-Ethnicity', *PMLA*, 113.1 (January 1989).

Hyam, Robert: *Empire and Sexuality: The British Experience* (Manchester: Manchester University Press, 1990).

Jaggi, Maya: 'Out of the Torrid Waters of Colonial Culture: Writer David Dabydeen Talks to Maya Jaggi about his New Reading of the Enigmatic Turner', *Guardian*, 23 April 1994.

Jameson, Fredric: *Postmodernism, or the Cultural Logic of Late Capitalism* (London and New York: Verso, 1991).

Kroeber, Karl: 'Experience As History: Shelley's Venice, Turner's Carthage', *English Literary History*, 41 (1974).

Lindsay, Jack: *J.M.W. Turner: His Life and Work: A Critical Biography* (New York: NY Graphic Society, 1996).

McIntyre, Karen: 'Necrophilia or Stillbirth? David Dabydeen's 'Turner' as the Embodiment of Postcolonial Creative Decolonisation', in *The Art of David Dabydeen* ed. by Kevin Grant (Leeds: Peepal Tree, 1997).

McWatt, Mark: 'His True-True face: Masking and Revelation in David Dabydeen's Slave Song', in *The Art of David Dabydeen*, ed. by Kevin Grant (Leeds: Peepal Tree, 1997).

Morrison, Toni: *Playing in the Dark: Whiteness and the Literary Imagination* (London: Picador, 1992).

Naipaul, V. S.: 'On Being a Writer', *New York Review of Books*, 34, 7 (1987).

Parry, Benita: 'Between Creole and Cambridge English: The Poetry of David Dabydeen', in *The Art of David Dabydeen*, ed. by Kevin Grant (Leeds: Peepal Tree, 1997).

Perloff, Margerie: *Wittgenstein's Ladder: Poetic Language and the Strangeness of the Ordinary* (Chicago: Chicago University Press, 1996).

Relich, Mario: 'A Labyrinthine Odyssey: Psychic Division in the Writings of David Dabydeen', in *The Art of David Dabydeen*, ed. by Kevin Grant (Leeds: Peepal Tree, 1997).

Rich, Adrienne: 'Split at the Root', *Blood, Bread, and Poetry* (New York: W. W. Norton & Company, 1986).

Riggs, Thomas (ed.): *Contemporary Poets*, 6th edn. (New York: Saint James Press, 1996).

Rushdie, Salman: 'V. S. Naipaul', in *Imaginary Homelands* (Harmondsworth: Penguin, 1992).

Ruskin, John 'Of Water as Painted by Turner', in *Modern Painters*, ed. by David Barrie (London: Deutch, 1978).

Ruskin, John: 'The Storm-Cloud of the Nineteenth Century', in *The Norton Anthology of English Literature*, 5th edn, (New York and London: Norton, 1986).

Said, Edward: *Orientalism* (London: Routledge & Kegan Paul, 1978).

Said, Edward: *Culture and Imperialism* (London: Chatto & Windus, 1994).

Searle, Chris: 'Naipaulacity: A Form of Cultural Imperialism' *Race and Class*, 26, 2 (1984).

Sivanandan, Ambalavaner: 'The Enigma of the Colonised: Reflections on Naipaul's Arrival', *Race and Class*, 31,1 (1990).

Spivak, Gayatri: 'Can the Subaltern Speak?', in *Colonial Discourse and Post-Colonial Theory: A Reader*, ed. by Patrick Williams and Laura Chrisman (New York: Columbia University Press, 1989).

Spivak, Gayatri: 'Three Women's Texts and a Critique of Imperialism', in *The Feminist Reader: Essays in Gender and Literary Criticism*, ed. by Catherine Belsey and Jane Moore (London: MacMillan, 1989).

Stoler, Ann Laura: *Race and the Education of Desire: Foucault's History of Sexuality and the Colonial Order of Things* (Cambridge: Cambridge University Press, 1997).

Suleri, Sara: *The Rhetoric of English India* (Chicago and London: University of Chicago Press, 1993).

Tiffin, Helen: 'Postcolonial Literatures and Counter-Discourse', in *Postcolonial Studies Reader*, ed. by Bill Ashcroft, Gareth Griffiths, Helen Tiffin (New York: Routledge, 1995).

Tinker, Hugh: *A New System of Slavery* (Oxford: Oxford University Press, 1974).

Tordorov, Tzvetan: *Theories of the Symbol*, trans. by Catherine Potter (New York: Cornell University Press, 1997).

Tuma, Keith: *Fishing by Obstinate Isles: Modern and Postmodern British Poetry and American Readers* (London: Faber and Faber, 1990).

Twitchell, James: *Romantic Horizons: Aspects of the Sublime in English Poetry and Painting, 1770-1850* (Columbia, MO: University of Missouri Press, 1983).

Walcott, Derek: 'The Antilles, Fragments of Epic Memory: The 1992 Nobel Lecture', *World Literature Today*, 67. 2 (1993).

Wallace, Robert: *Melville and Turner: Spheres of Love and Fright* (Athens and London: University of Georgia Press, 1992).

Walvin, James: *An African's Life: The Life and Times of Olaudah Equiano* (London: Cassell, 1998).

Warner, Marina: 'Cannibal Tales: The Hunger for Conquest', in *Managing Monsters: Six Myths of our Times*, The Reith Lectures (London: Virago, 1994).

Welsh, Sarah: 'Experiments in Brokennness: The Creative Use of Creole in David Dabydeen's *Slave Song*', in *The Art of David Dabydeen*, ed. by Kevin Grant (Leeds: Peepal Tree, 1997).

Williams, Raymond: 'Between Country and City', in *Reading Landscape: Country-City-Capital*, ed. by Simon Pugh (Manchester: MUP, 1990).

Young, Robert: *Colonial Desire* (London: Routledge, 1995).

CONTRIBUTORS

Tobias Döring is Professor of English Literature at the University of Munich, where he specializes in postcolonial studies and early modern literature. His books include *Caribbean-English Passages: Intertextuality in a Postcolonial Tradition* (2002), *Eating Culture: The Poetics and Politics of Food* (co-edited with Markus Heide and Susanne Mühleisen, 2003), *Performances of the Sacred in Late Medieval and Early Modern England* (co-edited with Susanne Rupp, 2005), and *Performances of Mourning in Shakespearean Theatre and Early Modern Culture* (2006).

Aleid Fokkema was a senior lecturer at the University of Utrecht for nearly twenty years, teaching contemporary literatures in English. She has published widely on postcolonialism and postmodernism, focusing mainly on the question of cultural identity and literary affiliation in writing the metropolis. The authors she has published on include Salman Rushdie, Derek Walcott, Grace Nichols and J.M. Coetzee. She recently left the University to become a full-time independent author and translator.

Pumla Dineo Gqola is a Chief Research Specialist in the Society, Culture and Identities research programme at the Human Sciences Research Council in Pretoria, and Extraordinary Associate Professor in Humanities at the University of the Western Cape. Her essays on topics in African, Caribbean and South Asian literature, African feminist discourse, and cultural studies have been published in journals and collections in Africa, the Americas and Europe. She guest-edited *Agenda* 63 on *African Feminisms II: Sexuality and Body Image* (2005), *Feminist Africa* 6 on *Subaltern Sexualities* (2006) with Elaine Salo, and co-edited *Discourses on Difference and Oppression* (2002). She is one of the three editors of the online feminist/womanist e-zine *fito*.

Heike Härting is assistant professor of English at the Université de Montréal and teaches postcolonial and Canadian studies. She presently holds a research grant from the Social Sciences and Humanities Research Council of Canada and is a participant in the Major Collaborative Research Initiative "Globalization and Autonomy" at McMaster University. She also holds a FQRSC research grant from the government of Québec for her project "The Politics of Corpses: Contemporary Anglophone and Francophone Narratives and Films of Global Conflict in Rwanda and Sri Lanka". She is presently finishing a book entitled *Unruly Metaphor: Nation, Body and Diaspora in Contemporary Fiction in English Canada*. She has published in various journals and books, including *ARIEL*, *Third Text*, *SCL/ELC*, *Essays on Canadian Writing* and *English Studies in Canada*.

Lee Margaret Jenkins grew up in Edinburgh, was educated at Cambridge University and has lived in Cork, Ireland, since 1994, where she is a Senior Lecturer in English at University College Cork. She is the author of *Wallace Stevens: Rage for Order* (1999), and *The Language of Caribbean Poetry: Boundaries of Expression* (2004). She is the co-editor of *The Locations of Literary Modernism* (2000) and of *The Cambridge Companion to Modernist Poetry* (forthcoming).

Kampta Karran, a Chevening Scholar and a recipient of the ORS Award is currently a senior lecturer at Nations University and is actively engaged in sugar cane farming in his home country Guyana. He has edited two books on ethnic studies, co-edited two volumes of poetry and has published several articles on issues ranging from ethnic conflict to multicultural music.

Gail Low teaches contemporary literatures in English at the University of Dundee. She is the author of *White Skins/Black Masks* (1996), the co-editor of *A Black British Canon?* (forthcoming) and is currently working on an institutional history of 'Commonwealth Literature' 1958-67.

Lynne Macedo teaches Caribbean literature and film at the University of Warwick. She is the author of a monograph: *Fiction and Film – The Influence of Cinema on Writers from Jamaica and Trinidad* (2003). She has published several articles including 'The Impact of Indian Film in Trinidad' in *Beyond the Blood, the Beach and the Banana* (2004) and '*Auteur* and Author – A comparison of the works of Alfred Hitchcock and V.S. Naipaul' in *Entertext* (2001). She is also a contributor to the *Oxford Companion to Black British History* (forthcoming).

Michael Mitchell teaches at a secondary school in Germany and has published a number of school textbooks, including *The Postcolonial Experience* and *Ethnic Diversity in the UK*. He has also edited a collection of Caribbean short stories (*I See These Islands*) and a school edition of Hanif Kureishi's screenplay *My Beautiful Laundrette*. He is the author of *Hidden Mutualities: Faustian Themes from Gnostic Origins to the Postcolonial* (forthcoming) and has published numerous articles on postcolonial literature. He divides his time between Germany and Stratford-upon-Avon.

Christine Pagnoulle teaches English literatures and translation at the University of Liege. She has published on African and Caribbean as well as British writers (monographs on Malcolm Lowry and David Jones, articles on Ngugi, Kamau Brathwaite and Wilson Harris). She has also published and edited books on translation issues (Les gens du passage, Cross-Words). She also translates poetry.

Mark Stein teaches postcolonial literatures at the University of Muenster. His publications include *Black British Literature: Novels of Transformation* (2004) and *Cheeky Fictions: Laughter and the Postcolonial* (co-ed with Susanne Reichl, 2005). He has published articles on parody, irony, visual culture, transculturation and on writers such as Dambudzo Marechera, Charlotte Brontë, William Thackeray, Olaudah Equiano and Aphra Behn.

Madina Tlostanova is a professor at Peoples Friendship University of Russia (Moscow), a member of ICLA and MLA and has published extensively in several different countries (USA, Poland, Estonia, Uruguay, Romania, Brazil and others). Her interest focuses on the multi-faceted problematic of globalization and culture. She is the author of *Post-Soviet Fiction and Trans-cultural Aesthetics* (2004), *The Janus-faced Empire* (2003) and *The Multicultural Debate and the US Fiction of the Late 20th Century* (2000).

ALSO FROM PEEPAL TREE

Slave Song
ISBN: 1 84523 004 3, 72pp., £7.99

Slave Song is unquestionably one of the most important collections of Caribbean/Black British poetry to have been published in the last twenty years. On its first publication in 1984 it won the Commonwealth Poetry Prize and established Dabydeen as a provocative and paradigm-shifting writer.

At the heart of *Slave Song* are the voices of African slaves and Indian labourers expressing, in a Guyanese Creole that is as far removed from Standard English as it is possible to get, their songs of defiance, of a thwarted erotic energy. But surrounding this harsh and lyrical core of Creole expression is an elaborate critical apparatus of translations (which deliberately reveal the actual untranslatability of the Creole) and a parody of the kind of critical commentary that does no more than paraphrase or at best contextualise the original poem.

It took some time for the displaced critics to recognise that this prosaic apparatus was as much part of the meaning of the whole as the poems themselves, that Dabydeen was engaged in a play of masks, an expression of his own duality and a critique of the relationship which is at the core of Caribbean writing: that between the articulate writer and the supposedly voiceless workers and peasants.

This new edition has an afterword by David Dabydeen that briefly explores his response to these poems after more than twenty years.

Turner
ISBN: 1-900715-68-6, pp. 84, £7.99

David Dabydeen's 'Turner' is a long narrative poem written in response to JMW Turner's celebrated painting 'Slavers Throwing Overboard the Dead & Dying'. Dabydeen's poem focuses on what is hidden in Turner's painting, the submerged head of the drowning African. In inventing a biography and the drowned man's unspoken desires, including the resisted temptation to fabricate an idyllic past, the poem brings into confrontation the wish for renewal and the inescapable stains of history, including the meaning of Turner's painting.

'Turner' was described Caryl Phillips as 'a major poem, full of lyricism and compassion, which gracefully shoulders the burden of history and introduces us to voices from the past whose voices we have all inherited', and by Hanif Kureishi as 'Magnificent, vivid and original. The best long poem I've read in years.'

The Intended
ISBN: 1 84523 013 2, £8.99

The narrator of *The Intended* is twelve when he leaves his village in rural Guyana to come to England. There he is abandoned into social care, but with determination seizes every opportunity to follow his aunt's farewell advice: '...but you must tek education...pass plenty exam'. With a scholarship to Oxford, and an upper-class white fiancée, he has unquestionably arrived, but at the cost of ignoring the other part of his aunt's farewell: 'you is we, remember you is we.' First published almost fifteen years ago, The Intended's portrayal of the instability of identity and relations between whites, African-Caribbeans and Asians in South London is as contemporary and pertinent as ever. As an Indian from Guyana, the narrator is seen as a 'Paki' by the English, and as some mongrel hybrid by 'real' Asians from India and Pakistan; as sharing a common British 'Blackness' whilst acutely conscious of the real cultural divisions between Africans and Indians back in Guyana. At one level a moving semi-autobiographical novel, *The Intended* is also a sophisticated postcolonial text with echoes of *Heart of Darkness*, its play with language and its exploration of the instability of indentity.

Disappearance
ISBN: 1 84523 014 0, £8.99

A young Afro-Guyanese engineer comes to a coastal Kentish village as part of a project to shore up its crumbling sea-defences. He boards with an old English woman, Mrs Rutherford, and through his relationship with her discovers that beneath the apparent placidity and essential Englishness of this village, violence and raw emotions are not far below the surface, along with echoes of the imperial past. In the process, he is forced to reconsider his perceptions of himself and his native Guyana, and in particular to question his engineer's certainties in the primacy of the empirical and the rational.

This richly intertextual novel makes reference to the work of Conrad, Wilson Harris and VS Naipaul to set up a multi-layered dialogue concerning the nature of Englishness, the legacy of Empire and different perspectives on the nature of history and reality.

'Richly layered with symbol and metaphor *Time Out*.
'An electrifying array of surmises about how the imperial past has affected everyone in Britain today.' *Scotsman*.

The Counting House
ISBN: 1 84523 015 9, £8.99

Set in the early nineteenth century *The Counting House* follows the lives of Rohini and Vidia, a young married couple struggling for survival in a small, caste-ridden Indian village who are seduced by the recruiter's talk of easy work and plentiful land if they sign up as indentured labourers to go to British Guiana. There, however, they discover a harsh fate as 'bound coolies' in a country barely emerging from the savage brutalities of slavery. Having abandoned their families and a country that seems increasingly like a paradise, they must come to terms with their problematic encounters with an Afro-Guyanese population hostile to immigrant labour, with rebels such as Kampta who has made an early abandonment of Indian village culture, and confront the truths of their uprooted condition.

"Beautifully written... Dabydeen's grace, as a poet turned novelist, is to give his characters' imaginations and inner lives voices in prose... This is a marvelous novel" – Michele Roberts, *Independent on Sunday*.

Ed. Kevin Grant
The Art of David Dabydeen
ISBN: 1 900715 10 4, pp. 231, £12.99

In this volume, leading scholars from Europe, North America and the Caribbean discuss his poetry and fiction in the context of the politics and culture of Britain and the Caribbean. These studies explore David Dabydeen's concern with the plurality of Caribbean experience, with its African, Indian, Amerindian and European roots; the dislocation of slavery and indenture; migration and the consequent divisions in the Caribbean psyche. In particular, these essays focus on Dabydeen's aesthetic practice as a consciously post-colonial writer; his exploration of the contrasts between rural creole and standard English and their different world visions; the power of language to subvert accepted realities; his use of multiple masks as ways of dealing with issues of identity and the use of destabilizing techniques in the narrative strategies he employs.

Bruce King writes in *World Literature Today*: 'Part of the usefulness is that the essays overlap, build on, and disagree with one another. They bring out Dabydeen's recurring themes, autobiographical material, and the links among his scholarly publications, interviews, and creative writings.'

NEW FROM PEEPAL TREE

Laurence A. Breiner
Black Yeats: Eric Roach and the Politics of Caribbean Poetry
ISBN: 9781845230470; pp. 302; £17.99

For readers of West Indian literature, a study of Eric Roach requires no justification. He is the most significant poet in the English-speaking Caribbean between Claude McKay (who spent nearly all of his life abroad) and Derek Walcott. Roach began publishing in the late 1930s and continued, with a few interruptions, until 1974, the year of his suicide. His career thus spans an extraordinary period of Anglophone Caribbean history, from the era of violent strikes that led to the formation of most of the region's political parties, through the process of decolonization, the founding and subsequent failure of the Federation of the West Indies (1958-1962), and the coming of Independence in the 1960s. This book presents a critical analysis of all of Roach's published poetry, but it presents that interpretation as part of a broader study of the relations between his poetic activity, the political events he experienced (especially West Indian Federation, Independence, the Black Power movement, the 'February Revolution' of 1970 Trinidad), and the seminal debates about art and culture in which he participated.

By exploring Roach's work within its conditions, this book aims above all to confirm Roach's rightful place among West Indian and metropolitan poets of comparable gifts and accomplishments.

Laurence Breiner is the author of the critically acclaimed *Introduction to West Indian Poetry*.

Stewart Brown
Tourist, Traveller, Troublemaker: Essays on Poetry
ISBN: 9781845230531; pp. 320; £14.99

Major essays on the work of Caribbean and African poetry, including Kamau Brathwaite, Frank Collymore, Olive Senior, Kwame Dawes, James Berry, Linton Kwesi Johnson, Niyi Osundare, Femi Oyebode, Jack Mapanje and others. With the subtext of a mistrust of postcolonial theory and its whole academic industry, Stewart Brown, as a practicing poet, both establishes the autobiographical grounds from which the essays are written and asserts that the poetry is more important than its criticism. This is a collection that is wide-ranging, provocative, intellectually rigorous – and eminently readable.

All the above titles (and a couple of hundred more) are available online at peepaltreepress.com.